Praise for *Ecommerce Analytics*

"Leveraging analytics to improve business results requires first knowing the questions that need to be answered. *Ecommerce Analytics* is the book to read if you are looking to use data to improve your online performance."

—**Josh James**, Founder and CEO, Domo; Cofounder and Former CEO, Omniture

"With U.S. ecommerce sales set to cross $450 billion in 2017, the opportunity in front of you is immense. Yet, it is likely your conversion rates are stuck at 2%. I'm excited about Judah's comprehensive tome because it is just what the doc prescribed to help unstick your ecommerce strategies. From cart abandonment to multichannel attribution to lifetime value… You'll get precise guidance to win big!"

—**Avinash Kaushik**, Digital Marketing Evangelist, Google; author, *Web Analytics 2.0, Web Analytics: An Hour a Day*

"Are you a digital analyst working for an ecommerce company? Or are you an ecommerce marketer and your boss just asked you to provide more data about your digital efforts? If you are, then you should check out *Ecommerce Analytics*!

"Judah does a great job of making digital analytics for ecommerce logical and easy to understand. If you're a digital analyst familiar with topics like attribution modeling, you'll love how Judah discusses the specifics for an ecommerce business.

"If you're new to digital analytics you'll find the content easy to approach and very actionable. But that doesn't mean that he cuts corners! Judah is really, really thorough! He takes the time to dive into all the different metrics and analysis techniques that you can perform on your ecommerce business.

"I put *Ecommerce Analytics* on my bookshelf and plan to use it whenever I work with an ecommerce company—you should, too!"

—**Justin Cutroni**, Analytics Evangelist, Google; author of *Google Analytics* and *Performance Marketing with Google Analytics*

"This important book is required reading for anyone who wants to understand how to deliver successful ecommerce analysis and data science. It's instructive and helpful, unifying the subject matter in way that is actionable for leadership, managers, technologists, and analysts."

—**Raj Aggarwal**, Cofounder and CEO, Localytics

"Judah has created a must-read book for all digital analysts. It's clearly framed and combines a comprehensive understanding of the topic with a practical flavor only the author can bring through decades of experience. This should be a hit in any college analytics class and will be on my graduate analytic course reading list in the future."

—**Rand Schulman**, Managing Partner, Efectyv Digital; Cofounder, DealSignal; Cofounder, Digital Analytics Association

"In *Ecommerce Analytics*, Judah has delivered a comprehensive survey of the field, covering a broad array of topics important to implementers, analysts, and executives. This book contains a wealth of information that will be valuable in successfully executing an ecommerce strategy."

—**Bob Page**, Director Emeritus, Digital Analytics Association; Internet entrepreneur

"Judah has done the impossible. In just a few chapters, he helps you understand the opportunity ecommerce retailers have in front of them, the monumental impact ecommerce analysis can have, the challenges you'll face from a management and socialization perspective, and most importantly, how to navigate all of it and get stuff done.

"This book is a must-read for those who want to elevate their ecommerce stores to the next level, for the data teams who are tired of shouting into the wind, and for the managers who want to make a more meaningful impact on the organization. It is well researched, carefully thought out, and covers all of the bases. Stop reading this and buy the book already; your company will thank you."

—**Tommy Walker**, Editor-in-Chief, Shopify

"Judah has delivered something critical in this remarkable information age—a broad, comprehensive summary of the essential elements of digital commerce. *Ecommerce Analytics* starts by showing what's possible, in stark terms: the size and growth of the market, along with metrics of the leaders. From there, it elaborates on the entire taxonomy—defining the end-to-end process, what data to collect—how to analyze it—and then most importantly how to interpret it and optimize from there. He even digs into some of the trickiest bits: attribution, governance, and how to organize the company around digital success. Finally, his consistent emphasis on asking business questions and defining the outcomes and measurements before starting to crunch the numbers makes the subject truly accessible—and actionable."

—**Sid Probstein**, Founder and CEO, RightWhen; Cofounder and former CTO, Attivio

"*Ecommerce Analytics* helps you understand each of the critical components needed to collect data, personalize interactions, and move customers through the funnel. It's the backbone of marketing automation and personalization. This is the best book for anyone who works in ecommerce or who wants a job in that field where they will have to use data to understand and drive the business."

—**Jonathan Corbin**, Director, Marketo

"Ecommerce: In 2016, everyone's doing it; few do it well; even fewer share what they've learned, and only one makes the top of that list. Judah Phillips is that person, and this is that book. I've learned a ton from Judah, and you will, too."

—**Cesar Brea**, Founder, Force Five Partners;
author of *Marketing and Sales Analytics* and *Pragmalytics*

"No one understands analytics more than my man Judah. This is a crucial read for anyone trying to step up their analytics game and who wants the tangible results that mastering data brings!"

—**Greg Selkoe**, Founder and CEO, Curateurs.com;
Founder and former CEO, Karmaloop

"*Ecommerce Analytics* is a must-read for anyone involved in ecommerce. Not only will you learn how to do different types of analysis, it also covers the hard topics like data modeling, data integration, attribution, and building data-driven teams. You'll even get some conversion optimization knowledge, too. You should read it before your competition does."

—**Bryan Eisenberg**, Cofounder and CMO, IdealSpot; coauthor of the *Wall Street Journal* and *New York Times* bestselling books *Call to Action*, *Waiting for Your Cat to Bark?*, *Always Be Testing*, and *Buyer Legends: The Executive Storytellers Guide*

"This book is a must-read for anyone interested in making the most of their ecommerce-related data. The author does an excellent job making complex concepts accessible as well as teaching the reader how to get to actionable insights."

—**Jesse Harriott**, CAO, Constant Contact

Ecommerce Analytics

Analyze and Improve the Impact of Your Digital Strategy

Judah Phillips

Publisher: Paul Boger
Editor-in-Chief: Amy Neidlinger
Executive Editor: Jeanne Levine
Editorial Assistant: Sandy Fugate
Cover Designer: Alan Clements
Managing Editor: Kristy Hart
Senior Project Editor: Betsy Gratner
Copy Editor: Cheri Clark
Proofreader: Debbie Williams
Indexer: Ken Johnson
Compositor: Nonie Ratcliff
Manufacturing Buyer: Dan Uhrig

For information about buying this title in bulk quantities, or for special sales opportunities (which may include electronic versions; custom cover designs; and content particular to your business, training goals, marketing focus, or branding interests), please contact our corporate sales department at corpsales@pearsoned.com or (800) 382-3419.

For government sales inquiries, please contact governmentsales@pearsoned.com.

For questions about sales outside the U.S., please contact intlcs@pearson.com.

Company and product names mentioned herein are the trademarks or registered trademarks of their respective owners.

2   16

ISBN-10: 0-13-417728-2
ISBN-13: 978-0-13-417728-1

Pearson Education LTD.
Pearson Education Australia PTY, Limited
Pearson Education Singapore, Pte. Ltd.
Pearson Education Asia, Ltd.
Pearson Education Canada, Ltd.
Pearson Educación de Mexico, S.A. de C.V.
Pearson Education—Japan
Pearson Education Malaysia, Pte. Ltd.

Library of Congress Control Number: 2016930328

To Lilah and Elizabeth and my mom and dad,
who all shop online and wonder what I do at work.

Contents at a Glance

Contents

Foreword

Let's say that you fit into one (or perhaps more) of the following categories:

- You work at a sophisticated ecommerce company—say you are a new employee at Amazon.com—and you know your employer is very analytical, but you aren't.

- You are a manager at a company with some ecommerce capabilities, and you have a nagging feeling that your firm could be better at analytics, but you don't know how to go about it.

- You have an analytics-oriented job, but you need to learn more about ecommerce analytics.

- You work at a brick-and-mortar retailer that has dabbled in ecommerce, but you and your colleagues know you need to get more serious about it.

- You want to start a new ecommerce company.

- You are a student and want a job in ecommerce.

If you resemble any of these people, this book is the answer to your prayers. It is the one-stop shopping destination for everything you need to know about ecommerce analytics. It will provide a short refresher course on statistics. (Perhaps you did not fully engage with your statistics class in college.) It will give you enough content on retail and selling stuff online to get you by in most meetings. It will help you through difficult and esoteric topics like customer behavioral flow analysis, customer lifetime value, abandoned shopping carts, and virtually anything else you will encounter in this field.

As I read this book, I was surprised at how thorough it was and how clearly Phillips presents the key concepts. I was a bit amazed at the breadth of topics represented and that a young guy like Phillips has accumulated the analytical wisdom of the ages in topics like exploratory data analysis and communicating effectively about analytics. But I was truly shocked to read early in the first chapter that this is the only book on ecommerce analytics. Given the importance of ecommerce to the economy and the importance of analytics to ecommerce, I couldn't believe that there are no other books on the topic. But I skeptically undertook a cursory search on "ecommerce analytics books" and found nothing in the category. There are books on digital analytics (Phillips himself has written a couple of good ones), specific topics like conversion, and tools that are related to digital and ecommerce analytics (Google Analytics, for example), but literally nothing directly targeted at ecommerce analytics.

So if you have an interest in ecommerce analytics, it's a no-brainer to buy and read the book. If you are reading this foreword in Amazon's "Look inside" preview mode, go directly to the shopping cart and buy it. If you have actually found this book in a physical bookstore (though they should probably refuse to carry it since it threatens their business), take it up to the cash register and get out your wallet. I don't know how much they will sell this thing for, but do you value your career? Do you want a promotion? You should not only buy the book but also send Judah Phillips 10% of your total compensation as a tribute.

You should also stop reading this foreword and get to the real content. But first, one more request. If you're like many people, your primary interest in this book is in the "hard" advice on ecommerce analytics—statistical methods, techniques for getting data, specific key performance indicators to employ, and so forth. These are certainly important and valuable, and attending to them here makes perfect sense.

However, the book is also replete with "softer" advice that will make you a much better ecommerce analyst. There is, for example, the general philosophy of "getting close to your data" by observing distributions and outliers. There is the focus on telling a good story about your data. Phillips also maintains a strong focus on understanding what your organization wants from analytics and on making analytical results as digestible as possible. These types of wise perspectives and suggestions are just as valuable as any method or tool prescription.

So buy and read this book—every page of it. Take its recommendations to heart. If you want to be successful at ecommerce, you need a heavy dose of analytics. And if you want to be successful at ecommerce analytics, you need a heavy dose of this fine book.

—**Thomas H. Davenport,** President's Distinguished Professor of Information Technology at Babson College; Research Fellow, MIT Center for Digital Business; Cofounder, International Institute for Analytics; Senior Advisor to Deloitte Analytics

Acknowledgments

This book is the first text written that is solely dedicated to explaining and exploring the subject of ecommerce analytics. The content is an unprecedented synthesis of experience and ideas, bringing together hard-learned knowledge about the business, technical, organizational, managerial, mathematical, scientific, artistic, and analytical aspects of delivering successful ecommerce analytics (and data science) in companies of all sizes. I wrote this book for analytics practitioners, managers, and leaders, as well as people who work with, who are studying, or who simply want to learn more about ecommerce and how to analyze it. It's a multidisciplinary text that crosses a range of topics and contextualizes them under the idea of "ecommerce analytics" and thus unifies the content into a cohesive whole. I cover analytical concepts and theory, to applied mathematical and statistical methods, to analytical processes and organizations, to specific types of ecommerce analysis, to data modeling, integration, collection, storage, security, and privacy. I tried to be as ambitious and innovative in writing this text as the ecommerce industry, its leaders, and its workers are daily in their jobs. Thank you for reading my book.

First I'd like to thank Jeanne Glasser-Levine, Betsy Gratner, Cheri Clark, Amy Neidlinger, and the staff at Pearson who helped me produce this book. I'd also like to thank the following people (in random order): Thomas Davenport, Jonathan Corbin, Jeff Bezos, Brian Massey, Sid Probstein, Julio Gomez, Sergio Maldonado, Sean Hickey, Sarabjot Kaur, Peep Laja, Harpreet Singh, Shail Jain, Nick Kramer, Ants Anupold, Dave Weineke, Peter Gibson, Deepak Sahi, Jeff Evernham, Gary Rush, Vishal Kumar, Eric Valyocsik, Mike Taubleb, Dennis Mortensen, Gillian Ahouanvoheke, Kevin Rowe, Patrick McGinley, Ali Benham, Feras Alhou, Eric Fettman, Sergei Dvoynos, Amit Shah, Dave Munn, Jesse Harriott, Bart Schutz, Ton Wesseling, Raj Aggarwal, Jim Levinger, Tommy Walker, Justin Cutroni, Avinash Kaushik, Brian Clifton, Eric Dumain, Cesar Brea, Brett House, Olivier Titeca-Baeuport, Bala Iyer, Eric Colsen, Julien Coquet, Bob Mould, Jeff Checko, Bob Page, Jascha-Kaykas Wolff, Gary Angel, Kim Ann King, Eric Hansen, Gary Angel, Rand Schulman, Andrew and Luchy Edwards, Jim Sterne, Mark Zuckerberg, Bryan and Jeffrey Eisenberg, Josh James, and you.

About the Author

Judah Phillips helps companies create value with analytics and data science by improving business performance. Judah has led analytics and data science teams for Fortune 500 companies and has improved their financial performance through the applied analysis of data, the management of analytical and technical resources, and the alignment and optimization of analytics strategy against short-term roadmaps and long-term strategic visions. Judah strongly believes that cutting-edge technology is critical and necessary but often becomes technical overhead unless strategy is aligned with excellence in organizational development, operational management, and delivery execution that is solidly tied to impacting material financial goals. Judah has worked for or been hired as a consultant by Internet companies, media companies, consumer product companies, financial services firms, and various types of agencies.

- He is the sole author of three books on analytics, including *Ecommerce Analytics*, *Building a Digital Analytics Organization*, and *Digital Analytics Primer*. Judah has also authored chapters, edited, or contributed to the development of other books: *Measuring the Digital World*, *Advanced Business Analytics*, *Sales and Marketing Analytics*, *Digital Is Changing Everything*, *The Complete Guide to B2B Marketing*, and *Multichannel Marketing Metrics*.

- He served on various boards of or advised established and start-up technology companies, including global leaders in digital analytics, mobile analytics, ecommerce, mobile apps, and advertising technology.

- He is an Adjunct Professor at Babson College and has guest lectured on analytics and data science at the business schools for New York University, Boston College, Northeastern University, and others.

- He is the former V.I.P. at Harvard Innovation Lab, where he advised Harvard start-ups about analytics and data science.

- He has spoken at more than 70 technology and industry conferences since 2006.

Judah holds a master of science in finance and a master of business administration from Northeastern University and a B.A. from the University of Massachusetts Amherst.

1

Ecommerce Analytics Creates Business Value and Drives Business Growth

The global ecommerce market is expected to grow at a compounded annual growth rate of 17% from $1.3 trillion in 2014 to $2.5 trillion by the end of 2018. In the United States in the third quarter of 2015, ecommerce generated $87.5 billion and accounted for 7.4% of all retail sales (Rogers 2015). Ecommerce has been growing annually on average between 14% and 15% quarterly since 2014, while retail growth has remained less than 3%. comScore estimated that U.S. consumers spent more than $57 billion online from November 1 through December 31, 2015, up 6% from 2014. On Cyber Monday, U.S. consumers spent more than $2 billion online (comScore 2016). Alibaba, in China, reported more than $14.92 billion in "goods transacted" on one popular shopping day (Denale 2015). Amazon's Q3 2015 ecommerce revenue grew 23% from 2014 to more than $25 billion (SEC 2015). Frost and Sullivan predict that by 2020, the business to consumer (B2C) ecommerce market will be $3.2 trillion and the business to business (B2B) ecommerce market nearly twice as large at $6.7 trillion. Nearly $10 trillion in ecommerce revenue will occur by 2020. Globally, the United State and China are the largest ecommerce markets, accounting for more than 55% of ecommerce sales in 2015. eMarketer estimates that by 2018, China's ecommerce marketing annually will be more than $1 trillion, with the U.S. likely reaching $500 billion, followed by the U.K. at $124 billion and Japan at $106 billion (Rogers 2015). Clearly, huge amounts of goods and services are being transacted between businesses to consumers and between businesses and other businesses globally.

Ecommerce analysis will continue to be an important activity for generating such growth and new levels of revenue. Puma generated a 7% conversion lift using analytics. PBS increased conversions and visits by 30% using analytics to track customer events in the funnel. WBC cited a 12% boost in conversion rate through customer segmentation. Watchfinder claimed a 1,300x increase in ROI remarketing based on analytics. Marketo claims a 10x higher conversion rate for personalized campaigns using analytics. BT used conversion testing to increase form completions by more than 60%. Amari Hotels increased online bookings and sales by 44% by using analytics to optimize online advertising (Google 2015). Companies that do ecommerce analysis increase their business performance.

Ecommerce is transacted on pure-play B2C ecommerce sites that have no physical storefront, such as Zulily, eBags, and Wayfair, and by omnichannel B2C retailers, such as Walmart and Staples, that have physical stores. Even pure-play ecommerce sites, like Amazon and Warby Parker, are opening stores. As a result, existing companies that already sell goods and services are now selling online and vice-versa. New companies are almost required by the market to have an online presence. Although some companies that sell physical products use an online presence only for branding to drive offline sales, that's increasingly rare. Even luxury brands are selling their goods directly to consumers on retail sites. B2B ecommerce is even larger than B2C ecommerce. Major global companies execute ecommerce, such as Ford, GM, Coca-Cola, Chevron, IBM, General Mills, Kraft Heinz, ExxonMobil, General Electric, and Microsoft. The largest 300 B2B ecommerce companies were projected by eMarketer to grow 13.3% this year to $547 billion (from $483 billion in 2014)—figures that easily eclipse the U.S. B2C ecommerce market.

Ecommerce isn't just about the site anymore. The most popular ecommerce sites have a mobile experience, whether mobile web or mobile app. 30% of U.S. ecommerce sales in 2015 were generated on a mobile device (Brohan 2015). Many ecommerce sites also have physical stores. And in the future, ecommerce will be embedded into "things" and pervasive in Internet-connected devices—with mobile payments just a touch away both online and in-store. *Internet Retailer* predicts that in 2015 the U.S. *mobile* commerce sales will total $104.05 billion, which is up 38.7% from $75.03 billion in 2014.

They estimate that mobile commerce in 2015 will grow 2.58 times faster than desktop ecommerce sales, which they predict will grow 15% this year to an estimated $350.64 billion globally. Note that 30% of mobile customers leave an ecommerce site when it is not optimized for mobile (Dorian 2015).

Ecommerce is an extremely competitive space. It takes huge amounts of capital to even try to compete with the major ecommerce players. This competition can create razor-thin margins or revenue that can be driven primarily through discounting. Ecommerce can be considered a zero-sum game. Thus companies are competing by creating digital experiences that enable a person to quickly and easily find and buy. Whether on a desktop, tablet, or mobile device, the companies that are winning in ecommerce make it easy and frictionless to find the product or service desired, understand how it fits the need, and buy it. Then these sites can compel their customers to come back again and again to buy more online and in-store. To do so, ecommerce companies use marketing and advertising that is tightly coupled with a user experience that ladders up to a prospect or customer's notion of the brand and works to meet their intent. People come to ecommerce experiences with certain goals in mind: to learn more about a product by reading product information and social reviews, to compare prices and promotions, and to purchase products. Ecommerce sites that win at this zero-sum game can match that intent to a product and create commerce.

Leading ecommerce companies use data and analytics to compete—and they use a lot of different data to do so. Data is collected and analyzed about who visits an ecommerce site, when they visit, what pages they view, and what site or source they came from (the referrer or marketing channel). Other information is also collected about user behavior, such as user interactions and events on the site, data related to products viewed, promotions used, pages visited, time spent, the different paths and clickstreams on the site, the queries entered in search, and many other data points, such as the order value, the price of products, the shipping method used, and the payment information. Customer data may be captured or inferred, such as who the customers are or could be, where they live, what they like and their preferences or propensities, what they've bought, and other demographic and psychographic information.

The idea of "conversion"—where a prospect transitions to a paying customer—is embedded into the analytical DNA of the world's leading ecommerce companies. They staff entire teams and run comprehensive programs for conversion testing and optimization. Marketing channels and sources of traffic, such as organic and paid search and various types of online advertising, are measured and tracked. Higher-order consumer research around brand awareness, favorability, and consideration is performed. Customer data is analyzed, segmented, grouped into cohorts, modeled, and understood using financial measures, like the cost of customer acquisition and customer lifetime value. Customer loyalty, retention, satisfaction, and churn are known and optimized. Merchandise, products, orders, and transactions are analyzed from the site to the warehouse through to shipping and fulfillment.

All this different quantitative and qualitative data about the entire ecommerce experience and operations can be captured, measured, and analyzed to improve business performance and make better decisions. Although tracking, measuring, and analyzing all of this data may sound challenging—and it is—it is possible to do. Of course, doing so isn't easy. It requires investment in people, first and foremost, who understand business, technology, and the process of doing analytics. It also requires investment into different types of analytical tools and technologies, including ecommerce platforms, business intelligence tools, analytical platforms, and data science sandboxes. It might even require the collection of new first-party data, the usage of second-party data, or the purchase of third-party data.

All of this data, the people and teams who work with and analyze it, and the technology supporting it represent powerful assets for ecommerce companies to use to help run their business. But the data must be collected and analyzed effectively and accurately for companies to use it to create better experiences, make better decisions, drive conversion, satisfy and retain customers, and thus increase revenue, growth, profitability, and value. The effective use of ecommerce data and related data requires investing in the analytics value chain—from the technology to the people to the processes, governance, and change management necessary. Doing so can provide a material return on investment from analytics by converting more users to customers and providing insights that can be used to improve the customer experience. The return from analytical investment can also come from improving marketing operations and tracking the cost and return of marketing and advertising. The impact of merchandising programs can be attributed to sales and other financial metrics. The details of transactions, the metrics around products, and the key performance indicators related to the shopping cart can be understood, benchmarked, and targeted with goals. These methods for competing with ecommerce data are entirely possible if you know how to succeed with ecommerce analytics.

Ecommerce analytics is the phrase used to describe business and technical activities for systematically analyzing data in order to improve business outcomes of companies that sell online. This broad definition incorporates business activities such as the gathering of business requirements, the execution of analytical programs and projects, the delivery and socialization of business analysis, and the ongoing management of the demand and supply of analysis. The range of business stakeholders demanding service in ecommerce companies will run the gamut from the C-suite to the leaders of merchandising, buying, planning, marketing, finance, user experience, design, customer service, inventory, warehousing, fulfillment, and more.

Ecommerce analytics also involves working with IT and engineering teams in the appropriate software and Internet development lifecycle. It requires the analytical team to participate and possibly lead technical activities that are required to deliver or support analysis, such as data collection, extraction, loading, transformation, governance, security, and privacy. Ecommerce analytics can include understanding and doing dimensional data modeling, working with databases, handling data processing, creating and executing querying, determining data lineage, participating in data governance committees, acting as a data steward, working with and defining metadata, and using tools to analyze data, create data visualizations, and do data science and advanced analytics. All of this work occurs within a corporate organization with its own culture and ways of working, into which the analytics team must integrate and learn to support and guide to drive data-informed business outcomes. Successful analytics often requires rethinking and reorganizing the way a company is structured, including new roles in the C-suite, such as chief analytics officers, chief data officers, and chief data scientists.

Companies that are successful and effective with ecommerce analytics ask business questions that can be answered with data, and then they employ analytical teams that can collect and acquire data, govern and operate analytical systems, manage analytical teams, and generate analysis and data science that inform stakeholders. These companies create value by asking questions, answering them with data, and changing the way they take action as a result. Business questions for ecommerce can include the following:

- **Customers:** What are the characteristics of my most loyal customers? Least loyal?
- **Marketing:** How do customers perceive our company and products?
- **Categories and products:** Which products drive the most sales or highest gross margin? Which products are frequently purchased together?
- **Price and promotions:** What impact do discounts and promotions have on overall sales?
- **Omnichannel sales:** How are my channels performing and how do they complement each other on the path to purchase? How does this differ from attribution?
- **Prospects and customers:** Which prospects should I target to convert into loyal customers? What products or offers would be most effective?
- **Optimization and prediction:** What parts of my site should I test? What products should I order now to match sales forecasts?

Many other questions can be asked to help guide and drive business performance; ecommerce analytics leads to asking a lot of questions. The analysis of ecommerce is complex not only because it crosses both business and technology, but also because it is on the forefront of digital experience and innovation. The site, mobile, and connected ecommerce experiences online in 2016 are innovative, fast, personalized, contextual, and powerful for guiding us to the right product, at an appealing price, and then leading us through a purchasing process that is easy and frictionless. But in certain cases, the opposite is true. Ecommerce sites and experiences have many opportunities to improve. They may be hard to navigate or may make it difficult to find product information. The trustworthiness of the site may be in question. The experience of selecting products, adding them to the cart, and stepping through the shipping and payment pages may be problematic, confusing, or in the worst case dysfunctional for the device or browser the person is using. In addition, the people working at ecommerce companies may largely be unaware of these problems because they aren't getting timely, complete, and relevant data and analysis to help improve the experience and increase conversion. Or ecommerce stakeholders might be suspicious of experiential or customer issues but can't prove them using data. Or there's the worst case, where no set of unified resources, technologies, or analytics team exists to help stakeholders. What's missing at these companies that aren't taking full advantage of the information and insights in their data is solid, focused ecommerce analysis that helps business stakeholders do their jobs better. Whether that job is to merchandise the site, improve the user experience, drive customer acquisition, increase conversion, manage orders and fulfillment, or maximize customer profitability and shareholder value, ecommerce analytics can be a successful competitive advantage.

This book was written to help both new and experienced analysts succeed with ecommerce analytics. It was also written with the understanding that people who work at ecommerce companies in non-analytical roles, or who are simply interested in the topic, may read this book. Thus it is structured to guide the reader into the topic by first reviewing ways to think about doing ecommerce analytics as part of what I call a "value chain." Methods and techniques for doing analysis are discussed in detail for both the new reader and experienced analyst. Reporting, dashboarding, and data visualization for ecommerce are explored. Data modeling is reviewed, including a discussion about dimensions, facts, and metrics. Several chapters are dedicated to detailing the what, why, and how of useful types of ecommerce analysis executed for marketing, advertising, behavior, customers, merchandising, orders, and products. The sciences of conversion optimization and attribution are discussed. Guidance on building effective and high-performing teams is provided. Data governance, security, and privacy of ecommerce data and what the future holds for ecommerce analytics are deliberated. The comprehensive scope of this book offers an experienced practitioner's perspective and viewpoint into ecommerce analytics across multiple dimensions: business, management, technology, analytics, data science, and the ecommerce domain. Although more content and detail can always be added in future volumes, the broad and ambitious subject matter discussed is unprecedented. This book offers a view into ecommerce analytics that hasn't before been consolidated nor unified into one source. Whether you read this book as a standalone text or in combination with my other books, *Building a Digital Analytics Organization* and *Digital Analytics Primer*, you will develop and enhance your understanding of ecommerce analytics, the business and competitive opportunities it enables, and how to use analytics to take advantage of them.

2

The Ecommerce Analytics Value Chain

Achieving successful analytical outcomes requires thinking of analytics as a value chain. In my book *Building a Digital Analytics Organization*, I postulate a phased approach to doing analytics, which I called "the Analytics Value Chain." I suggested this concept to describe, in a simple way, how to think about the nature of analytical work from a managerial perspective. The value chain suggests a way to abstract an activity-based categorization of what is generally required, in most cases but not all, to do professional analytical work. The value chain answers the question, "What activities does my analytics team need to do to ensure quality analytical output and outcomes?" The value chain envisions analytics as a set of phases that suggest a logical flow for executing analytics work. The phases can be recursive—and you can enter a phase based on your capability level. These activities in the value chain can occur in a linear sequence or non-sequentially. Each activity could be carried out by an analyst, the analytics team, or a supporting team. Companies are likely to be simultaneously working in one or more of the phases to execute analytics work in any project—especially in globally distributed companies that have matrixed organizations working on multiple concurrent projects or that have different teams executing analytical activities. As such, the value chain phases support one another by providing the input necessary for the next phase to continue. What's important to understand about the value chain is it suggests a starting point to begin or points of entry to continue analytical work. It was created to help analysts, managers, and leaders who are building or running analytical teams to understand what to do to execute and to increase maturity when building a team or capability. The Analytics Value Chain is summarized into the following phases:

- **Understanding what to analyze:** The first phase requires gathering business requirements and goals, understanding the current data environment and the data within it, and developing a plan to execute work.

- **Collecting and verifying data:** The second phase involves determining if data is available and accurate and, if not, making it so. This work generally involves data engineering and implementing new data collection, data models, or databases. Data governance and master data management are implemented.

- **Dashboarding, reporting, and verifying:** The third phase is when dashboards, reports, and other artifacts that show data are created, verified, and made available.

- **Analyzing, communicating, and socializing:** During the fourth phase, the team analyzes data beyond the creation of reports and dashboards. Business questions are answered. Insights are generated. Analysts talk to stakeholders, meet with them, and ensure they understand the analysis. Narratives and stories are constructed and presented for discussion.

- **Optimizing and predicting:** The fifth phase is when the "data science" occurs and advanced analytical methods are applied and used to predict what could happen and recommend what should be done next.

- **Demonstrating economic value:** The sixth phase is when the analytical outcomes are gathered, and the business impact is quantified financially. The value of the analytics team and work is demonstrated by showing how it increased revenue or reduced cost.

The value chain represents the specific phases and work performed by an analytics team. It suggests the types of activities that managers want to align with when building organizations. It applies to ecommerce analysis because it is generalized in nature and at a high level. For ecommerce analytics, the value chain can be made even more specific because of the targeted nature of the ecommerce work. Thus, in this book, I suggest a new Analytics Value Chain: the Ecommerce Analytics Value Chain, which represents the phases suggested to deliver analysis in ecommerce environments. The phases of the

Ecommerce Value Chain expand and incorporate the overall analytics value chain previously described. The phases in the Ecommerce Analytics Value Chain are as follows:

- **Identifying and Prioritizing Demand** requires the analyst to determine the business questions, requirements, and goals to define a set of projects that can be prioritized based on financial impact, resourced, and then executed and delivered.

- **Developing an Analytical Plan** enables the analyst to document details specific to the projects and define the analytical approach to delivering against the business objectives.

- **Activating the Analytics Environment and Collecting and Governing Data and Metadata** refers to deploying, using, managing, and maintaining infrastructure, technology, and tools and the governance of data within those systems and architectures.

- **Preparing and Wrangling Data** provides the analyst the opportunity to clean data and ready it for analysis.

- **Analyzing, Predicting, Optimizing, and Automating with Data** involves using applied methods, data science, and advanced techniques.

- **Socializing Analytics** enables the analyst to communicate answers to business questions, including conclusions, recommendations, insights, actions, and next steps.

- **Communicating the Economic Impact of Analytics** proves that the outcomes of the analysis created quantifiable business value.

Identifying and Prioritizing Demand

Analytics is done for an audience of business stakeholders who operate across multiple lines of business and have different needs and requirements to do their jobs. For example, you may be tasked with creating analysis for the merchandising team, or you may be tasked with delivering analysis for the marketing team. In still other cases, the main thrust of analytical activities may be around the finance team. The audience of stakeholders who require analytical work can be as numerous as the different titles in an organization. That is why, in order to successfully deliver ecommerce analysis, you must identify the most important demand for your work so that you have the highest impact to your organization. Analysts must be tied to the business goals and questions, so it's important to identify what those are. These areas of important analytical interest are generally not defined by the analyst, but the analyst must identify them by extracting them from the minds of stakeholders. In other words, you can't simply hire an analyst; give her access to tools, data, and resources; and then expect her to fully deliver value. Although it is definitely possible for an analyst to deliver value-generating analysis when asked to simply "come up with it," that isn't the best way to operate. Companies that use data to inform operations and drive critical decision making initiate analytical demand in a different way. They have analysts who work with stakeholders to identify what needs to be done. They work with stakeholders to define the business goals, questions, and concerns they want to solve for using data. And then they prioritize them and execute based on maximum business impact. That means that the projects that help the company succeed financially get done. That is why, in the Ecommerce Analytics Value Chain, the first step is initiating and prioritizing demand to ensure analytical work is creating value and not overhead.

Demand is the work required to execute the projects people want the analytics team and analysts to perform for them. Consider demand to be the business requirements that frame an analytical project or request. For analysts to do their jobs, the demand for analytics needs to be communicated as a work activity that centers on answering a business question. When an analyst elicits business questions from stakeholders, the questions can be deconstructed into business requirements. The requirements can be aggregated into projects (or epics or stories). The business impact of those projects should be financially understood and prioritized by maximum impact, and then resources (the supply) can be allocated to support the team, and the work executed and delivered. Take, for example, a merchandising executive who asks the analytics leader to answer the business question "What brands should I merchandise to in order to maximize profit?" From this question, it is possible to begin to frame what the business requirements for analysis are. And then a project can be created named "The Merchandising Brand Analysis." When thinking about this analytics demand, first, it's clear that the domain of the analysis will be around merchandise and brands and their products, margins, and discounts. It will be important in this analysis to understand the cost, retail price, sales prices, discounts applied, and the margin for each brand (and perhaps each product sold within each category for each brand). It's also clear that this analysis will require a historical understanding and synthesis of past performance. It will also require a prediction about the budget allocation across the brands discovered and analyzed. These fundamental elements of an analysis are easily teased out of a business question. It is harder to tease out business requirements if a merchandising stakeholder simply says, "Tell me what brands to buy."

Starting the analytical process with an understanding of demand is crucial. Detailed business questions can be used to frame business requirements that can be formed into projects. Make sure that business stakeholders who request analytical work define some detailed business questions before the analytics team begins any work. These questions must relate to financial concerns and be answerable with existing analytical data and team capabilities. If you don't do this, you will be unlikely to succeed. It sounds simple, right? But getting people to provide detailed, explicit, and relevant business questions is not as easy as it sounds. People might not understand the data, have the time, nor want to commit to knowing the answer. However, it is definitely possible to do. Start by asking your ecommerce analytics stakeholders for one of the top-five or top-ten business questions that they answer for which data is required as part of that answer. Write them down. Elaborate on the details with the business stakeholders. It may be necessary to reframe their original question and ask them to improve the business question. By following this guidance, you will soon have a list of business questions that are agreed upon from key stakeholders that you can use to identify demand, understand the requirements of the demand, group it into projects, prioritize the business impact, resource the demand, and then execute and deliver it. The next step for delivering on the demand is developing an analytical plan for each project that is specific and detailed enough to act on. In fact, that is the next step in the Ecommerce Analytics Value Chain.

Developing an Analytical Plan

An analytical plan is a written document that identifies the analytical approach that you or your team will execute in order to deliver an analytics project that answers business questions. The plan provides information to key stakeholders that synthesizes their business challenges, goals, questions, and requirements. The plan then reviews what analysis is going to be performed, the purpose of the analysis, the data to be used, the models to be applied, the audience for the analysis, the timeline for delivery, and more detail and information as necessary. By creating an analytical plan, you define your future work in a formal artifact that is referenceable, traceable, and actionable. After your plan has been socialized, agreed upon, and signed off on, you have a mandate to execute the work.

Although it can be argued that the creation of a detailed analytical plan increases the time it takes to produce analysis, a clear plan can actually reduce the time to deliver successful analysis. Just as a clear statement of work in the consulting industry frames the expected delivery effort and deliverables, so does the analytical plan for an analytics project. An analytical plan does the following:

- **Demonstrates a rigorous commitment to a systematic, scientific** approach by starting with a question, articulating a hypothesis, and explaining the logical approach and timeline for the analysis to be performed.

- **Lists the business questions to be answered and the data set to be examined** in a formal, structured way, such as a bulleted list or descriptive table. The goal of the list of questions is to ensure the right frame for the future data analysis.

- **Provides a high-level, yet transparent road map, for the analytical work.** The plan should suggest the objectives, data, resources needed, technology required, capabilities achieved, and the timelines for doing so.

- **Defines the analytical objectives and the decisions made to deliver them.** The objective cited in the analytics plan should tie back to financial impact—and should list the reasons why stakeholders chose these objectives as important.

- **Aims to be objective** by not introducing bias or opinion into the plan. The goal is to be consultative and helpful with analytical work. You might know the answer already or think the work request is not helpful. Although those conclusions and feelings are helpful and should be explored with fellow analysts, the analytical plan sticks to the facts and is objective. It shouldn't be politicized.
- **Provides a centralized artifact for focusing work as the work progresses.** Some analytics teams will continue to update an analytical plan as work commences, as sprints ensue, and as decisions are made that change the scope or objectives of the work. Important decisions that impact analytics documented in a formal project management plan may be cross-referenced or cited in the analytics plan.

Before creating an analytical plan, you need to consider the following:

- What is the business question?
- What is the business impact and how will it be financially qualified?
- What is the purpose of the analysis for the business question?
- What is the timeline?
- What analyses will be provided?
- What resources are available in terms of people and technology?
- How large is the total data set or sets?
- What types of data are available?
- Who is the audience and who are the stakeholders?
- What is the best way to deliver analysis to the audience?
- How will the audience judge the effectiveness of the analysis?

An analytical plan may contain the following:

- Business question(s) and hypotheses about potential answer(s)
- The purpose of the analysis
- The sources of data and the specific data sets you want to use

- The way you will integrate data
- Business rules used to include and/or exclude data about the analysis
- Specific key data elements to be used as variables in the analysis
- An indication of the type of analytical method that may be used

The ultimate goal of the analytical plan is to communicate the answers to questions like these in order to present the plan to stakeholders so they approve it. The plan shows that you understand the business goals and know what to do. Keep in mind that in almost all cases, the analytical plan should communicate the approach to analysis and how the work will be delivered, why, and for whom, and what the outcomes could be (Guest 2011).

Activating the Ecommerce Analytics Environment

Activating the analytics environment means ensuring that the right systems, infrastructure, architecture, tools, and technology are in place to succeed with analytical work. Although many readers will already be working in a company that has figured out (or at least attempted to create) the best possible technology to build the ecommerce site, fewer companies have built solid ecommerce analytics environments. Certainly the big companies in the category, such as Amazon, eBay, Zappos, and others, appear to have strong analytical capabilities—from customer research, to digital analytics, to site optimization and testing, to data science and predictive analytics. They have set up the appropriate analytics environment to accomplish their business goals. The analytics environment can be simply defined as *the set of tools and technologies, including the underlying systems architecture and infrastructure, that analysts use to analyze data and communicate analysis.*

The distinction between what is a tool and what is a technology is arguable. For purposes of this book, tools are what analysts use hands-on, and technologies support the function of tools. Similarly, architecture is the conceptual model of the way tools and technology are structured to support analysis. The infrastructure includes the underlying systems, such as storage or servers, that are part of the architecture and that support the tools and technology. These distinctions will vary by how a company envisions the role of the analytics team. What is a technology to a team of nontechnical data analysts may be a tool for more technical or engineering-minded analysts and data scientists. For example, popular analytics languages such as R or Python are technologies that programmers and data scientists may use to analyze data—but they also populate models that result in output used in tools that less-technical analysts may include as input to focused business analysis. It is understood that the roles and responsibilities assigned to the analytics team dictate what is considered a tool and/or technology. Architecture and infrastructure may be defined, maintained, and controlled by an analytics team or by IT partners. It is not uncommon for companies to have multiple or redundant tools, technology, systems, infrastructure, and architecture within different business units. In larger and older companies, more of this "baggage" exists.

Companies' analytical leaders and analysts must deal with an ever-new emerging set of tools, technology, and techniques for data analysis. As such, the infrastructure must be consistently maintained and enhanced, and the architectures evolved to support new needs. Whether the new requirement is doing analysis in R or Python on data in an RDBMS, a data warehouse, Hadoop, Spark, a cloud database, or some other technology, what's certain is that an analyst will be asked, at some point, to analyze data that may not exist in the current analytics environment. In this case, an analyst will have to activate a new analytics environment or integrate data or functionality into an existing environment to do the work needed to use or deploy new production-ready tools and technology. For a company to make an investment in capital—whether that investment is time, people, or technology—the analyst must take a business-based approach that includes these actions:

- **Defining the technology requirements.** Working alongside technology and business partners, the analyst can help to document functional requirements and expected outcomes, which can be used to frame the technology needed.

- **Justifying the investment.** Typically companies have models derived from financial planning and analysis (FP&A) that can be used to account for the costs, return, and payback period for a technology investment.

- **Bringing the request to IT.** This can be done by formally meeting with leadership and presenting your financially justified and business-necessary requirements for IT investment.

- **Defining required resourcing commitments and expectations.** This means working with leadership, program and project management, and other stakeholders to allocate appropriate human and technical resources to deliver on the project.

- **Allocating investment to build, buy, and maintain.** This can be a decision made at the beginning of an investment request or as a result of new learning once requirements are known. The point here is that the way technology gets created has a financial impact the analyst must consider—and there is a political implication, too. Some companies prefer to buy or build. It's up to you to determine if that preference is suitable for analytics.

- **Building and configuring and testing.** Do this once you have gained the investment, allocated resources, and kicked off the project. This is when the software development lifecycle, whether Agile or waterfall or somewhere between, will be done and aligned with business and analytics teams to deliver.

- **Going live and maintaining and supporting.** This means releasing and communicating the results of the investment and project to the company—and engaging the necessary teams (or your team) to maintain and support what has been delivered. Rollout can also include training and change management.

Elements of an Ecommerce Analytics Environment

The elements of an ecommerce analytics environment are not entirely controlled by the analyst or analytics team. In some cases, the analytics team "owns" it all, and, in many cases, the IT team maintains responsibility with the analyst as a "customer" of IT. Regardless, it is expected that the analysts will understand the environment enough to use it—and if they don't, to learn it. The tools and technologies within an analytics environment will include the following:

- **Data collection** refers to the systematic and technical approach for gathering specific data about ecommerce. This data could be about prospective customers and their behavior, current customers and their behavior, transactions, products, marketing channels, and more.

- **Data sources** are the systems in which data is collected in whatever format it exists: log files, databases, data warehouses, cloud technologies, data lakes, and so on, including the ecommerce platform.

- **Data processing, storage, and virtualization** are important components of building data pipelines that move data from source to analysis. At the time of writing, Hadoop and Spark can be used for big data analytical processing for ecommerce. Other technologies, such as Cloudera Impala, may perform SQL-based analytics when massively parallel processing on Hadoop data. Mahout has favor for machine learning. Giraph has popularity for graph processing. Spark is faster with data that fits in memory, and Hive is better at data that doesn't fit in memory (where Impala may have issues) and is more SQL-compliant.

- **Data administration** includes the tools and technologies that enable technologists to understand the environment in which data is being collected, stored, processed, analyzed, and used by the business. Data administration tools can include technologies for understanding the speed of queries, the queries used and by whom, the load on the server as a result of various operations, and other technologies for operating, cataloging, and working with data.

- **Data querying and data preparation** require tools and technologies that enable analysts to retrieve, write, update, join, and delete data residing in different databases, formats, and systems.

- **Data analysis** tools enable analysts to apply methods to the data in such a way that new information can be discovered. Data analysis tools may have features and functionality that are as simple as listing frequencies, like the top products, or more complex, like automatically clustering customers based on their attributes.

- **Visualization** tools and technologies are used to graphically and visually represent data to illustrate relationships, patterns, and outliers that would be harder to identify or determine looking at raw data or data tables.

- **Presentation** tools are the technologies used for presenting data—from PowerPoint to Prezi to Word and other tools that support narrating and story-telling.

Collecting and Governing Data and Metadata

Modern ecommerce environments have multiple tiers: the Data Tier, the Analytics Tier, and the Integration Tier. Each tier represents a logical grouping of components that provide an important function for creating an ecommerce experience. The **Data Tier** is extremely important for analytics. In this tier are the relational databases, NOSQL components, and other legacy systems that contain data to analyze. Another tier is the **Analytics Tier**, where the in-memory systems and other systems for data analysis reside. These two tiers are enabled by another tier, named the **Integration Tier**. The Integration Tier stitches together the various operational and transactional data so that it can be analyzed. Although the details of the components of a multitiered ecommerce analytics architecture are beyond the scope of this book, it is important for an analyst to have this knowledge to work with IT. A multitiered environment can be helpful for tracking data lineage and defining and working with metadata to ensure that data is secure, searchable, and accurately defined. Managing data by committee, maintaining good data stewardship, and implementing data governance should ensure that ecommerce data remains accurate and useful for the desired purposes over time, fitting well into this multitiered architectural framework.

Preparing and Wrangling Data

Ecommerce data comes in many forms, formats, and markups. It can be structured data like transactions, or semistructured data like log files, or unstructured data like text. In today's distributed environments, all of this data likely exists in separate locations and may often be analyzed in silos. Increasingly, however, ecommerce analysts are being asked business questions that require crossing these different data silos to join data for analysis. Data about marketing, customers, and transactions must be unified together to answer omnichannel business questions or questions across businesses' value chains. Traditionally, the analyst would unify and join data by working with engineers and IT to load new data into a data warehouse or into a standalone database. Today, however, the analyst has many other options, which may not require the need to work with IT or data engineers. Newer technologies for data preparation are available for both business analysts and data scientists. These tools have changed the work analysts do to integrate data together to form new, unified data sets from multiple sources. Employing a data preparation tool, often called a "data wrangling" tool, requires less IT support, engineering, and database expertise after the tool is set to work. As a result, business analysts with little technical expertise can access data and work with it, even in "big data environments" that use Hadoop. The data is replicated, joined together, and made available for analysts to analyze.

The next step in data preparation is for the analyst to use his domain expertise to assess that the new data set is suitable to use for the analytics purpose. Modern data preparation tools guide the analyst by offering methods for cleaning data via visually profiling and examining the data to show distributions, find outliers, identify erroneous or suspicious data, recommend suitable join keys, and so on. As an analyst cleans the data, each step in the cleaning can be recorded as a script, and the script can be reused. The data preparation process, once scripted, can be automated and run again and again, ensuring that the new data set is always ready for use. In other words, you can write instructions (scripts) in data preparation tools that can be reused on similar data sets, thereby reducing the time to prepare similar data in the future.

Thus, one of the responsibilities of the ecommerce analyst in 2016 is to ensure that the data preparation process is sufficient for enabling analysis. Whether the analyst uses a data preparation tool, defers to Excel, or uses other technologies (like R and Python) to clean and prepare data, it is critical to ensure that the data preparation function is understood and resourced with people and technology. That way, the analytics and data science team spends most of its time on generating analysis not on preparing data to do analysis.

Analyzing, Predicting, Optimizing, and Automating with Data

Analysts are required to understand business concerns, work with stakeholders to determine the business questions to answer with data, create an analytical plan, and then execute the plan by doing analytical activities to answer those questions. Of course, to do so, it is implied that the data is sufficient for answering the business question and doing the analysis. If it is not, data needs to be collected within the analytics environment you activated. The type of analytical work to be done may be exploratory, explanatory, confirmatory, or predictive in nature. Exploratory analysis is inductive in nature. During exploratory analysis, the data is observed and explored to understand and explain it, perhaps using descriptive methods, against known premises. Explanatory analysis can be both deductive and inductive in attempting to explain why something happened. Confirmatory analysis seeks to accept or reject a conclusion or pre-conceived idea, hypothesis, or belief. Predictive analysis attempts to identify what could happen given a set of data. It is deductive in nature but may include inductive thinking. Prediction may also lead to "prescriptive" analytics, in which recommendations or suggestions about the best course of action to take based on prediction are determined. Optimization is analysis that attempts to improve the current performance of a goal, often revenue-related. In many cases, optimization (and other types of analysis) can be automated. Take, for example, personalized landing pages that are automatically created based on a prediction of a user's preference or propensity as inferred from already-collected data about the products he or she purchased.

When data is available, an analyst may look at data already collected and provide a viewpoint on that data, hopefully answering the business question and communicating helpful insights to stakeholders. This type of descriptive analysis will answer "What has happened?" or "What is happening?" In other cases, business questions may require the use of predictive analytics to answer "What will happen?" or "What is likely to happen?" In ecommerce environments where recommendations are actively being made, the use of prediction as an input to prescriptive analytics answers the question "Given what I know, what choice should I make?" Prescription occurs when products are recommended and up-sells and cross-sells are made. Regardless of the type of analysis or the work required, the majority of analyst time should be spent producing analysis and working with and communicating to stakeholders, not cleaning data and being concerned about technology. The value in analytics is created by analyzing data and helping people make decisions and create digital experiences based on data. There isn't much value in analytics technology without business-focused analysis, so concentrate on creating analysis, not only on technology. Companies must focus on having analysts produce analysis as an outcome and not having analysts (or IT people named analysts) working with technology.

Socializing Analytics

The best and most helpful ecommerce analysis is useless unless it is socialized and shared with key stakeholders. Thus, a critical objective for analysts is to set up the right opportunities to socialize analysis. It's always a good idea to set up a regular cadence of analytical review meetings with the different lines of business and stakeholders who depend on your analysis or want your data. These meetings provide the important opportunity to gather business requirements, refine existing requirements, decide or clarify scope, update on demand or supply issues, and ensure work alignment. Analysis can also be socialized directly within analytics environments via collaboration features such as chat rooms, threaded discussion, and direct messages. But the most powerful collaboration in analytics comes from people in the same room reviewing data together and agreeing on the decisions to be made based on the data. Some companies even set up entire "analytics rooms," where large screens allow workers to explore dashboards and work directly with analytics teams to explore data and product analysis. Other companies set regular weekly, biweekly, or monthly meetings between the analytics team and lines of business. Office hours, where analysts carve out time to be available to stakeholders, is another method. It is common for companies to create intranet sites, help desk queues, or, less commonly, call center support for analytics.

Regardless of how you choose to socialize analysis, the key is that you continue to socialize it. Remember that unless people perceive the output of analytics teams as helpful and important, no matter how awesome you think your analysis is, it is meaningless. The positive perception of stakeholders about the helpfulness and support of analytics is enabled through socialization and talking to people. You can't sit in your office and send spreadsheets, emails, and links to dashboards. You need to talk to people, answer their questions, and build a consultative relationship with them. If you successfully socialize analysis so that people come to you and have a perception of satisfaction in your analytical work, then you have succeeded. Your clever fat-tailed autoregressive model is overhead, unless someone perceives it as valuable and acts on it. Socialize to survive, analysts!

Communicating the Economic Impact of Analytics

Analysts must demonstrate the financial impact that their work has had on the business. This impact must be quantified by understanding the decisions made, actions taken, risks mitigated, pitfalls avoided, and opportunities taken as a result of the analysis. An analyst can quantify the financial return on analytics in various ways:

- **Log the actions taken and decision made as a result of analysis.** The analyst can keep a running log of actions and decisions made by stakeholders and the estimated financial impact.

- **Ask business stakeholders to estimate the financial impact.** Stakeholders can be asked to identify how analytical work has helped them and to financially quantify the impact.

- **Track the revenue or cost data and resulting derivatives, such as margins.** Simply tracking the cost reduced or revenue generated when the business acts on analysis is another method. For more automated ecommerce processes, in which data is used like recommendations for up-sell or cross-sell, the recapture of revenue from abandoned shopping carts, or the lift in terms of conversion or revenue from personalization and optimization, tools may report the financial impact. For example, conversion testing tools will report metrics like the "average revenue per user" or "average order value" for each test and then identify the best performers.

- **Use a financial model for capital budgeting, like Net Present Value (NPV) or Internal Rate of Return (IRR).** Business models that are financially rigorous may have been used in your analytical plan (or not). The end of a project is a good time to revisit and tune these models to reflect reality. Capital budgeting models quantify financial impact against the investment made, and discount the financial return by a reasonable cost of capital (the hurdle rate or weighted average cost of call, WACC). The benefit of using a financial model is that it can be compared against other enterprise projects and its output will be understood by executives.

As you continue to read this book, keep in mind the Ecommerce Analytics Value Chain and the phases and activities within it. The value chain emphasizes business understanding, stakeholder alignment and technical sophistication, and analytical propriety. It requires data governance and quality and focuses on analytical excellence. It suggests, and even requires, communication and socialization and tangible proof of financial return from analytical activities. As an abstraction of the type of work that ecommerce analysts and ecommerce analytics teams perform on their own and with supporting teams, this conceptual framework will be helpful for putting into context the other chapters in this book.

3

Methods and Techniques for Ecommerce Analysis

This chapter reviews several concepts that are useful for applied analysis of ecommerce data. The review here is at a higher level focused on an audience that has had an introductory level of exposure to analytical concepts, such as data visualization and mathematical and statistical methods. It's written for analysts and those who are analytically inclined and want to learn more about how to analyze data. The analyst should be producing and communicating helpful analysis that creates value by helping people make better decisions. This chapter discusses some of the methods for doing so by:

- Overviewing past and current academic theory on analysis, which is useful and applicable to ecommerce analysis
- Discussing the techniques for examining and interrogating data after it has been extracted from sources using tools
- Reviewing important and helpful data visualizations for applying to ecommerce data
- Providing a high-level review of useful statistical data mining and machine learning techniques for data analysis

By the end of this chapter, you should have confirmed and expanded your knowledge on the fundamentals of analysis and the techniques and methods applied in many types of ecommerce analysis.

Understanding the Calendar for Ecommerce Analysis

Ecommerce analysis frequently involves comparing data across different time periods. Time series data is common. Stakeholders want to know how sales and margin compare to last week, last month, last year, and so on. Day over day (DoD), week over week (WoW), month over month (MoM), quarter over quarter (QoQ), and year over year (YoY) are standard comparisons. Seasonal periods and the impact of seasonality is necessary to track and measure when analyzing ecommerce. Unfortunately, comparing time periods in ecommerce isn't as simple as it seems. The same numerical day from last year does not occur on the same day of the week. For example, July 4, 2016 occurs on a Monday, but July 4, 2015 occurred on a Saturday. Thanksgiving may always occur on the fourth Thursday in November, but the holiday is on a different numerical day. Cyber Monday is always the same day of the week, but it is infrequently on the same numerical day. The National Retail Federation (NRF) realized that data comparisons could be problematic and invented a retail calendar. The NRF calendar eliminates the problem of confused date range comparisons because it standardizes the way weeks are counted and thus compared. It's called a 4-5-4 calendar. For ecommerce analytics, the adoption of the National Retail Federation's 4-5-4 calendar is a common, though entirely voluntary, industry practice. It is especially useful for companies that also operate traditional retail businesses offline and also online.

The 4-5-4 calendar divides the year into months based on 4-week months, then 5-week months, then 4-week months. It solves for the problem of weekend days (Saturday and Sunday) through division into standard week increments. The NRF calendar aligns holidays so they can be compared across time. It also ensures that the same number of weekend days occurs during each month. In this way, time can be compared accurately. Fluctuations and changes in data aren't misinterpreted or misunderstood simply by date confusion. This calendar also accounts for leap-year changes and what is known as the "53rd week," occurring in 2017.

Storytelling Is Important for Ecommerce Analysis

At the end of the day, being successful with analysis involves more than just technology, data, reports, dashboards, and applied methods. The analytical deliverable, whatever that is, needs to be understood sufficiently by stakeholders. Communication creates understanding, and storytelling creates understanding of communication. In fact, narrating a compelling story to stakeholders about what the data tells you or is being used to do is one of the last steps in the delivery of analysis. Use stories to communicate the answer to a business question. Keep in mind that the applied methods and techniques discussed in this chapter may be interesting to analysts, but other businesspeople may have a low tolerance for new, unfamiliar, or difficult concepts. I once had a colleague tell me she writes her analysis so that a 12-year-old or her grandmother could understand it. The takeaway is that the story and the way you deliver the message behind the analysis may in fact be more important to successful outcomes than the techniques or data.

Keep in mind that if you present analysis that in any way differs, changes, or presents a perspective different than is commonly understood or if your analysis shows business performance in any way that is not positive, it is likely that your data and analysis will be challenged. The analyst must ensure that analysis is presented in the most humanistic way possible focused on organizational behavior, motivation, and human emotion. Storytelling is an inherently human activity, so communicating narratives is a natural way for people to understand things. Thus, instead of blasting up data only with numbers and slides with charts and graphs, fancy PowerPoints, and glitzy data visualizations—which are all important—also make sure to weave a narrative through the data to tell a story about what the data says. Do not make the mistake of presenting only data and visualizations. Tell stories with the data. It's easy to say "tell stories." It's harder to do. Some people invent pretend characters to represent customers and internal and external actors. Others use personas or customer segments as the basis for storytelling.

Following are several guidelines for use when forming a story to tell from data. Consider applying these techniques when socializing analysis in the form of story-based narratives:

- **Identify why the analysis has occurred and why the story you are about to tell is important.** Businesspeople are incredibly busy and require context for reporting and analysis. Explain why they should care.

- **Indicate the business challenge you want to discuss and the cost of not fixing it.** By clearly stating what business issue catalyzed the analysis and framed the recommendations, you can eliminate confusion.

- **Identify any forewarnings.** If there are any errors, omissions, caveats, or things to discuss, clearly indicate them in advance.

- **Depersonalize the analysis by using fictional characters to help humanize the data you are reporting.** Using fictional characters helps to depersonalize analysis and lowers political risk. Aliasing scenarios and abstracting eliminate the risk of offending a specific stakeholder or group.

- **Cite important events that help to illustrate a narrative.** Annotating externalities and things that happen in the business as the data is collected or when the behavior occurs can help to clarify analysis.

- **Use pictures.** They are worth a thousand words. And they can save you time explaining concepts in writing. Charts, graphs, trend lines, and other data visualization techniques are helpful.

- **Don't use overly complex, wonky vocabulary.** Esoteric and scientific vocabulary is best left within the analytics team. No one will really be impressed if you use words like *stochastic*. It really means "random." Try to make the communication and presentation of analysis as simple as possible.

- **Identify what is required.** Clearly indicate what you think needs to be done in written language using action-oriented verbs and descriptive nouns. Say what you think and what you want to do.

- **Identify the cost of inaction.** Clearly indicate the financial impact of doing nothing and compare it against the cost of doing something. It may help to present comparable costs from other alternatives.

- **Conclude with a series of recommendations that tie to value generation (either reduced cost or increased revenue).** Although you may not be an expert at the same level as the person requesting the analysis, analysts should express their ideas and perspective on the data and business situation. Recommendations should be made that are clearly and directly based on data analysis—and these recommendations must be able to withstand the scrutiny and questions.

Tukey's Exploratory Data Analysis Is an Important Concept in Ecommerce Analytics

John Tukey authored the (in)famous book *Exploratory Data Analysis* in 1977 and was the first person to use the term "software" and the word "bit" or "binary digit" in the modern lexicon.

Exploratory data analysis (EDA) is more of a mind-set for analysis than an explicit set of techniques and methods; however, EDA does make use of several of the techniques contained in this chapter. Tukey's philosophy on data was one that favored observation and visualization and the careful application of technique to make sense of data. EDA is not about fitting data into your analytical model; rather, it is about fitting a model to your data. As a result, Tukey and EDA created interest in non-Gaussian and non-parametric techniques in which the shape of data indicates that it is not normally distributed and may have a fat head with a long tail. The idea of the long tail is a Pareto concept that Tukey probably would have favored for understanding big data. After all, some ecommerce behavioral data is not normally distributed, so using basic statistics that expect a normal distribution would not be optimal.

The reason Tukey is referenced in this text is not only because he has been hugely influential in using mathematics and statistics to understand what the data is saying, but because his paradigm for data analysis is based on a set of philosophies or tenets that involve data visualization, pattern analysis, contextual understanding, hypothesizing, and simply looking at the data. Tukey recommends the following:

- **Visually examining data to understand patterns and trends:** Raw data should be examined to learn the trends and patterns, which can help frame what is possible using analytical methods.

- **Using the best possible methods to gain insights into not just the data, but what the data is saying:** Tukey espouses getting beyond the data to what the data is saying in the context of answering your questions. This approach is integral to ecommerce analytics.

- **Identifying the best performing variables and model for the data:** Ecommerce analytics is ripe with so much data, but how do you know what is the right data to use to solve for? EDA helps ascertain what is important.

- **Detecting anomalous and suspicious outlier data:** Digital data has outliers and anomalies that in and of themselves may be important or just random noise.

- **Testing hypothesis and assumptions:** The idea of using insights derived from data to make changes within digital experience is crucial to EDA.

- **Applying and tuning the best possible model to fit the data:** Predictive modeling and analysis can benefit from an EDA approach.

Tukey's principle helps to simplify the creation of analysis because it first emphasizes the visual exploration of the data instead of first applying statistical methods to the data.

The philosophy of EDA is aligned with ecommerce analysis. One of the first things an analyst may do when examining a data set is to identify key dimensions and metrics and use analytical software to visualize the data before applying any statistical method. This way, the analyst can use pattern-recognition abilities to observe the data relationships and unusual data movements to focus his or her work. Then after taking a look at the data, determine how to analyze it and apply the appropriate analytical model and method. Tukey's EDA approach (or modality) to data analysis can be used separately or with other analytical techniques. EDA can be used in combination with other, perhaps more well-known, modalities for understanding data, such as classical statistics and Bayesian methods. Fortunately, all three modalities for data analysis provide frameworks for finding insights in data that can be applied to ecommerce analytics. EDA, however, imposes less formality than either classical or Bayesian approaches. This flexibility is helpful when analyzing all the different types of ecommerce data.

EDA advocates that you look at the data first by plotting a data visualization and then analyzing the data using the best possible techniques for that data, which may be classical or Bayesian. Classical statistics, unlike EDA, would first instruct the analyst to fit the data to the preferred model, perhaps trimming data to make them fit. A Bayesian approach is an extension of the classical approach in which you would first look at prior data. EDA recommends creating data visualizations first before selecting a model or reaching any conclusive insights. Classical and Bayesian analysts would likely view data visualization as a supporting artifact created during or after analysis (not as the first step to start an analysis). EDA would consider Gaussian and non-Gaussian techniques equally valid based on the data and would encourage the analyst to explore the data and make simple conclusions based on useful visualizations. The advanced applied analysis in EDA comes after the simple conclusions.

When conducting digital analysis, keep classical, Bayesian, and EDA approaches in mind and remember what Tukey said. The following is a short suggestion of exploratory data analysis from Tukey:

> *It is an attitude AND a flexibility AND some graph paper (and transparencies, or both).*
>
> *No catalogue of techniques can convey a willingness to look for what can be seen, whether or not anticipated. Yet this is at the heart of exploratory data analysis. The graph paper and transparencies are there, not as a technique, but rather as recognition that the picture-examining eye is the best finder you have of the wholly unanticipated.*

Types of Data: Simplified

Data typing is a useful concept. *Data type* refers simply to the types of data that an analyst runs into in the ecommerce world. My goal here is to not overwhelm you with complexity nor confuse you with unusual and uncommon words. Data type doesn't refer to the common computer science and engineering terms (integers, Boolean, floating point, and so on). I review that, lightly, in Chapter 5, "Ecommerce Analytics Data Model and Technology." Instead, what I describe here is a simple way to understand data types and data subtypes in a practical business-focused way for ecommerce analysis:

- **Quantitative data:** Data that is numeric. The data is a number, such as 2 or 2.2 whole or floating-point integers, in engineering parlance. Quantitative data can be further subdivided into these types:
  - **Univariate data:** Like the prefix "uni," this data type deals with one single variable. The analyst uses this variable to describe the data to stakeholders using methods to examine distribution, central tendency, dispersion, and simple data visualization techniques like box plots. A question of univariate data might be "How many unique visitors have we had on the site by month for the past 24 months?"
  - **Bivariate data:** The prefix "bi" means "two"; thus this data type deals with two variables. The analyst uses these variables to explain the relationship of one to another. The method's uses include correlation, regression, and other advanced analytical techniques. A question of bivariate data might be "What is the relationship between marketing spend and product purchases?"
  - **Multivariate data:** This data type covers data that has more than two variables. Many advanced analytics techniques, from multiple linear regressions to automated tested, targeting, and optimization algorithms and technologies, use multivariate data. Most if not all analytics systems create multivariate data. Big data is multivariate data.
- **Qualitative data:** Data that is not numerical but text-based. Traditionally, qualitative data could be pass/fail (P/F) or

multiple choices (A, B, C, D) or text-based, verbatim answers derived from market research.

Quantitative and qualitative data can further be divided into sub-types such as these:

- **Discrete data:** Data that can be counted separately from each other; for example, the number of unique customers.

- **Nominal data:** Data in which a code or variable is assigned as a representation. Nominal data can be quantitative or qualitative; for example, using Y or N to represent whether a particular marketing campaign was profitable.

- **Ordinal data:** Data that can be ranked and has a ranking scale attached to it. For example, Net Promoter Scores and the star rating on a mobile application are examples of ordinal data.

- **Interval data:** Data that is based on two points; where the count starts does not matter. Interval data can be subtracted and added but not divided or multiplied; for example, the recency of two distinct segments of data (as expressed in days).

- **Continuous data:** Data that can take any value with a specific interval; for example, the amount of time customers spend on a mobile device on weekdays compared to weekends. Or the size over time of your web site's home page.

- **Categorical data:** Data that is, as the name implies, represented by categories. Think of search categories, inventories, taxonomies, and other classification systems that need to be represented in analysis; for example, the brands and products in your product catalog.

The reality in ecommerce analytics is that an analyst runs into each type of data often when solving for the same business problem. Take, for example, the analytical project in which a search-referred visitor's online opinion data about a mobile application is joined to his digital behavior. In this case, the search keyword (and related ad group) is known, as is the person's either positive or negative opinion about the relevancy of the digital content to his intent—and the person's behavior that led him to his conclusion. Taking on an analytical challenge like this example requires the analyst to work with multiple data types (and sources).

Looking at Data: Shapes of Data

When first beginning an analysis project, it helps to look at the shape of the data to understand what method may be appropriate. You can use data visualization tools to look at the shape of data. *Data shape* is likely a familiar concept to you due to the popularity of concepts like the bell curve in the normal distribution. A perfect distribution is normally shaped like a bell. In ecommerce reality most data is not perfectly shaped; instead, it is usually skewed *negatively* to the left or *positively* to the right.

At the ends of the distributions, you can find outlier data. Outliers are data values that fall outside of where most of the data is located. The traditional statistics rule is that an outlier is indicated by a data measurement at or more than two standard deviations away from the average. When data has many outliers, they are considered to have *kurtosis* such that the ends of the distribution may be fatter and turn up at the ends. Kurtosis can be mesokurtic (like a normal distribution), leptokurtic (high peak in the middle, flat ends), or platykurtic (low peak and flat ends).

Shape is important when data is analyzed because it is an easy way to immediately infer the type of data and the possible methods or approaches for dealing with the data. For example, if you notice that the shape of your data is Pareto with a long tail, it may not make sense to use a model for normally distributed data. Perfectly symmetrical data would be ideal to work with, but it never exists; thus, analysts attempt to use various techniques to turn skewed data into symmetrical data.

Understanding Basic Stats: Mean, Median, Standard Deviation, and Variance

Ecommerce analytics uses classical statistics, like those taught in business schools throughout the world, to make sense of ecommerce data:

- **Mean or average of the data is understood by mostly everyone.** By summing all the observed values in a data set and dividing by the number of observations, you can calculate the average. Averages are perhaps the most commonly used technique for making sense of data. They can also be one of the most misleading because the mean can be skewed by the outlier data.

- **Median is the term used to describe the middle point in the data.** Stated another way, half of the observations were above the median and half were below. The median basically takes the statistical midpoint in the data. It is the middle of the data set, the median.

- **Mode is the often neglected or forgotten concept.** Generally speaking, mode is the value most frequently in distribution. For example, if 29 out of 50 people got a score of 82 and 21 people got scores that were not 82, then the mode would be 82 (because it is the most frequently occurring value).

- **Standard deviation is a measure of the spread in a data set.** The standard deviation measures the dispersion of the values in the data. For example, if analytics showed that people spent between 3 and 27 minutes on web site A and between 13 and 15 minutes on web site B, then web site A would be considered to have a larger standard deviation because the data is more dispersed.

- **Range is another useful concept used in digital analytics.** It is the measure between the highest and lowest values in a data set. As such, it is highly influenced by outliers. For example, if one month a mobile app has 200,000 downloads and the next month the app has 500,000 downloads, the range would be 300,000 (500,000–200,000).

- **Outliers is a common term in data, measured by an observation in a data set that is equal to or larger than two times the standard deviation.** In real-world practice of ecommerce analytics, some analysts choose to trim outliers from the data set to shape the data for application in the model. Other analysts think this is not correct. In a true EDA-esque approach, outliers may be investigated to determine whether an unusual insight may exist in the outlier. Take the 2016 water crisis in Flint, Michigan. It was reported that the highest lead levels recorded in the town's data set were trimmed, which caused the lead level to fall below the threshold where the town was required to report to the federal government. Now imagine if EDA had been used. The data would not have been trimmed; the federal government may have investigated sooner. Trimming data has real-world implications in practice. Be careful.

Another example of outlier detection is common in the financial services. If a person deposits $1 million into her bank account instead of her usual $10,000 paycheck, the $1 million deposit would be considered an outlier. Banks use outlier data detected by analytics systems as input for targeting and promotional offers. For example, the person's bank may offer a financial instrument for investing those million dollars upon next login. If a customer starts spending more money on your ecommerce site than historical norms indicate, then outlier detection can help you realize it, so you can respond.

These basic statistical concepts are the foundation for understanding how to analyze quantitative data. Make sure to comprehend these concepts and their definitions, and apply them in your ecommerce analysis.

Plotting Ecommerce Data

One of the simplest, lowest risk, quickest, and highest value analytical activities is plotting data. Plotting data is an approach to data visualization. In fact, some of the plots described in this chapter are referred to in the next chapter on data visualization. Plotting data is data visualization, but the goal and purpose can be different. EDA requires plotting data as input to analysis, whereas beautiful data visualizations put into PowerPoints are the output of analysis. By taking the data in raw or detailed form and applying it to a set of coordinates and related visualizations, prior to doing any analysis, an analyst can see what the numbers say. That's core to EDA. In EDA, the graphical interpretation of data is central and primary. EDA requires data visualization at the start of the process, not at the end of an analytical process. In ecommerce analytics, plotting data using the techniques described next can help the analyst identify the best model for analyzing the data. These techniques may reveal outliers and other anomalous data that should be closely investigated as a part of an ecommerce analytical plan. These plots are the block, lag, spider, scatter, probability, and run sequence plot discussed here.

Block Plot

The *block plot* is an EDA tool that attempts to replace the Analysis of Variance (ANOVA) test used in Bayesian statistics. The block plot is a graphical technique that enables the comparison of multiple factors on a particular response across more than one group. Block plots are useful in ecommerce analytics for comparing data generated from testing and experimentation where multiple combinations of elements on a goal are being analyzed.

The block plot can help you determine whether a particular variable impacts your goal and whether the impact is significant. By using a block plot to visually examine the results of testing and experimentation, you can identify the best possible combination of variables meeting a goal and how much current performance may be impacted by the various experiments.

For example, you can use a block plot to visualize the impact of a business plan on an average order value (a common ecommerce metric) where the plot experiments with marketing channel, site speed, time of day, and the user's persona. You can then use the block plot to determine whether the average order value is significantly impacted by the people being exposed to different advertising at different times of the day and the impact of speed.

The block plot helps you quickly identify the impact of your experimentation without using ANOVA or another method. The challenge when trying to employ this basic EDA technique is that most commercial software can't create block plots, so you may need to use data science.

Lag Plot

A *lag plot* is a more complicated type of a scatter plot. It is used for visualizing whether a data set is random (stochastic) or not over a particular lag (time). After all, random data should look random and not actually take any noticeable and definable shape. For example, if you plot data and notice that the lag plot shows data points in a pattern (like a line), you could quickly surmise that the data was linear or quadratic and apply the appropriate analytical method. The lag plot is one easy way to check for randomness—and also notice if any outliers exist in the data. Use a lag plot to check the shape of data and visually inspect it to determine a suitable model to apply for analysis.

You may ask what is the difference between a scatter plot and lag plot? The difference is that the two variables measured in a lag plot are plotted over time displacement. If you don't understand what time displacement means, use a scatter plot.

Spider/Star/Radar Plot

A *spider plot* is a type of plot for multivariate data in which the analyst wants to understand the impact of one variable against others. This visualization can also be called a *star* or *radar plot.* In this plot, each variable is connected by lines between a set of spokes. Each spoke is a variable, and the length of the angle is in proportion to the impact of that variable (against all other variables). As such, the data looks like a star or spider. This type of data plot is especially useful when you compare a number of observations across the same scale. The angles visually demonstrate whether any variables have more of an impact than others and can also help in comparing whether similarities or differences exist when different subjects are compared across the same attributes. Just remember not to use too many variables, or the plot can get messy and unreadable. A spider plot could be used to visualize the performance of a web site. Each geography could be compared by visits, visitors, time spent, and conversion rate. Spokes would be drawn between these dimensions to create different shape per geography. This shape would help to quickly show differences in the data.

Scatter Plot

A *scatter plot* is a fundamental data visualization that quickly helps to show relationships between variables. You would plot one variable and all observations on the x-axis and the other variable and values on the y-axis. Metrics such as conversion rate and dimensions such as marketing campaign and time can be scatter-plotted to reveal relationships, such as linearity or nonlinearity. As with most EDA visualization, the noticeable relationship between the data in the scatter plot can help the analyst understand correlation (visually) and help in selecting the best analytical model to use for analysis. As with other analytical techniques, be careful not to over interpret a correlation noticed in scatter plots.

Probability Plot

The *probability plot* is a powerful EDA technique for determining the type of distribution of your data. For example, it is helpful to know whether you are working with a normal distribution or another non-Gaussian type of distribution. The mechanics and mathematics of creating a probability plot are well beyond the goal of this book; however, probability plots are easy to understand and interpret. The analyst plots each data point in a straight line (or at least attempts to do so)—and any data point that falls outside of the line is considered to not fit the hypothesized distribution based on a correlation coefficient. Because of the flexibility of seeing whether the data fits into the plot (and thus the hypothesized distribution), this technique enables the analyst to run tests on the same data against different distributions. The probability plot with the highest correlation coefficient indicates the best-fitting distribution for the data.

Run Sequence Plot

The *run sequence plot* is among the most common data plots because it is applied to univariate data. That is, an analyst needs only one variable plotted across time to create this simple, but powerful, data visualization. It is the data summarization technique that helps to detect changes in the data. This plot enables a data set to be examined on a common scale and across the distribution to determine outliers, the scale of the data, the location of the data, and the randomness.

The response variable, such as conversion rate, is always plotted on the y-axis.

Four Plots and Six Plots

Four plots and *six plots* are, respectively, sets of four and six EDA techniques for graphically and visually exploring your data. The main difference in the presentation is that a four plot uses the run sequence plot, and the six plot uses scatter plots. The four-plot technique is more frequently associated with univariate data, whereas the six plot is more associated with multivariate data. Both visualizations are in fact useful for ecommerce data. Table 3.1 shows the four- and six-plot techniques.

Table 3.1 Types of EDA Plots

Plot Grouping	Methods
Four Plot	Run sequence, lag, histogram, probability plot
Six Plot	Three scatter plots (independent, dependent, and residuals), lag plot, histogram, probability plot

Histograms (Regular, Clustered, and Stacked)

Histograms are graphical representations that show scale of one or more observations to summarize the data distribution. They help an analyst visually comprehend the spread of a distribution along with its center, skew, and any outliers. Typically, the y-axis shows the measurement and the x-axis shows the variable measured. Histograms are flexible visualizations in that you can custom define both measurements you want to show. Showing more than one measured variable is simple with a histogram because the analyst can create the groupings (called classes) based on their own rules—or using classical statistical methods (such as dividing into ten equal classes).

Histograms show scale on the y-axis and different data on the x-axis based on type. Histograms can be any of the following:

- **Regular histograms** show one or more similar measurements, for example, displaying the count of customers and orders by month for 2016.

- **Clustered histograms** show scale on the y-axis and a grouping of variables along an interval. For example, you may use a clustered histogram to show the count of customers per month acquired by different marketing channels.

- **Stacked histograms** show the components (the detail) in a distribution. For example, you may stack marketing spend by month by campaign.

Pie Charts

Pie charts are an extremely common visualization in data analysis. They are circular and divided into sections such that each section represents a portion of the total measurement. Pie charts do not, however, make all analysts happy. The pie chart is quite disdained as an insufficient or unnecessary technique. Pundits claim that a data table can show, more easily, the slices of pie. A histogram shows the exact same data as a pie chart—these two visualizations are interchangeable. The pie chart starts to get messy and hard to read when divided into more than six sections.

Pie charts are easy to understand and are a common dessert metaphor, which explains their popularity. Everyone understands how to slice up a pie, and it's an easy leap for students and new analysts alike to put their data into this familiar image. Pie charts are of four types:

- **Standard pie charts** are circular and show the proportion to scale of each piece in the total measurement.

- **Expanded pie charts** are where the sections of the pie are dislocated from the entire pie and then shown adjacent in space. By using whitespace to separate sections of the pie, the analyst is visually highlighting the data.

- **New types of pie charts,** such as the *3D pie,* the *pie ringchart,* and the *doughnut chart,* are evolutions of this visualization and have their own parameters and applications that further break down the pie chart to communicate and highlight more data.

- **Harvey Balls** are not actually pie charts according to the traditional definition, but are highlighted because of their similarity of shape. A Harvey Ball uses a hollow, solid, or sectioned circle to communicate information about the applicability of an object to criteria. For example, you could use Harvey Balls to illustrate whether the speed of a web page meets a given threshold.

Line Charts

A *line chart* is a visualization for communicating trends in data that occur, most typically, over time. Because the chronology of experience can be charted using a line, this chart is frequently employed by analysts to show trends and time series. By plotting data points in a distribution and then connecting them with a line, you can communicate the scale and pattern in a trend and the temporality. Outliers, trends, and anomalies can be seen using a line chart. By comparing lines representing the same measure across different intervals, changes in data can be observed. Line charts are created by plotting the measure for which you want to trend on the y-axis, and time on the x-axis.

The "line" in the chart in most cases represents the trend exposed by connecting the data points. In other cases, an analyst may present a line on a chart that "fits" that data. The "best fitting" line when plotted, typically within another type of chart, is meant to show the general trend in a large number of data points where it is not possible to draw a meaningful line by connecting the data points. In these cases, the best-fitting line can be created using many statistical methods, such as linear regression or other methods in which the best-fitting line may not necessarily be a straight line, such as quadratic or exponential techniques.

The most common line charts an analyst will produce are the following:

- *Area charts* are used to show portions of a total or to compare more than one variable across the same measures (generally scale and time). Like the stacked bar, the area chart can be used to show the distribution and movements of sections of data against other sections and the whole.

- *Sparkline charts* are popular because they are so simple to understand, visually powerful, and easy to create. Unlike the standard line chart, the sparkline is never bivariate or multi-variate. It's always univariate. In application, the sparkline is loosened from the "chartjunk" and "infoglut" such as axes, grid-lines, words, and numbers to concisely and quickly communicate a small amount of information.

- *Streamgraph charts* are an evolution of the area chart in which more than one variable is trended across time (or another measure) against some scale. Each "stream" in the graph represents a portion of the total in the same way that a bar in a stacked bar chart represents a portion of the total. The difference in the stream is that the axis is displaced such that the lower and upper bounds of the chart are not limited or trimmed. Each stream touches the bottom of the higher stream and the top of the lower stream.

Flow Visualizations

Flow visualizations have their roots in operational management and other phased processes that result in an outcome. The metaphor of a "flow" is suitable for ecommerce analytics in which customers are coming and going from many channels, on many devices, to many different digital experiences. As these prospects and customers flow through an ecommerce experience, it is important to understand whether the customer is creating value by measuring whether the customer completes the goals you have defined either in one visit or across time. You can read more about flow analysis in Chapter 7, "Analyzing Behavioral Data."

The idea of "flow" should sound familiar to those who already work in the ecommerce industry. One of the most common constructs for representing customer flow is a data visualization that shows the discrete steps in a user's behavior that makes money. Take the well-known notion of the "conversion rate" in which three to five pre-identified steps, such as entry page > search > product page > checkout > thank you page, define the conversion flow on your web site. Customers may not convert when they begin the conversion process, or they may jump between steps, abandon the process, or complete it at a later date via different marketing channels.

To help visually communicate these complex digital experiences and the customer flow over time, the following flow visualizations are useful:

- **Bullet chart:** A bullet chart is a flow data visualization technique whose closest offline analog is a thermometer you might have found in the Austrian Alps in the 1960s. Bullet charts not only display the scale of a univariate observation, but also use color to highlight a qualitative judgment of success and enable plotting a goal. Bullet charts are a type of histogram—and could be categorized as such; however, because they can be associated with a goal and a target; they can also be used to visualize conversion—and thus can be considered flowcharts. By showing multiple bullet charts in an adjacent space, you can illustrate a sequence of steps.

- **Funnel chart:** A funnel chart is a graphical technique for illustrating the sequence of steps that lead to a macro or micro conversion within a digital experience. Funnels can be custom defined to begin at any point in the customer lifecycle. For example, a multichannel funnel may start with exposure > acquisition source > landing page > product page > checkout. A site funnel might simply represent the steps taken to purchase a product or to sign up for a newsletter. Other funnels may be in-page funnels representing the fields a user must fill out to complete an action.

  Funnel charts are often represented linearly such that each step in the funnel immediately occurs sequentially before the others. It is also valid to show a nonlinear, nonsequential funnel in which steps are jumped, skipped, or entered from other parts of the site. The funnel has no formal structure or creation rules except that the last step in the funnel is the conversion point at which value is created. Advanced funnel visualizations, such as those found in some tools, attempt to visually demonstrate funnel linearity and nonlinearity including step-jumping, interpolation, and abandonment in a single chart.

- **Tumbler chart:** A newer concept, which you may be reading about for the first time here, is the Tumbler. The Tumbler expresses flow as a series of step-jumping in and out of various states. In the context of ecommerce, a person goes through the following states: seeking (when they look for a product); shopping (when they buy the product); and sharing (when they talk about the product with other people). The Tumbler is a visualization that shows the flow as people move in and out of these purchasing states.

Analyzing Ecommerce Data Using Statistics and Machine Learning

The next section moves away from the discussion of the philosophy behind and techniques important and helpful to ecommerce analytics—which is exploratory, observational, visual, and mathematical—to a business review of data analysis methods used in today's analytical companies. These quantitative techniques can be applied judiciously to data to answer business questions. Statistics and machine learning are complex topics beyond the technical scope of this book. The quantitative techniques that form the algorithms for advanced analytical tools are numerous and, without a background in statistics, can be esoteric.

When you're executing on an analytical plan, certain techniques exist for understanding the order of the data to determine what is important and represented in a distribution. You can determine whether there is a correlation between two or more data points. An analyst can use tools to automate different types of regression analysis to determine whether certain data can predict other data. The details of distributions and assessments of probability can be calculated. Experimentation can be evaluated, and the hypotheses on the data can be tested to create the best-fitting model for predictive power.

Correlating Data

The statistics adage is that "correlation is not causation," which is certainly true. Correlation, however, can imply association and dependence. The analyst's job is thus to prove that observed associations in data are truly dependent and relevant to the business questions, and ultimately to determine whether the variables caused the relationship determined. Correlation is whether two variables move together. For example, if every time a visitor comes to your site he buys something, you could consider a strong positive correlation between a site visit and a purchase. This insight may lead you to conclude that all a person needs to do is visit a site and he will always buy. Although you might want this relationship to be true, it's more likely that the person has already decided to purchase the item before coming to the site and is just fulfilling his desire. Thus, although the mathematics may show a positive correlation between data, common sense indicates that correlation does not imply causality—and that there is only an association between a site visit and revenue. Thus, there is no true causality, and the conclusion that a site visit always creates revenue would be a specious and arguable conclusion at best.

The most common measure of correlation you find in an analytics practice is a type of correlation named Pearson's correlation. Pearson produces a measurement between 1.0 and −1.0. The closer the measure is to 1.0, the stronger the positive correlation; whereas the closer the measure is to −1.0, the weaker the positive correlation, such that a negative correlation coefficient indicates that the data move in the opposite direction from one another.

In a world of linearity, Pearson's correlation is useful; however, if the data relationship for which you are calculating causality is not linear, Pearson's correlation should not be used because the conclusion based on the measure will be wrong. Test for linearity (using a number of methods) on your data set before using Pearson's correlation. If you determine that the relationships in your data are not linear, the world of statistics has other quantitative methods for determining correlation.

Rank correlation coefficients, instead of Pearson's correlation, can be applied to data sets in which the distribution is not linear. If you use correlation on a set of predicted variables, you can use a partial rank correlation to understand the data. Rank correlation also indicates the relationship in which one variable increases or decreases in proportion to another.

Nonlinear dependent correlation calculations, such as Kendall's and Spearman's coefficient, express the same type of positive or negative data relationship but for non-normal distributions. An analyst, however, should be careful when testing data to determine the correct correlation coefficient. Although it may be possible to substitute a linear correlation measure for a nonlinear correlation measure, these calculations are measuring differently. Such difference needs to be understood in the context of data and explained in your analysis.

Regressing Data: Linear, Logistic, and More

The phrase *regression analysis* means the application of a mathematical method to understand the relationship between one or more variables. In more formal vocabulary, a regression analysis attempts to identify the impact of one or more independent variables on a dependent variable. There are many different approaches to completing a regression analysis based on all sorts of well-known and not-so-well-known methods. The more common methods are based on Bayesian statistics and probability distributions, such as single linear regression and multiple linear regression.

Analytics professionals and the people who ask for analytical deliverables often talk about regression, regression analysis, the best-fitting line, and ways to describe determining or predicting the impact of one or more factors on a single factor or multiple other factors. For example, the impact of various marketing programs on sales may be determined through regression analysis. The most common regression that you see in business is the linear regression. It's taught in business schools worldwide, and many of the widespread spreadsheet and data processing software programs support regression analysis. In the ubiquitous Excel by Microsoft, the complexity of calculating a regression is reduced to a simple expression on a data set.

In ecommerce analytics, the regression analysis is used to determine the impact of one or more factors on another factor. As in formal statistics, regressions in ecommerce analytics have one or more independent variables and at least one dependent variable. In some cases the application of a multiple linear regression analysis is possible with digital data. It is far more likely that one of the other types of regression analysis, such as exponential, quadratic, and logistic regression, is a much better fit for your data. With regression analysis in digital analysis, your mileage can vary due to the interplay of relationships in big data.

Although this book, and particularly this chapter, is not meant to give exhaustive coverage, by any means, of the mathematical principles behind the application of various models to digital data, a true understanding of the application of advanced applied analytical techniques such as regression, ANOVA, MANOVA, and various moving average models requires comprehending the underlying small data.

In the purest form, as explained in the discussion of correlation, the type of distribution impacts the model you select. In true EDA fashion an analyst must first look at each factor proposed to be used in a potential regression analysis. Multicollinearity, kurtosis, and the other shapes and measures of dispersion help the analyst determine whether classic, Bayesian, or nonparametric techniques are the best fit for the data.

For ecommerce data derived from digital experiences, such as the keywords and phrases from search engines to the frequency of purchases of various customer segments, data is most often not normally distributed. Thus, much of the classic and Bayesian statistical methods taught in schools are not immediately applicable to digital ecommerce data. That does not mean that the classic methods you learned in college or business school do not apply to digital data; it means that the best analysts understand this fact. Fortunately, so do the engineers and product managers who create analytical software whose applications assist analysts in preprocessing non-normally distributed data to fit classic methods all the way to applying the best nonparametric model to the data.

The remainder of this chapter discusses frequently mentioned types of regression analysis. It also exposes newer thinking by current academics and gives overviews of techniques that you can explore to understand how to fit your data to a model if you choose to go that route—or if you choose to fit your model to the data. Remember that regression analysis is not appropriate with all types of variables, such as discrete variables for which alternative regression must be used.

Single and Multiple Linear Regression

The underlying math behind simple and multiple linear regression can be studied in detail in books such as *Applied Regression: An Introduction (Quantitative Applications in the Social Sciences)* by

Michael S. Lewis-Beck (August 1, 1980). For the purposes of ecommerce analytics, a simple linear regression is used when an analyst hypothesizes that there is a relationship between the movements of two variables in which the movements of one variable impact, either positively or negatively, the movements of another variable. See the "Correlating Data" section earlier in this chapter for more information.

Multiple linear regression and other forms of regression in which the dependent variable—that is, the variable for which you are predicting—is predicted based on more than one variable are used in ecommerce analytics. Understanding the marketing mix and how different marketing channels impact response is often modeled using multiple logistic regression.

Logistic Regression

Logistic regression predicts a dependent categorical variable based on several independent (predictor) variables. The output of a logistic regression is binomial if only two answers are possible or multinomial if more than one answer is possible. A 0 or 1 may be the result of a binomial logistic regression, whereas an output of "yes," "no," or "maybe" may be the output of a multinomial logistic regression. The predictor variables are used to create a probability score that can be used to help understand the analysis.

Logistic regressions are used frequently in predictive modeling for ecommerce analytics and, particularly, marketing analytics data. The best predictors should be tested for their impact on the model; however, the output is easy to understand. Take, for example, how a logistic regression could be used to segment data into a 1 or 0, in which 1 meant to sell that product online and 0 meant to sell it only in stores. Logistic regression is one type of predictive data analysis.

Probability and Distributions

Observing the shape can help an analyst understand it and select the right analytical method to use on. After all, the way an analyst applies a method to a normal distribution is different from the way an analyst applies a method to a non-normal distribution.

Probability, simply stated, is the study of random events. In analytics you use statistics and math to model and understand the probability of all sorts of things. In ecommerce analytics, you are concerned about probabilities related to whether a person will buy, visit again, or have a deeper and more engaging experience. And using analytics tools, you can count and measure events related to marketing and customer purchasing behavior and patterns. Measures of probability are used to determine whether events will happen and then to help identify or predict the frequency of those events.

Probability analysis in ecommerce analytics can be done mathematically (using existing data) or experimentally (based on experimental design). Simple and compound events occurring discretely or continuously, either independent of or dependent on other events, are modeled in probability.

An ecommerce analyst should be familiar with the following concepts:

- **Modeling probability and conditionality:** Building a model requires selecting (and often, in analytics, creating) accurate data, the dimensions, and measures that can create your predictor variables. Central to the tendency to create models is statistical aptitude and an understanding of measures, probability, and conditionality. *Conditional probability* may sound complicated (and it can be), but the term simply means understanding the chance of a random event after something else has occurred previously (that is, a condition).

- **Measuring random variables:** A random variable is a type of data in which the value isn't fixed; it keeps changing based on conditions. In ecommerce analytics, most variables, whether continuous or discrete, are random. Because the nature of random is not possible in mathematics, random variables are understood as probability functions and modeled as such using the many techniques discussed in this chapter.

- **Understanding binomial distributions and hypothesis testing:** A common way to test for statistical significance is to use binomial distribution when you have two or more values (such as yes or no, heads or tails). This type of testing considers that the null hypothesis is done using Z and T tables and

P-values. The types of test are one-tailed and two-tailed. If you want to understand more than two variables, you would use a multinomial test and go beyond simple hypothesis testing to perhaps chi-squares.

- **Learning from the sample mean:** Measures of dispersion and central tendency (such as those discussed in this chapter: mean, median, mode, and standard deviation) are critical to understanding probability. The sample mean helps you understand the distribution and is subject, of course, to the central limit theorem, which states that the larger the sample population, the more closely the distribution will approximate normal. Thus, when modeling data (especially smaller data sets) the sample mean and the related measures of standard deviation and of variance can help you understand the relationship between variables.

Experimenting and Sampling Data

Experimenting with ecommerce data means changing one element of the experience to a sample of prospects or customers and comparing the behavior and outcomes of that group to a control group who received the expected ecommerce experience. The goal of experimentation is to test hypotheses, validate ideas, and better understand the audience/customer. In reality, though, ecommerce data is not biology, and it is often impossible to hold all elements of digital behavior equal and change just one thing. Thus, experimenting in ecommerce means controlled experimentation.

A *controlled experiment* is an experiment that uses statistics to validate the probability that a sample is as close as possible to identical to the control group. Although the boundaries of a controlled experiment may be perceived as less rigorous than a true experiment in which only one variable changes, that's not actually true because controlled experiments, when performed correctly, use the scientific method and are statistically valid.

The data collected from controlled experimentation is analyzed using many of the techniques explored in this chapter, such as applying measures to understand and work with distributions. The type of data analysis you do on the data can be as multivariate as the experimental data itself; however, controlled experiments typically have the following elements:

- **Population:** The aggregate group of people on which the controlled experiment is performed or for which data already collected is analyzed. The population is divided into at least two groups: the control group and the test group. The control group does not receive the test, whereas the test group, of course, does.

- **Sampling method:** The way you select the people, customers, visitors, and so on for your experiment. It depends on whether you want to understand a static population or a process because different sampling methods are required. Sampling is important because a poorly or sloppily sampled group can give you poor results from experimentation.

  Ultimately, you want to randomly sample your population to create your test group. Every person in your group should have the same probability of being selected as the other. When there is an equal potential for selection in the data, you have created a truly random *sample*.

  You can also break down a population into segments that each have their own attributes you define, for example, all customers who are male, below the age of 30, and make more than $100,000 a year. Breaking down a population by its attributes is called *stratified sampling*.

  When you are measuring processes in ecommerce analytics, such as a conversion process, it is likely that the process will change over time. Thus, you can't hold the population static. In cases like these, in which you analyze a process, you must consider process-based sampling methods, such as systematic sampling.

  In *systematic sampling*, the first datum is chosen randomly; then the next one is chosen based on some algorithm, such as every 25th or 50th or 100th visitor is selected for the test. This type of sample selection method approximates random and incorporates the dimension of time, which, of course, is important in the analysis of ecommerce behavior. An analyst can also look at sampling subgroups. Basically, the analyst finds a common dimension in a set of customers, and then picks the population from various subgroups according to best practices for sample size and at a sampling frequency that creates the necessary sampling size.

- **Expected error:** When analyzing the results of experiments by applying the methods discussed in this chapter, you need to go into your experiment with an idea of the expected amount of error you are willing to tolerate. There are various types of errors (such as type 1 and type 2). Confidence intervals and confidence levels are applied to understand and limit expected error (or variability by chance) to an acceptable level that meets your business needs.

- **Independent variable:** What you are holding static in the population or what is shared among the population or subgroups are the independent variables. Not all of them matter, but some (hopefully) will.

- **Dependent variables:** These are the predicted variables that are the outcome of the data analysis. For example, the conversion rate is a common dependent variable around which experiments in ecommerce analytics are intended to inform.

- **Confidence intervals:** Confidence intervals are commonly stated at 95% or 99%. Other times they could be as low as 50%. The meaning of a confidence interval is generally said to be that "99% of the population will do X or has Y," but that interpretation is incorrect. A better way to think of confidence intervals in ecommerce analysis is that were you to perform the same analysis again on a different sample, the model would include the population you are testing 99% of the time.

- **Significance testing:** This testing involves calculating how much of an outcome is explained by the model and its variables. Often expressed between 10% and 0.01%, the significance test enables you to determine whether the results were caused by error or chance. When this testing is done right, analysts can say that their model was significant to 99%, meaning that there's a 1 in 100 chance that the observed behavior was random.

- **Comparisons of data over time:** Comparisons such as year over year, week over week, and day over day are helpful for understanding data movements positively and negatively over time. Outlier comparisons need to be investigated.

- **Inferences:** What ideas are conceived or what thoughts are generated as a result of the analysis? Inferences are the logical conclusions—the insights—derived by using statistical techniques and analytical methods. The result of an inference could be a recommendation and an insight about the sampled population.

Experimentation in ecommerce analytics is often executed through advanced testing and optimization, which are discussed in more detail in Chapter 8, "Optimizing for Ecommerce Conversion and User Experience."

Three Useful Techniques for Building Models

Here are three useful techniques to use when analyzing complex and large data sets:

- **Discard outliers that you can prove are erroneous:** The common rule in statistics is that an outlier is any data observed to be two times the standard deviation. Techniques like the box plot can help you visualize outliers you have identified by applying descriptive statistical measures. Because outliers can skew data to the left or to the right and generally pull the distribution in one direction or the other, you may want to remove them to focus on the center of the distribution. But be careful! Although this best practice is useful in many cases where erroneous data is found, you don't want to do it in all cases. For example, in ecommerce analytics, if you remove outliers without actually thinking about the implication or knowing they are errors, you may be throwing away the most important data. Remember that there is a chance for outliers and anomalies in data to have meaning! Outliers may be worthy of deeper analysis, but first you need to prove that the outliers were not created by error. Don't just throw out outliers without heavily considering the implication on the analysis—and without having absolute certainty the data isn't an error.

- **Pick the best variables:** In ecommerce analytics, there are so many different data types, dimensions, measures, and values that it can sometimes be overwhelming to determine the best variables. Every variable could be an independent one, so how do you select the right variables? One common approach is to use stepwise regression to determine which variables are best for the model. That being said, stepwise regression is a garbage-in/garbage-out approach. Dimension reduction is becoming a feature in data science tools.

- **Don't overfit models:** Overfitting a model occurs when it becomes too complex by having too many variables. As a result, the output of the model yields questionable results and, in many cases, can produce inaccurate results. When you are creating a model, it is better to be as simple as possible, not as complex as possible. The principle of Occam's Razor should be applied to ecommerce analysis. The idea is that simplicity in analysis creates better outcomes and insights than being complex.

- **Don't let the model dictate the data; let the data dictate the model:** As Tukey's concept of EDA commands, the model should fit the data. You don't want to just apply a model because it's the one you know, it's the easiest, it's good enough, or because it is new and/or interesting. Make sure the model fits the data, not vice versa. Sure, the other way can work, but it's not preferred.

The best analysts take the time to study the data and understand the relationships in the dimensions and measures not only within the data itself but also against the business questions from stakeholders and the overall strategic business context. Data visualization before applied analysis is the right order of work for ecommerce analysis. As such, these best practices and ideas presented in this chapter are suggested and can be helpful for you; however, your mileage could vary. Regardless, it is certain that by focusing on the business questions, visualizing and exploring the data, and determining the best model and most appropriate set of analytical techniques, the analytical outcomes and insights resulting from your analysis will be highly effective, useful, and profitable (Adams 2015).

Using Key Performance Indicators for Ecommerce

Key performance indicators (KPIs) are metrics and ratios that represent important data to measure and track over time in order to understand business goals. They are created from the basic and complex techniques, methods, models, and analysis discussed earlier in this chapter. KPIs are typically descriptive in nature. They quantify data already collected over time and put them into context by comparing KPIs to past periods, such as month over month. KPIs can be segmented by cohort, customer segment, marketing campaign, and other rational business segments. KPIs often form the dependent variable in predictive models. Thus KPIs are thought of as also being leading or lagging indicators for performance. What this means is that certain KPIs may start to change before a key business event occurs, whereas other KPIs change only after an event occurs. Keeping track of what happens in a business, from promotions and marketing campaigns, to seasonality, to other impactful events, helps to understand why KPIs change.

When creating KPIs, you want to ensure that the data definitions for them address three audiences: technical, operational, and business. Business goals need to be identified from each audience. Dashboards should be created for the audiences such that each KPI is tied to the business goal. Each dashboard should have a communication plan for communicating KPI analysis to the audience. The expected actions people may take when the KPI changes and the potential outcomes expected from movements up or down are identified. Finally, creating KPIs involves mapping out the systems and integrations necessary to calculate, analyze, and report them.

In ecommerce there are many KPIs that represent behavior, events, interactions, conversions, orders, products, promotions, campaigns, costs, and revenue. The list of possible KPIs is large. Recommending a set of KPIs as "best practice" for every ecommerce business is difficult, because KPIs should help to guide against business goals, which are different for most businesses. Of course, there are a few shared goals across all ecommerce businesses: rates, averages, derivatives, percentages, cost and revenue-per metrics, and other useful ecommerce quantifications, which are described next.

KPI Metric Example: Page or Screen Views

Page views are simply a metric that measures the number of times a page or screen was seen by a user. This metric is used to understand the popularity of content in an ecommerce site. As a standalone metric, this measurement is almost entirely useless. I almost didn't include it in this book, but it is a core metric related to what content on a site is actually seen by people. It can help to put page views into context by looking at the number of users and number of sessions with more than one page view. The derivative KPI, page views per session or per user, can be created, which begins to indicate how engaging the content on your site is by tracking how many pages people view in one visit to your site. This KPI tends to be used in both executive and line of business KPI dashboards (although it can have limited utility).

KPI Metric Example: Visits or Sessions

Another common metric and core to many digital analytics tools is the concept of a visit or session. A visit or session is a set or group of interactions and events that occur during a given period within an ecommerce experience. When a person visits a web site or opens a mobile app and begins to look at pages and use the features, a session is counted. The session lasts for a duration defined by the company's data definition for visits or sessions. Most commonly a session ends after 30 minutes of inactivity or after 30 minutes. There are many challenges to accurate session measurement, which most businesspeople don't care about but analysts find interesting. These nuances include tabbed browsing, starting an expired session by a move of the mouse, time and date crossovers (i.e., what happens when the visit lasts past midnight and goes into the next day), and the inherent challenges of measuring time using cookies (i.e., single-page visit duration and the duration on the last page of a multipage visit are not counted). This KPI tends to be used in both executive and line of business KPI dashboards.

KPI Metric Example: Returns

The number of returned items and orders is important to measure in ecommerce. Because returns have a cost associated with them, which erodes margin, it is important to track the total number of returns at both an overall order and an item level. The return KPI can also be expanded to include other metrics, like returned revenue, and the derivative cost per return. This KPI tends to be used in both executive and merchandising KPI dashboards.

KPI Metric Example: Total Revenue and Revenue by N

Revenue is the sum of all the money collected by customers from purchasing goods or services during a given time frame. The results of all your efforts—from site operations, user experience, marketing, buying, merchandising, analytics, conversion optimization, and management—are reflected in this important metric. Simply having an accurate count of revenue earned is an important goal. Keep in mind that third-party payment processing puts transactions through states of approval (authorized, charged, approved, settled and so on), so you need to have your definition for what is revenue accurate and consistent across all channels where you sell. You want to avoid situations in which the revenue data is not defined identically. For example, if you want to track as a KPI a daily revenue total of all purchases authorized on that day, then you need to make sure what you are reporting is authorized purchases. If you choose to report as a KPI daily settled revenue, this is an entirely different revenue metric. Although the idea of revenue is quite simple to understand, it has nuance when it is being tracked in ecommerce environments. Be aware of the definition of revenue when you report, analyze, and reconcile it.

KPI Metric Example: Gross Margin

Gross margin is the amount and percentage of the total that remains when you subtract the cost of goods sold (COGS) from net revenue. This financial metric may be important enough to your business to track as KPI, or another margin metric, such as Contribution Margin or Net Profit Margin, may be tracked. The point of margin-based metrics is that they put context on revenue by adjusting it to include costs. In this sense you can see the financial performance of the business before other costs are accounted. Sales, promotions, and discounts all impact margin, so it's important to analyze, model, forecast, and predict gross margin impact.

KPI Metric Example: Lifetime Value

Lifetime value is a measure of the predicted revenue and profit of a customer across the expected duration of his relationship with the ecommerce site. See Chapter 9, "Analyzing Ecommerce Customers," for more information. Lifetime value (LTV) puts cost into context because, when modeled and analyzed correctly, it can predict the value of a customer over time. This prediction allows for costs to be allocated such that profitability is maximized. By looking at lifetime value overall, in the context of cohorts and segments, and of particular marketing campaigns, a business can fine-tune its spending to deliver maximal return. When this metric is tracked in a KPI dashboard, LTV can be understood as it changes. This KPI is frequently used in executive and marketing KPI dashboards.

KPI Metric Example: Repeat Visitors/Users/Customers

Repeat customers is a metric that counts how many customers of total customers have visited your ecommerce site in the past. This measurement is related to recency and frequency (discussed later in this chapter). Repeat customers are brand-aware customers who likely have an intent to shop. By understanding and tracking the volume of repeat customers across time, you can use other data related to their past purchases and preferences to target them. If you consistently notice a downward trend of repeat customers in a business in which customers tend to purchase frequently, then there could be an issue. When the number of repeat customers is in a rising trend, one needs to figure out why they continue to visit but not purchase again. For ecommerce companies that track time between customer purchases, it is possible to know when a return customer is near their next purchase, and then target appropriately. To begin to get this level of managing one-to-one repeat-customer experiences with data for understanding, detecting, and targeting, it all starts with measuring the number of repeat customers you have coming back.

KPI Rate Example: Conversion Rate

The concept of *conversion* and the associated derivative, *conversion rate,* is one of the most enlightening KPIs in ecommerce analytics. Conversion is when a purchase occurs on your site. For example, in an ecommerce experience, conversion can be defined as "ordering a product." Overall conversion occurs when an unknown visitor becomes a customer who may or may not be known; in the case of step completion, discussed later in the text, the conversion may occur when an event occurs after a user completes a series of predefined steps.

The key takeaway regarding the digital concept of conversion is that it occurs when a person does something that the owner of the ecommerce experience thinks is valuable—and thus creates material, financial business value in some way. In that context, there are several mathematical definitions for conversion.

For example, conversion can be measured based on a visitor or visit or customer or audience basis. Various camps exist about the usefulness of each numerator. Visitor measurement has inherent challenges with accuracy due to cookie deletion and externalities of the Internet (such as cookie blockers), social media, and mobile. Some analysts argue that using "visits" is a better denominator for conversion than "visitors" because a visit represents a unique opportunity to convert, whereas the visitor metric could include more than one visit. Other people argue that conversion should be unique people, not visitors or visits. While the discussion can be academic, it has implications. Due to the technical and conceptual challenges with measuring and understanding all the derivatives of conversion, visit conversion is most commonly measured, followed by visitor, by customer, then by person.

Regardless of your preference for the numerator in a conversion calculation, the larger point is that conversion occurs when a person does something that is considered valuable. And as such, conversion and the movements in conversion rates can be tied to financial measures, such as revenue and profitability.

KPI Rate Example: Step Completion Rate

Step completion rate, sometimes called *micro conversion* or even *waypathing,* is similar to conversion in that a step is a transitional point in an ecommerce experience that is part of a conversion flow. The idea of moving across a shipping experience from one page to another is a *step.* When a person completes the final step, the conversion is tracked.

Step completion can best be understood as an example. Say, an ecommerce site's goal is to sell products. Products are sold via orders. To get to the order page, a person must access a landing page (like the home page), search for a product, view the product page, and complete an order. The conversion steps would be as given here:

1. View a landing page.
2. Search for a product.
3. View a product page.
4. Order the product.

CONVERSION = View the order thank-you page.

In the example, steps 1 through 4 begin with the customer arriving on the landing page and then taking the next steps to complete the purchase. Step completion measures how many visits or visitors complete each step in the path. Drop-off in each step is quantified and known. Each step has an associated completion rate. The worst performing steps can be tested and optimized, which helps the overall conversion rate.

KPI Rate Example: Abandoned Cart Rate

An abandoned cart occurs when a person adds one or more products to a shopping cart and then doesn't buy them. Cart abandonment can be measured on a visit basis: The number of abandoned carts is divided by the number of total visits to calculate a rate. This rate represents what percentage of carts are left with items unbought. This metric can get complicated to measure when you consider that users can create an account, add products to the cart, and buy them later. The cart items are not necessarily tied to a cookie; they are stored on the back end in a persistent cart ready to be bought when the user comes back. Thus, it's difficult to say whether carts that are abandoned by known users are really abandoned or whether they are just delayed. It's these types of use cases that make abandonment measurement nuanced. That said, many companies define abandonment to occur whenever a session ends with unbought products in the cart. Regardless of your definition, by tracking abandoned carts, you have the ability to recognize how much revenue is being abandoned and then implement programs to recapture that abandoned revenue.

KPI Average Example: Average Order Value

One of the standard metrics in ecommerce experiences in which a purchase occurs is average order value (AOV). Simply constructed, AOV is the sum total cost of the items purchased, divided by the number of items. It's the average cost of all the items purchased—easy and informative. Even small sites that sell only one product benefit from tracking AOV. After all, AOV helps to identify inventory and purchasing trends as well as influence marketing, advertising, and promotions. Related to that is median order value, or MOV, which is less common. MOV is useful where ecommerce transactions create data with a large range in cost.

KPI Derivative Example: Bounce Rate

Bounce rate is a visit-based metric that identifies the number of single-page visits on a landing page. When a visit begins on a page and the visitor does not view another page, a bounce is said to have occurred. A lot has been written about "bounce rate"—so much that I thought of excluding it. My friend and colleague Avinash Kaushik, whose books I encourage you to read, has a good definition of bounce rate: "I came, I saw, I puked." In other words, the bounce rate measures the percentage of people or visits that came to your site and immediately left the site without doing anything. They simply looked at one page, made a decision that the site wasn't helpful to them, and left the site. In mobile applications, when a user goes to the background after opening the app, a bounce has occurred. Again bounce rate is most typically associated with landing pages on a site such that the rate measures how many people didn't view another page after starting their visit on that landing page. Any entry page on an ecommerce site has a bounce rate. Bounce rate is a visit- or session-based metric. Related to bounce rate is the concept of exit rate, which measures how frequently a particular page is the last page viewed before the visitor leaves the site. Exit rate is page-based. Bounce rate is visit-based. That nuance is important to understand.

KPI Derivative Example: Percentage of Orders with Promotions or Discounts

This derivative KPI identifies what percentage of orders have a promotion or discount applied to them. Track discounted orders and their volume and also measure the gross margin of orders to add more color to understanding promotional effectiveness. Of course, if you can track promotional discounts at the order level, you can consider tracking them at the item level in each order to understand the impact of discounts.

KPI Derivative Example: Inventory Turnover

The measurement of inventory turnover is very important for ecommerce companies that maintain inventory. Quite simply, this measure lets you know how many times during a given period the site's inventory can be expected to sell out and be replaced. For more information, see the discussion in Chapter 10, "Analyzing Products and Orders in Ecommerce."

KPI Derivative Example: Return on Investment

Return on investment (ROI) is a standard business calculation for which revenue is subtracted from cost of goods sold and that number is divided by cost of goods sold:

ROI = (Revenue – Cost of Goods Sold) / Cost of Goods Sold

This metric indicates the financial impact from the particular investment you have made—and is general enough that it can be applied to almost any business activity. For example, the creation of a set of conversion tests has a cost and it has a demonstrable revenue impact; thus it has an ROI. Marketing activities have a cost and a return, and thus can be held to an ROI as can the management of promotional and merchandising activities. Any business activity with a cost that can be tied to revenue (or not) can have an associated ROI calculated.

KPI Derivative Example: Loyalty—Time Since Last Visit (Recency)

Customer loyalty is what businesses with short, repeat purchasing cycles (toothpaste) strive to create. Even businesses with longer usage cycles (appliances such as washing machines and home windows) between new purchases benefit from loyal customers. One way to measure loyalty is with a concept derived from traditional marketing named recency.

The concept of *recency* is simple to understand. It is the time since the last visit or purchase by a customer. As a time-based metric and one tied to individual customers, it is a metric most easily measured in experiences and transactions in which the visitor is known via login, registration, unique ID, full name, or some other identifier. In environments with more anonymity, recency is identified on a segment level for identifiable customer segments—and at an object or event level; for example, time since the last download in a mobile application. Recency can be a helpful metric for tracking how loyal your customers are to your brand, products, or services.

KPI Derivative Example: Retention—Time Between Visits (Frequency)

Retention is another common concept in traditional marketing that is reused in ecommerce analytics. *Frequency* refers to how often a known person or an anonymous or mostly anonymous person comes back to an ecommerce experience she has visited previously.

Frequency, like recency (previously discussed) is also a time-based measure. As such, in ecommerce experiences in which people are identified by some mechanism, the ability to time-stamp when that person last came and then recently came to a site can be straightforward. Frequency in anonymous or mostly anonymous environments, such as those dependent on browser cookies, is harder to pinpoint. Cookie deletion and the inability to persist an association between one cookie and another over time can impact the accurate calculation of frequency.

Frequency is important to track in businesses for which repeat visits are important. For example, for news sites or social media sites, a decrease in frequency could indicate an issue with content relevancy. On ecommerce sites, the cause of an increase in frequency around a particular product or by a particular customer is something to investigate.

KPI Percentage Example: Percentage of X from Source N

In the section heading above, X is meant to be some measure from a source named N—for example, the percentage of customers from paid search or the percentage of revenue generated from marketing campaigns. As such, the abstraction of the percentage of something X from some source N is helpful to apply to the concepts in ecommerce analytics: distributions of the sources where people come from when they begin a site visit or the percentage of revenue from different brands, product categories, and so on.

The many ways in which a person enters a digital experience can be tracked in percentage terms and against the key metrics you want to segment by source. As a result, you can derive KPIs such as percentage of visitors from online advertising, or percentage of profit by marketing campaign. Percentages as a KPI are widely used in analysis.

KPI Percentage Example: Percentage of New Customers (or N Metric)

Percentage of new customers is a helpful KPI for sites that want to measure customer growth rate or market share—for example, the percentage of new customers from search, the percentage of repeat customers from display advertising, the percentage of customers visiting on both mobile app and desktop, and so on. Site owners want to know the percentage of new customers or the percentage of new customers in the past 12 months or year over year.

KPI "Per" Example: Cost and/or Revenue per Visitor

The highest value of a KPI is when it can be tied directly to a financial metric. In the case of advertising, the "cost per" metrics are numerous and their usage is widespread and well understood. The most common advertising-based "cost per" is the CPM or the cost per thousand (in the context of display advertisements). Ecommerce analytics uses "cost per" metrics in similar ways. The cost can be any object in the ecommerce analytics data model, such as cost per visitor or cost per conversion or cost per action or cost per lead or cost per engagement or cost per Facebook like or cost per user-generated tweet. These metrics may be too vague, so again segmentation or further derivation can be helpful, as are time-series comparisons of the cost metrics. The analog, revenue per visitor, can be calculated by summing total visitors and dividing by revenue. Subtracting "cost per" metrics from the comparable "revenue per" metric can be financially insightful. It is common to see "average cost per" metrics in use. Revenue per customer is discussed next.

KPI "Per" Example: Revenue per Customer

The counterpoint to the cost metrics reviewed in the preceding section are revenue-based metrics. The ultimate link to the business is when KPIs are joined with financial data. Helpful insights can be found when ecommerce analytics teams focus on bringing together financial data related to the "revenue per" with the "cost per" data. Thus, a useful KPI to track for measuring business performance is the "revenue per" metric. As the counterpoint metric for "cost per" metrics, the "revenue per" metric indicates how much money was generated. The most common usage of a "revenue per" metric is the revenue per customer KPI or revenue per product or revenue per product category. Also related are the "revenue per customer segment X or Y" and derivatives "revenue per new customer" or "revenue per repeat customer" and so on.

If your KPI strategy can execute to the level where "cost per X" and "revenue per X" KPIs are known, such as the "cost per paid search campaign" and the "revenue per paid search campaign," then you can calculate the "gross margin per paid search campaign" and "net profit per paid search campaign." Taking this to a deeper level, the analytics team could tell you "profit per keyword in search campaign X" and related comparative and time-series views of the KPI. As you may conclude, the power of such insights in transforming the profitability of a business using ecommerce data and derivative KPI analysis cannot be underestimated.

KPI "Per" Example: Cost per Customer Acquisition

A very important derivative KPI is named cost per customer acquisition. This KPI shows how much money it takes to generate one new customer. It's an important metric because it shows the effectiveness of your marketing spend and other customer acquisition strategies and tactics. When compared to lifetime value, you want to see a relationship such that the lifetime value is higher than the cost to acquire that customer. For more information, see the discussion in Chapter 6, "Marketing and Advertising Analytics in Ecommerce."

4

Visualizing, Dashboarding, and Reporting Ecommerce Data and Analysis

One of the most critical activities for an analyst is the presentation of data and analysis. The best analysis won't be used if it is not presented adequately to stakeholders. Analytical presentation is like "plating" in cuisine. It's not enough just to prepare and cook the food; the best restaurants know how to present their cuisine in a way that appeals not only to the palette, but also to the senses. The best analytics appeals in a similar way—whether to fill the need to look at detailed data in reports or to view a visualization. Stakeholders appreciate data in reports, but reports are not easy to understand. They provide the data and leave the difficult task of analysis, insight, and recommendation to the stakeholder, instead of the analyst.

When the analyst presents easier-to-digest analytical deliverables that make the data more clearly understood and insightful to the audience, the analyst helps the business create value. Excellent dashboards and visualizations that are backed up with accurate reports containing detailed-level data are what analytics teams should strive to create as deliverables to complement written analysis. These deliverables can stand alone without written analysis or act as complementary analytical artifacts to written analysis. Reports, dashboards, and visualizations are used to guide storytelling with the data.

The details presented in this chapter have applicability across all use-cases and approaches for ecommerce analytics presented in this book. All types of ecommerce analysis can be complemented by accurate reporting, carefully constructed dashboards, and well-designed and thought-through visualizations. In fact, it is imperative that analytics organizations develop the people and talent to deliver these types of artifacts, the processes to support their development and delivery, and the technology to enable creation and execution.

Reports, dashboards, and visualizations are used for the following purposes:

- **Comparison** refers to examining data to find similarities and dissimilarities. Comparisons are made over time or against items. You compare data across time periods or two rows in a report. When comparisons are made over time, they are made across one or more periods using cyclical or noncyclical data or across one or more categories. Comparisons of items can be based on one dimension or metric across one or more categories that contain one or more items. Note that dimensions are context, so you might compare conversion rate by the dimension (context) of geography.

- **Relationships** refer to how data is connected or could be connected to demonstrate applicability for a given purpose. Relationships can be shown across two or three dimensions and sometimes more dimensions. For example, the relationship between server response time and conversion rate by day by city.

- **Distributions** refer to the frequency of occurrence of values across an entire data set. Distributions are generally analyzed across one, two, or three dimensions and a few to many data points. For example, lifetime value by city by customer.

- **Compositions** show the elements or pieces of a whole. Compositions either are static and don't change or are dynamic and change over time. When compositions are dynamic, they are examined across a couple of periods or many periods and analyzed to show relative and absolute differences. Static compositions, of course, are a snapshot that can show totals, accumulations, subtractions, components, and more. For example, marketing-generated revenue is attributed 43% to paid search and 57% organic search.

Reports can show data that compares, shows relationships, elucidates distributions, and identifies compositions. It is common to see reports as simple data tables of comparisons of multiple items, across one or more categories by a single dimension—for example, conversion rate by day, average order value by customer type, and so on. Reports often show change over time and may contain multiple dimensions, different categories, and possibly relationships across a few variables. Showing how the composition of data over time changes across periods or as a static snapshot is a goal of some reports. Other reports provide data about distributions cross-tabbed by multiple dimensions. Reports show all of these things, but few business stakeholders truly dig into reports, which is why they have limited use in analytics. Reports show data. Stakeholders want insights. They want to see key themes, highlights, patterns, observations, and insights from the data about composition, distribution, relationships, and comparisons. They want to know how it all impacts their job and what to do about it to improve their business performance.

Dashboards and forms of data visualization provide more of what stakeholders require to easily and quickly understand data in reports—and make use of it. Executives love dashboards, and they love them more when analysts tell them what the movements and changes of the data mean in business context. By building visualizations that illustrate key performance indicators (KPIs) and other metrics related to business goals, end users no longer need to look at reports. The analytics team can then, instead, deliver and use dashboards and visualizations to help the business drive performance. Dashboards can underpin written analysis and content for presentations.

Data visualizations, like bubble charts, scatter plots, stacked area charts, and histograms, can stand alone or as a complement to analysis. Visualizations are used to create dashboards. Two or more visualizations (and perhaps a data table) can be combined to create dashboards that help stakeholders rapidly understand data to find insights.

Because reports, dashboards, and visualizations are all related—reports provide the data for visualizations that go on dashboards—it's important to determine how to maximize your opportunities with these types of analytical deliverables:

- Use reporting for operational work and cases when it is necessary to look at specific, item-level data.

- Use dashboarding for periodic reporting, especially to senior management, to highlight changes in trends and patterns related to goals measured by key performance indicators.
- Use visualization to begin exploring analytical data, as a complement to reports and dashboards, or as a final deliverable.

Ecommerce analytics teams will take the following roles when creating reports, dashboards, and data visualizations:

- **Brokers/intermediaries between IT and the business** function to align inputs and outputs in order to set the expectations and outcomes of analytics projects. Brokers could be appointed from program or project managers, relationship managers, and other teams if needed to help the analytics team.
- **Creators of reports, dashboards, and visualizations** may be analysts, IT, and business stakeholders operating in self-service analytics environments. In most cases, the analysts and IT team will have access to full data and more tools, whereas business stakeholders may have limited access to data and features in tools for working with data.
- **Providers of reports, dashboards, and visualizations** are teams whose functions are to provide access to the tools and technologies that enable the creation of analytical artifacts for stakeholders.
- **Validators** are teams that ensure the data accuracy of new and existing data sources and data within them. They may be part of the data governance team—or this function may be done part-time, ad hoc.
- **Investigators** are people or teams assigned to investigate data anomalies and "bad data." They will root-cause the source of the variation in data by testing the data pipeline to see where the problem exists. Then they will work to progress the fix and ensure the accuracy.
- **Stewards** are appointed members of teams who are responsible for ensuring data is accurate and managing it to maintain accuracy. They may validate and investigate data too, but their primary role is to ensure that data is defined and follows the right rules to make it accurate. It is said that data stewards ensure "data fitness" for a purpose.

Understanding Reporting

Reporting is the most common analytical artifact that you will see in a corporation. The formal structure of a report is a basic and core way information is communicated in most businesses. There are so many reports in every business—from the income statement, to the balance sheet, to data tables about metrics related to customers, brands, products, orders, merchandise and so on. Reporting, however common and standard, can be a very poor way of communicating information. Reports lack analysis—even when changes in data are shown using indicators. Reports are usually built to business requirements, which, if delivered to scope, are relevant until they aren't. Strategy changes; tactics evolve and the reports created for yesteryear may not be applicable to this year or next year. Since reports exist in isolation—often sent over e-mail or retrieved via a self-service system—they may not be used frequently by stakeholders too busy to open e-mail or access data systems. Reports may be accurate, but often they can drift in accuracy in companies that don't have data governance or data stewards—and in large environments where people can build their own reports, reports can sometimes be just plain wrong. The systems that house reports can proliferate, and redundant or confusing reports exist in multiple systems. For business-critical reporting in regulated environments, the level of effort spent verifying data accuracy before release can be considerable, considering data governance and master data management. Reports have utility; they complement analysis but are not substitutes or replacements for it. Keep in mind the two universal truths about data in reports:

- If the data does not meet expectations, it will be challenged.
- If the data does not show positive performance, it will be challenged.

Reporting is provided in a format and form factor appropriate to the business stakeholder. The form will be the rows and columns defined by the business from the available data. The form factor can be a printed document, in a software application, delivered in a browser, or via a mobile device, smartphone, tablet, or application. Reports have two macro purposes:

- **Sustaining reporting:** This reporting is produced in an ongoing manner, sometimes manually, but often can be generated through automation. It may be delivered to stakeholders or made available in self-service environments accessed via unique logins. Sustaining reporting is created to be used on an ongoing basis to support the reporting needs of programs, projects, and initiatives on the road map. It may be created to support the operations of various business functions. The hourly sales report, the daily sales report, the margin by promotion report, and the current inventory report are all examples of sustaining reporting. This type of reporting is operational in nature and is usually verified across systems to ensure that the data is of the highest quality. Sustaining reports are heavily governed and use master data derived from master data management systems. From sustaining reports, business stakeholders can understand their current performance and answer relevant business questions. Interesting or unusual data in sustaining reports may be investigated using other tools and explored in more depth.

- **Ad hoc reporting:** These are the reports created for one-time use as requested for helping solve a particular business challenge. For example, the CEO asks for reporting on margin by product category, or the warehouse manager asks for the recent inventory report for a specific brand. The nature of an ad hoc report is that it occurs once and only once. It may have occurred based on a trend or pattern observed in a sustaining report. Teams will create ad hoc reports often manually or they may be autogenerated. Sometimes queries will need to be written to retrieve the data for reports. Self-service analytics and business intelligence environments may be rolled out to enable the analytically inclined stakeholders to create their own reports. When an ecommerce stakeholder keeps asking for the same report on a periodic basis, it is no longer an ad hoc report (and should be transitioned to be a sustaining report). Ad hoc reports are done once and should be archived so they can be used again.

Reporting is elemental in a business. It has to be done. You really can't run a business without, at the very least, a few core reports. As a result, reports provide a central artifact to consult in the business process. They are custom built to business requirements and thus let stakeholders anchor on data to help put perspective on their performance. Reports can also help guide conversation by acting as a center of discussion. But, again, they complement written analysis but are never a substitute or replacement for written analysis.

Explaining the RASTA Approach to Reporting

As with all things in analytics, it helps to have an approach that frames a reference point for entering into an activity, like reporting in ecommerce. Whether you have to gather business requirements, rationalize existing reporting, or create new reporting to already-developed specifications, the RASTA method for reporting can help you. RASTA stands for

- Relevant, meaning the report is appropriate for the business question or goal
- Accurate, meaning the report is correct and precise with "good data"
- Simple, meaning the report is streamlined to show only the necessary data
- Timely, meaning the report is delivered to stakeholders when it has maximum utility
- Annotated, meaning the report has written annotations to help the viewer understand it (often in addition to other written analysis)

Understanding Dashboarding

Dashboards are analytical artifacts that contain numeric, textual, and visual representations of key performance data and written analysis. Dashboards are created from detailed data shown in reports that is summarized and distilled into simplified metrics and KPIs that are necessary to track, trend, and monitor over time. They contain individual sections of information that show important data related to a topic. Dashboards are meant to be understood quickly by busy businesspeople who monitor them on a periodic basis. When you are creating dashboards, it is important to ensure that the dashboard can be maintained with minimal effort and manual supervision. Automated and self-service dashboarding tools are useful, as is creating a data pipeline specifically for dashboarding purposes.

The data in dashboards is typically represented using data visualization. Different metrics are represented alongside text that guides the reader on what the data means (i.e., analysis). The data and KPIs in dashboards are represented using statistical and mathematical methods. For example, averages or the mean of the data set may be presented. Percentages that show the makeup of distributions are commonly displayed. The rate of occurrence of something, such as the number of orders to users—the conversion rate—and other volume ratios can be included on dashboards. Frequently, derivatives or calculated metrics resulting from combining other metrics are placed on dashboards. For each KPI on the dashboards, the data may come from master data aligned with data definitions from data governance. Targets for business goals may be compared against the movements and changes in KPIs to track performances to goal. Qualitative and descriptive data and explanatory narration and text on a dashboard can be used to communicate recommendations, insights, and suggestions about how to achieve expected actions and outcomes. Managers and leaders are typically the audience for dashboards. Hence, there are fewer dashboards than reports in a business. When forming a dashboarding strategy for ecommerce, keep in mind who the audience is and what that audience's goals are. Stephen Few, a notable author and thinker in the field of data visualization, describes the following types of dashboards:

- **Strategic dashboards** are focused on executive audiences and getting them the key performance indicators that identify important information about the current and, perhaps, future health of the business. The metrics in a strategic dashboard will trend over time, showing data by various time periods. Leading indicators may be highlighted to show future impact on the business. It is common for forecasts or predictions about the future movement of data to be included. These dashboards will be periodically updated but do require real-time data and the creation of a streaming data pipeline.

- **Operational dashboards** contain data that is necessary for "keeping the lights on." Information on operational dashboards relates to the current, immediate state of the business. This information is often streamed and provided in real time or near real time. This type of dashboard can contain technical data related to ecommerce site performance, and it can also contain information about customer behavior, shipping times, product unavailability, current promotional health, margins, and financial performance, and other information relevant to the day-to-day operations of an ecommerce business.

- **Analytical dashboards** contain strategic and operational data about a particular business question, product or project, a line of business, or a particular team, group, or role. The data will include current, leading, and lagging indicators. Aggregate metrics such as sales or revenue may be provided at the top line, and other sections of the dashboard may break down the metric, for example, sales by geography. Analytical dashboards also provide users with a way to work with and manipulate the data using filters, search features, and other methods to drill up and drill down on the data. Analytical dashboards can be provided in self-service environments where users have various permissions to access certain data and tool functionality. Real-time, or daily data, is often required.

Each section of a dashboard should ideally provide an answer to one or more business questions or business goals, regardless of audience or orientation. It may be necessary to group the information in the dashboard to relate to the other information. One example would be showing a marketing conversion dashboard starting from left to right with acquisition KPIs, behavioral KPIs, and conversion KPIs, like you would see in tools such as Google Analytics.

Explaining the LIVEN Approach to Dashboarding

The phrase "going live" means that a software or technology application has been released for use. Dashboards "go live" when they are rolled out to stakeholders. But how do you ensure that the dashboard you went live with is actually useful? You want to, metaphorically, "liven it up" for stakeholders, so they use it and consider it an informative and helpful analytical output. I created a simple mnemonic, LIVEN, to describe some of the key important properties that good dashboards tend to have that, well, liven them up. I call this approach LIVEN dashboarding. Applying this approach will certainly liven up your dashboards and ensure they are more likely to be accepted at go-live and used thereafter. The LIVEN acronym attempts to bring together several important concepts helpful to designing dashboards:

- **Linked** refers to linking to the data underlying a KPI or metric. This link might enable viewing the raw data, drilling-down into it, or linking to another system.
- **Interactive** describes dashboards that have features for data exploration, such as filtering.
- **Visual** dashboards have data visualizations. They aren't just data tables in Excel or what Avinash Kaushik calls "data pukes."
- **Echeloned** means organized in a structured way so that the top-level executive data is the highest data layer. Data in subordinate dashboards relates to the executive level dashboard—with the executive as the highest echelon.
- **Narrative** dashboards contain written analysis adjacent in space to the data visualizations that explains the story behind the data and KPIs, including relevant insights and recommendations.

What Data Should I Start With in an Ecommerce Dashboard?

A basic ecommerce dashboard lets the viewer see a trend and do data range comparison on the following concepts (Few 2015):

- **Key performance indicators relevant to your business:** Example metrics and KPIs include data and derivatives such as cost per acquisition, orders, revenue, customers, visits, path length, conversion rate, and average order value. Remember that a KPI is a metric that helps you understand your business objective (often against a goal you set).

- **The conversion funnel that represents the linear path to buy:** An example funnel might be abstracting by tracking the people who follow a path such as the following: Visits > Shoppers > Added to Cart > Purchased.

- **Abandoned cart data that is helpful to understand what the site is leaving on the table:** Helpful metrics include total abandoned cart revenue, total abandoned carts, and cart abandonment rate, as well as the top abandoned products and their abandoned revenue and carts. Returns and rate of returns across certain brands, categories, and promotions might be presented.

- **Lists of frequency, rank order, or popularity:** Examples include top product, brands, categories, and marketing channels with the number of users, shoppers, revenue, revenue per user, conversion rate, and average lifetime value per user.

Understanding Data Visualization

Data visualization is the phrase used to describe the creation of a visual or pictorial representation of data in a way that enables the viewer to quickly and intuitively understand and explore it. Data visualization uses illustrations and graphics to assist the viewer in identifying and communicating relationships, patterns, and outliers in the data. The best data visualizations communicate complex analysis in an easy-to-understand manner—and often include interactive, self-service features for the user to explore the visualization. As a replacement for data tables and reports or even as supporting or standalone materials, data visualizations convey information in a way that nontechnical and even non-numeric learners can understand. Instead of forcing the user to look through many pages of data, a solid data visualization will represent key data elements in ways that simplify the data to make its interpretation simpler to understand. A data visualization can be annotated with descriptive text or be adjacent in space to written analysis.

According to Vitaly Friedman (2008), the "main goal of data visualization is to communicate information clearly and effectively through graphical means. It doesn't mean that data visualization needs to look boring to be functional or extremely sophisticated to look beautiful. To convey ideas effectively, both aesthetic form and functionality need to go hand in hand. That way, a data visualization provides insights into a rather sparse and complex data set by communicating its key-aspects in a more intuitive way. Yet designers often fail to achieve a balance between form and function, creating gorgeous data visualizations which fail to serve their main purpose—to communicate information."

Data visualizations are used in ecommerce to

- Communicate complex information using commonly understood graphical formats
- Highlight unusual changes or movements in data
- Identify patterns, changes, and trends in data
- Discover new data relationships and ways to understand data in the context of other data

The Process for Data Visualization

Data visualization is another process for an analytics team and the analyst. The process starts with business understanding and ends with the distribution and socialization to stakeholders of an appropriate data visualization that answers the business questions asked. The process that analysts go through to develop a data visualization is as follows:

1. **Determine the business questions to be answered.** This is step 1 in the value chain described in Chapter 2, "The Ecommerce Analytics Value Chain."

2. **Define the data needed to answer the question.** This could involve data collection, movement and transformation, or aggregation.

3. **Evaluate the data to understand the thresholds and benchmarks in it.** The applicability, relevancy, and appropriateness of the data to the business purpose need to assessed.

4. **Create the appropriate data model to build the visualization.** Visualizations and data visualization tools require data structured in the appropriate way. It's helpful to create a conceptual data model that supports the visualization—and then confirm the source data matches it.

5. **Build wireframes and mock-ups based on the data and the data model.** This step in the process can be done after the data is evaluated—or it is possible to do this earlier in the process. If you do mockups too soon, you may realize that you don't have the data you need or that you need to do a lot of work to collect or prepare the data. Mocking up after data evaluation can reduce the risk that you ideate something not feasible in a timely manner.

6. **Access or replicate the source data in a governed and managed way.** This step requires alignment with your data steward and governance team (if you have one).

7. **Load the real data into your system and apply it to the wireframes and mockups.** Depending on the level of technical acumen in the team, this step can require support from data engineers or IT.

8. **Test the data visualization and any functionality embedded in it.** Depending on the level of support the analytics team or analyst receives from a quality assurance team, this step requires the analyst to ensure the output matches requirements.

9. **Do user acceptance testing.** Do this by releasing the visualization to your stakeholders. Get feedback and iterate to acceptance.

10. **Release the visualization once accepted by stakeholders.** The release step includes a formal communication and may even include change management in the form of training and guidance

11. **Analyze and interpret the visualization.** Do this using your experience and expertise to communicate answers to the business question, other insights, recommendations, and perspectives.

Maximizing Impact with Data Visualization: The SCREEN Approach and More

The communicative power of data visualization is maximized when the best possible visualization is applied (see the end of this chapter for a review of common visualization types). Fortunately there are several guiding principles that you can use to maximize the impact of data visualization regardless of how you illustrate the data. Here are some tips:

- **The best data visualizations show the data.** This may sound obvious. But Tufte-ian "infoglut" exists in the visual communication of information. Keep it as simple as possible and make the key data pop out and stand out.

- **Include only the relevant key data elements and supporting metrics and derivatives that are necessary to communicate the information pertinent to the data visualization.**

- **Don't bother the user with esoteric technical details.** As much as possible, the user should be isolated from the underlying connections and configuration needed to generate the data visualization.

- **Do not distort conclusions by creating visual relationships that deceive or delude.** Make comprehension easy and encourage the user to visually compare different data to both reveal fine-grained details of the data and give a broad understanding of the available data and its structure.

- **Include verbal explanations of the data in order to focus the data on delivering a message that has a clear purpose.**

The purpose might be describing the data, trending the data, exploring the data, calculating new data, or forecasting and predicting with the data.

The acronym SCREEN helps me ensure that the visualizations I produce are sufficient for release. SCREEN stands for the following:

- **Specific** refers to the relevance and fit for the visualization to the business purpose and the audience. When the visualization is specific to the audience, it reduces any cognitive dissonance. Does the visualization answer the business question? Does it contain enough information and suitably rich features for discovery?

- **Considerate** speaks to accommodating the needs of the audience. Can the audience easily access the visualization? Does it accommodate for color-blindness and handicaps? Does it render on the device and in the form factor on which the audience wants to see it?

- **Required** references whether the data and functionality of the visualization are essential for communicating the information and ensuring relevancy to the stakeholder. For each data point, you want to ask whether it is required to drive home the point and enable comprehension. Anything not required should be removed.

- **Explanatory** indicates that the visualization can be interpreted to sufficiently explain the data shown in a way that enables the stakeholder to answer the business question. It can be helpful to show the visualization to people who haven't seen it before, and ask them to explain it to you and answer the business question.

- **Exploratory** refers to the requirements for visualizations to have features and functionality for exploring the data. The exploration may be driven by filters, search and select boxes, or other interactive elements. The visualization may be annotated and the data described using words and narratives embedded directly in the visualization.

- **Nimble** relates to the potential to reuse the visualization and the underlying data and data model with necessary modifications to fit other business purposes. Having a common library of visualizations that you can nimbly reuse for other business purposes can be helpful when you are doing new analytical work.

Why Use Data Visualizations?

Data visualization isn't just buzzworthy; it's also important for helping people understand data when they aren't highly quantitative or when they have a low tolerance for ambiguity. The simplest data visualization may only have one dimension and metric—and the most complex may have four, five, or even six dimensions. Professionally, I became enamored with data visualization in late 1990s when Edmund Tufte came to my city and talked about how the Challenger explosion in 1986 could have been prevented, basically, with better communication of information. After applying the lessons learned at his seminar to my work, I found people to be more receptive of my analysis. It's as if adding a picture added extra weight to my analysis. Another well-known example of data visualization in action is the work of Hans Rosling and his Trendalyzer software, which converts trend data into interactive illustrations and graphics. I took away from the work of Tufte and Rosling that a picture is indeed worth a thousand words (at least). Stephen Few cites the following eight rationales for building data visualizations:

1. **To compare data across the same or different time series.** Time-series visualizations show the movement of a single data point (variable) over time—for example, the daily conversion rate shown as a line chart and trended over every day in the current year.

2. **To compare numbers or nominal, numeric data.** Number or nominal comparisons are visualizations that show the volume or count of one or more variables. They compare data in no specific order, but are helpful in visually comparing the magnitude of the numbers presented. For example, you could compare revenue by promotional code, or margin realized by promotion code.

3. **To show part-to-whole relationships.** Part to whole visualizations show the sections of the whole as measured in

increments or a ratio. The often-disdained pie chart can show parts of a whole. You may want to show what brands generate what portion of profit.

4. **To show geography and geolocation.** Geographic or geo-spatial visualizations use a map of a geography or a blueprint or outline of a structure to compare one or more data points across geography. For example, you may see a heat map that shows the cost of customer acquisition by state, city, DMA, or MSA.

5. **To rank order data.** Ranking visualizations order variables based on their relationship to the main category. By subdividing a category and ranking the data in it from highest to lowest, new insights can be realized. In ecommerce, you may use a ranking to illustrate the highest revenue-generating products from within a specific brand, or what product categories generate the most profit.

6. **To indicate frequency.** Frequency distributions are common to statistical analysis and certainly can be represented with data visualization. When you show the variables observed, deeper knowledge can be easily realized. For example, you may want to show the number of customers who bought over time after first registering on your site. You would bin the groups into deciles and show the count of each decile member. A histogram can be used, or you can even have a box-and-whisker plot to show statistical information, such as average, median, and other binning (like quartile ranges).

7. **To demonstrate correlation.** Correlations shown in visualizations identify the relationship between two variables to determine whether they move identically, partially together, or in opposite directions. The variables are plotted on a coordinate graph—for example, plotting customer lifetime value (X) and cost of customer acquisition (Y) for customer segments. A scatter plot is a common way to visualize correlation.

8. **To identify deviation and outliers.** Deviation visualizations show a variable against a reference point so that they can be compared visually to illustrate the difference. For example, you might want to show revenue targets by brand against the actual revenue generated.

Types of Data Visualization

Many types of data visualizations exist in ecommerce. They are often combined with statistical approaches to analysis, such as Tukey's Exploratory Data Analysis (EDA) reviewed in Chapter 3, "Methods and Techniques for Ecommerce Analysis." Several standard and commonly encountered data visualizations can be easily created using analytical, data science, and business intelligence tools and technology. Developers can use technology such as D3.JS, AngularJS, or Chart.js. Data scientists can use technology such as R, Matlab, Dygraphs, or Leaflet. Business analysts can use Excel, Tableau, Qliksense, Qlikview, or Spotfire. All these tools have pros and cons and better applicability to certain projects. Beyond these specialized software applications and technologies, some companies have analysts work alongside graphic designers to create visualizations. The many types of data visualizations are limited only by the creativity of analysts and designers and the features and functionality to support the integration of data and the creation of the visualization. In ecommerce, the following data visualizations are common:

- **Bar charts** are used to compare a group to a measurement. Bar charts present grouped data plotted on a scale horizontally or vertically. They are usually scaled so that all the data can be shown. When ordered, they are referred to as Pareto charts. Variants also include stacked bars and grouped bars. For example, you might show lifetime value by customer segment on a bar chart.

- **Line charts** order a series of data points that are connected by line segments. Most frequently, the line shows a chronological trend and is called a run chart. For example, you might show revenue by day on a line chart.

- **Radar charts** plot three or more numeric dimensions around a circle and use spoked lines, called radii, to illustrate the value of a metric related to all dimensions. For example, you might want to compare the budget to the spend of different departments in your ecommerce company.

- **Pie charts** show a distribution of data as sections of a circle. Each "pie" segment is relative in size to the contribution of that piece to the whole. For example, the sources of traffic to your ecommerce site might be expressed in a pie chart.

- **Tree charts** can be used to visualize hierarchical relationships and part-to-whole relationships. Each dimension is sized in a rectangle relative to the others and the whole. Tree charts can be used to show large numbers that can't be shown in a bar chart. Labels on tree charts can include values from other metrics related to the primary dimension. For example, you might show gross margin by promotion and net margin by brand.

- **Waterfall charts** show the series of positive and negative values that start from an initial value. For example, you might show the range of revenue by product category.

- **Network charts** show the connections between related data points based on one or more inferred or expressed similarities or attributes. For example, a network chart could be used to show customers who have bought the same products or brands or used the same promotions.

- **Scatter plots** are used to represent data points on two different scales. For example, you could create a scatter plot that shows conversion rate and revenue with the size of data points scaled relative to gross margin.

- **Heatmapping** uses colors to indicate values. For example, you might create a heatmap showing the links on the homepage that get the most clicks, the areas of a landing page where people move their mouse, or the space on a mobile screen where people's eyes look and focus.

- **Geovisualizations** plot data points on a cartographic map, such as a physical land map, road map, political map, climate map, or topographical map. The data may be overlaid on these maps using numbers or iconography. Heatmapping is often used on geolocation. For example, the cost of customer acquisition by country, region, state, city, and so on.

5

Ecommerce Analytics Data Model and Technology

Ecommerce analysis requires having the appropriate data to analyze in order to answer business questions. Whether the goal of your company is to use ecommerce analytics to better understand what's working (or not) on your site to drive conversion optimization or to build a customer profile to power targeting and personalization, it is extremely important that you have the data to achieve your goals. "Data model" is the phrase used to describe the way data is organized, standardized, and related to one another. Thus, in order to analyze data, you must have a data model that represents the data you want to analyze. Businesspeople help identify the data to collect and analyze in what is called a conceptual data model that expresses the data elements. Analysts and data engineers create a logical data model in software, which is then implemented by data engineers as a physical data store supported by hardware.

Analysts live and die by the flexibility and applicability of the data model and the data in it. To align a data model with the business, the analysts must work with the stakeholders responsible for ecommerce operations to help them ideate and/or define the ecommerce data needed to be stored, processed, and collected/analyzed. When you're using off-the-shelf tools, the data models come prebuilt and may be extensible (for example, the Google Analytics "custom metrics" feature), but it is rare that one tool or even a combination of paid tools will have the specific data model necessary for all ecommerce analytics use cases. It is common for an ecommerce company to create their own data model and implement it in a database they own and control outside of the off-the-shelf ecommerce analytics technologies. It may be that your company has many different data models for each function, such as merchandising, promotions, orders, fulfillment, and customer service. Regardless of the technology containing the data or the siloed nature of ecommerce data, the most forward-thinking companies bring together required ecommerce data by creating their own unified ecommerce analytics data model.

Many ecommerce sites use an "ecommerce platform," which is discussed in more detail in Chapter 4, "Visualizing, Dashboarding, and Reporting Ecommerce Data and Analysis." The data collected and generated by an ecommerce platform may not contain the data needed to be analyzed, or that data may not be wholly sufficient for deep analysis of the ecommerce experience. It depends on your platform. But in many instances, today's ecommerce platforms may provide a limited data model for capturing data for ecommerce analysis, which your company will need to augment with data derived from outside the platform. Fortunately, the data in ecommerce platforms can be very useful—and tools such as Jirafe were specially created to provide reporting and analytics on top of popular ecommerce platforms. The data captured by an ecommerce platform often includes detailed information about products, orders, promotions, and transactions; however, the same platform may have a very limited amount of data available about customers, marketing campaigns, conversion, and other concepts and behavior related to ecommerce.

Ecommerce analysts may choose to purchase ecommerce analytics software that can augment and extend the data in ecommerce platforms. For example, a digital analytics platform, such as Google Analytics or Jirafe, may be configured to recognize tagged marketing campaigns and track the onsite behavior of the people referred from a campaign—and may have built-in integration features to join data from ecommerce platforms (like Jirafe does) or other methods to integrate custom dimensions (like Google Analytics does). In this way, digital analytics tools can be used to measure conversion rate by marketing campaign—and deeper conversion metrics by product, brand, and category when the data is made available through integration. Going a step further, the elements of the user experience—from the text entries in form fields to the use of check boxes to the selected values in drop-down boxes to specific click-based interactions (such as the use of Zoom on a product page)—can also be tracked (and integrated). All of these data are then related to one another via the data model and processing logic and rules underlying the digital analytics tools.

Other digital analytics technologies that have ecommerce functionality may go a step beyond tracking behavior and marketing campaigns. Some analytics technology may enable data collection and reporting via integration with a company's merchandising platforms and inventory management or warehouse replenishment systems. Still other technologies may allow for data collection that occurs off-site, such as in Google's Product Listing Ads or in Amazon Marketplace. All this digital data may be stored separate from the ecommerce platform. Or the digital data may be passed back to the ecommerce platform for reporting via a pre-built integration. Alternatively, digital data collected from digital analytics tools can be integrated with ecommerce platform data with business intelligence and analytics tools. See Chapter 13, "Integrating Data and Analysis to Drive Your Ecommerce Strategy."

In the best case, a comprehensive, unified ecommerce data model supported by an analytics implementation that integrates data from the platform and first, second, and third party data will enable data analysis across the entire ecommerce experience and for many different stakeholders. The right data model makes it possible to track customer behavior in third-party experiences, the click-through back to the site, and to purchase. The right data model enables you to build a detailed user profile, or track a customer's browsing behavior and relate it to available inventory in order to suggest items that the customer may be interested in. The right data model specific to your business and relevant to your stakeholder's business questions is necessary and critical for ecommerce analysis.

Understanding the Ecommerce Analytics Data Model: Facts and Dimensions

The optimal data model for an ecommerce company depends on the ecommerce site's requirements, which can extend beyond only analytics requirements. For example, the choice of an overall data model will look to address technical concerns, such as transaction rate, reliability, maintainability, scalability, and cost, as well as business concerns. It is common for a "relational data model" to be chosen for ecommerce. The most common relational model for analytical processing is a dimensional data model. Of course, in today's world of big data, there are "post-relational" data models (such as graphs and multivalue stores) that may be used. But this book is not meant to and will not explore the reasons for implementation choice behind data models. Instead, readers need to understand the dimensional data model and its logical representation. It is from the dimensional data model that analytics can be extracted, new data can be joined, and detailed analysis can be done. The ecommerce data model focuses on facts/measures and dimensions. A fact can be a business measurement, a quantity (an amount), or an event that is part of a business process. A fact is typically a continuous numeric value that is additive, but it does not have to be. Facts can be additive (summable), semi-additive (summable under certain conditions), and non-additive. Facts are used to answer questions such as "What were sales last month?" Facts are identified in a construct named a "fact table." Without getting into data model design, it's important for an ecommerce analyst to know that measures are calculated values that are based on facts. A measure points to a fact and also specifies the aggregation on the value (such as a sum or median). For example, you may have a fact named "Order Transaction Fact Table." In that table, you may have some measures, such as sales price, sales quantity, cost (as well as foreign keys to dimensional tables, such as time/date, product ID, category ID, and promotion ID). A measure is usually an additive numeric value for representing a business metric. You may have multiple measures associated with a fact (Chen 1976). For example, if your fact table is used to store data related to international purchases, you may have measures for each type of currency based off of one fact (i.e., the international purchase). For ecommerce you might also have measures related to product cost, list price, sale price, average sale price, and so on.

Dimensions provide context about a fact, such as what or to whom the fact would apply, when it can be used, under what conditions the fact can be measured, and where. Dimensions correspond to people and objects. Facts correspond to events and numbers. Dimensions are typically discrete variables that can represent a character, string, or number value. Dimensions that do not change are called static dimensions; those that change are called slowly changing dimensions. For example, you may have a dimension named "brand" that represents the brands you sell. In many businesses the brands do not change over time, but in others they can change slowly over time. Slowly changing dimensions have special methodologies, referred to as Type 0 to 6. In ecommerce analysis, dimensions are used to identify and group data, such as customers, locations, marketing campaigns, and categories. You may use a dimension to answer the question "What products did we sell last holiday season?" For example, you may have a dimension named "Customer Dimension" that references the fact "Customer ID" (as the primary key). In this Customer Dimension, you might want to track the customer name, address, and other attributes of the customer profile. Other types of dimensions, beyond the scope of this book, include conforming dimensions, junk dimensions, degenerate dimensions, and role-playing dimensions.

You may be asking yourself, "What is a primary key?" A primary key is a database construct that is identified in a dimensional table, and is thus part of a dimension. It is a column or set of columns in a table where the values uniquely identify a row in the table. The primary key is unique for each row in the dimension table. The value of the primary key is what's stored in the fact table. Within a fact table, you will have another type of key named a "dimension foreign key," which is the key whose values correspond to the values of the primary key. Primary keys are related to dimension foreign keys in the sense that the foreign key enables the relationship between the fact and the dimension by enforcing referential integrity between the two tables (Agrawal 2001). The primary key can be a "surrogate key" that joins the dimension to the fact.

When you are doing ecommerce analytics, it is important to understand the facts, measures, dimensions, and keys in your database (if they are made available) in order to query the database. In some tools, esoteric details related to the dimensional model and the query language can be abstracted and hidden from the user via drag-and-drop interfaces or interfaces in which you visually select a dimension or measure as, respectively, the rows and columns in a report. Google Analytics' "custom reporting" feature is an example of this type of visual query abstraction.

As an analyst, you likely will have to query databases or express, in somewhat technical terms, the data you are looking to analyze. Understanding facts, measures, dimensions, and the types of keys will help you navigate through the data and get your bearings in order to get the data you need for analysis.

Explaining a Sample Ecommerce Data Model

Now that you have a general understanding of dimensional data models and the concepts applied to them, it is possible to define a sample ecommerce data model. Your ecommerce data model will be custom to your company. Analysts work with technologists to define the conceptual data model and then implement it logically (with keys) and physically (in a database so it can be with data from site activity). Although the model will vary by company, it can have facts similar to those in the following list. Each of these facts will have dimensions and measures and at least one primary key for joining data across facts to create new combined data:

- **Inventory fact** contains data about the products within your inventory wherever it exists, such as in your warehouse or, in the case of drop-shipping, at the manufacturer. The information contained in this fact will include dimensions about the inventory, how long it has been at the company, and other information about cost and sales.
- **Products fact** represents information specific to particular, unique products, such as the product name, the SKU, the retail price, the brand, the category, the department name, and other data and metadata related to specific products.
- **Order fact** indicates data related to the cost and profit of orders, the number of orders, the number of items in an order, the date the order was created, and more.
- **Order Items fact** contains data about the item's brand, the identifiers, the sale price, the data purchased, and information related to whether the item was returned and details about the return.

- **Customer fact** identifies data about customers, including the customer ID, the name, the address, the e-mail address, and other personally identifiable and mostly anonymous data (such as gender).

- **Customer Order fact** represents data about customers after they place an order. It can contain information about how long the user has been a customer, when she first and last ordered an item, whether she is a repeat customer, and other derivative information. Some data modelers may include this data in the customer fact and not create a separate fact.

In this simplified data model we have users who order products that are in inventory. As you can see, this sample model is elegant in its simplicity (Occam's razor, anyone?) but may not be sufficient in all business cases. These facts will contain data that can be represented as dimensions and measures, which are used for analysis. When working with a technical team to model this data, you must identify the data you need and relationships necessary to perform analysis that answers your business questions. The following sections expand on these facts and define the dimensions and measures you may want to create within them, or use as a basis for understanding or evolving your company's data model.

Understanding the Inventory Fact

"Inventory" is a collection of goods that an ecommerce company retains for the purpose of reselling them for profit. An Inventory fact will have different dimensions and measures. An Inventory Identifier will always be created to uniquely specify the inventory item. Dimensions such as Cost of the inventory as paid by the ecommerce company are included. The Date Created and Sold Date dimensions are used to specify the calendar date when the inventory was first available (in the warehouse or the site) and then sold. Days in Inventory and Days Since Arrival may be used. Measures in an Inventory fact could include cost metrics, such as Average Cost and Total Cost. The Number on Hand and Number Sold are useful Inventory measures, as is the Sold Percent.

Understanding the Product Fact

A Product is a specific inventory item that is sold on the ecommerce site. Products are managed and marketed. Promotions and discounts are offered on products. Products are, of course, very important to track and understand. Thus, having a comprehensive fact is helpful. A Product Fact will have a Product Identifier to uniquely specify it and also a Product Name. The Shop Keeper's Unit (SKU) may be assigned. Price-based dimensions such as Wholesale Price, Retail Price, Sale Price, Gross Margin, and Discount Percentage might be used. The product's Brand, Category, and Department can be dimensions, as might be the Sale Rank representing the popularity of the product.

The Product fact can have measures, most commonly, counts of dimensions, like Total Count, Brand Count, and price and discount-based measures, like Average Sales Price and Average Promotional Discount. If you sell services online, then you would have a Services Fact, which will have similar and probably slightly different dimensions, like Provider.

Understanding the Order Fact

The Order is a request for one or more products (or services) that occurs as the result of the purchasing process. Order analysis is a core activity in ecommerce; thus, the Order fact has many possible dimensions. An Order Identifier, Order Created Date, and the Order Status are all necessary. Financially derived dimensions, like the Order Cost, Order Total Amount, Order Gross Margin, and Order Profit are helpful. Dimensions related to marketing programs, like Campaign Source and Traffic Source, could be used. Dimensions that flag specific concepts may be created, such as First Purchase Flag, Days Since Last Order, and Repeat Order Within X Days (when order data is joined with customer data).

The Order fact has measures such as the Count of Orders, the Purchase Date, the Average Order Amount, Average Profit, and Total Profit. If orders can be "pending," then measures to determine the Maximum Days Pending or Average Days Pending could be calculated, as could the Repeat Purchase Rate for identical orders. Measures related to customers and their orders can be created as Order measures, like the Count Percent Change (the change in the count of orders compared across periods) and the Count Percent Total (the total percentage of orders). New Customer Revenue, New Customer Orders, Repeat Customer Revenue, and Repeat Customer Orders may be modeled.

Understanding the Order Item Fact

The Order Item fact is related to the Order in that the Order contains the Order Item. It's awkward to write, but simple to understand. When you place an order on a site, you buy things. The item is the thing you buy. You may buy many items in an order. The Order Item has dimensions, such as the Order Item Identifier and many financially based dimensions, such as the Wholesale Price, Retail Price, Sales Price, Gross Margin Total, Gross Margin Percentage, Gross Margin Tier, Contribution Margin Total, Contribution Margin Percentage, and Contribution Margin Tier.

The Order Item fact also has measures, such as the Count of Order Items (people order more than one individual item in the order). Financially based metrics should be included, such as Average Gross Margin, Total Gross Margin, Average Contribution Margin, and Total Contribution Margin (and Percentages). Of course, you can also include Average Sales Price and Total Sales Price.

Understanding the Customers Fact

A Customer is a user who has ordered one or more products from your ecommerce site's inventory. The Customer fact has many dimensions, which should seem familiar to you. The Customer Identifier uniquely identifies the customer. Dimensions are included such as Name, Email, Address, City, State, Zip Code, and Country. The Gender of the customer may be a dimension. Marketing-focused dimensions in the Customers fact could include the Campaign (attributed to acquiring the customer), Marketing Channel (attributed, again). Value-based dimensions include Number of Orders, Lifetime Value, and Cost to Acquire. Lifecycle dimensions include Days as Customer (that is, customer age), Days Since Last Purchase, Distinct Months with Orders, and Customer Segment. Revenue-specific dimensions based on time periods are possible, such as 24-Hour Revenue, 30/60/90/180 Revenue, and Yearly Revenue. The Users fact can also have measures such as the Count, Average Customer Age, Average Days to Next Order Estimate, Total 24-Hour Revenue, Total 30-Day Revenue, Total 90-Day Revenue, and Total 365-Day Revenue.

Understanding the Customer Order Fact

A Customer Order fact is related to both customers and orders. Some data modelers may choose not create this fact and instead make this data part of the Customer fact. Like all facts presented so far, a Customer Order fact will have a Customer Order Identifier. Dimensions can include the First Order Date, Last Order Date, Lifetime Orders, and Days Since Last Order. Measures include the Count of Orders, Days Between Orders, and Lifetime Order Value.

Reviewing Common Dimensions and Measures in Ecommerce

By this point in the chapter, I hope you understand more about ecommerce data models, the concepts of facts, dimensions, and measures, and how they can be applied in ecommerce. As you can imagine, the data model for an ecommerce company can get complex and can include much more than we've reviewed so far. One of the more common tools I've seen used on many ecommerce sites is Google Analytics. It's free and may be the first tool many ecommerce analysts see. Google has elegance in how they approach ecommerce and enhancing ecommerce data. They focus on the following six facts:

1. **Transactions** represent the totality of the purchase event, the entire transaction, within an ecommerce experience. Transactional data is collected when someone buys a product. The data about a transaction includes a Transaction Identifier, Revenue, Shipping, and Tax.

2. **Items** represent the individual products that were in the shopping cart. Items are the individual products that a user placed into the shopping cart. An item is a container for a product and is thus a higher-level abstraction. Item data can contain an Item Identifier, Item Name, SKU, Category, Price, and Quantity.

3. **Impressions** represent information about a product that has been viewed. It is data about the product that has been seen by a user and examined within your ecommerce experience. Viewing a product is akin to viewing an advertising impression in ecommerce. Thus, similar approaches to analyzing advertising can also be applied to product impressions. The dimensions and measures in an impression include an Impression Identifier, Impression Name, Variant, Price, Quantity, and Position.

4. **Products** represent individual products that were viewed, added to/removed from the shopping cart, and generally interacted with by users. Products are specific, unique, named items sold in ecommerce that are associated with a brand, category, and possibly department. A deep understanding of how users engage with, perceive, conceive, browse, and buy products is at the heart of ecommerce analytics. Data to model about products includes the Product Identifier, Product Name, Product Variant, Price, Quantity, and more.

5. **Promotions** represent information about a discount or marketing promotion that has been viewed. A driver of commerce, especially in periods of high seasonality, is discounts. Promotions are those discounts, which are typically offered via promotional codes. Promotional data represents information about available promotions, such as the Promotion Identifier, Promotion Name, Promotion Creative, Promotion Position, and Promotion Discount.

6. **Actions** represent information about an ecommerce-related activity in which the user has engaged. An action represents information about the key activity performed by users. In an ecommerce experience, actions to model include activities such as Click, View Product Detail, Add to Cart, Remove from Cart, Checkout from Cart, Checkout Completed, Checkout Option, Purchase, Return, Refund, and Promotion Used.

The ecommerce analyst must keep in mind that the ecommerce data model contains facts, dimensions, and measures. The underlying requirements to frame the data model must first be elicited by the analysts from businesspeople in merchandising, marketing, user experience, analytics, and customer service. Many of these groups will have no familiarity with ecommerce data models, or even the constructs of dimensions and measures. But their experience is essential to aligning the data they need with a data model that allows you to analyze it. Because the analytics team often stewards or works as an intermediary between the business and IT, it is necessary to understand data models and related concepts. They are crucial for being a successful analytical participant in a data modeling project as a broker in analytics projects between IT and the business. Analysts will also work with IT and engineers to ensure that logical and physical database implementation represents the information needed by stakeholders. This data you collect to populate your data model(s) will be used as variables to build data science models, as the metrics and numerators and denominators for key performance indicators, the detailed data in operational reports, and the information illustrated in data visualizations. Do not underestimate the importance of defining, creating, and understanding a data model—it forms the container for the data, relationships, and information you need in order to analyze and communicate analysis.

6

Marketing and Advertising Analytics in Ecommerce

Marketing is the business activity of communicating the value of a product such that a consumer recognizes that value and performs a value-generating transaction for the business. Advertising is the vehicle by which marketing communicates that value. Marketing and advertising analytics, thus, involves conducting analysis to support the marketing function and make recommendations that improve advertising performance. The information and recommendations are used by managers to make decisions about what to do next to run the marketing function, more efficiently allocate spend, or make decisions about marketing investment, both tactically and strategically. The ecommerce analyst's job may include analyzing the impact of marketing spend overall on revenue, brand value or equity, specific types of campaign channels and their performance, and even down to the impact of individual ad units. Customer analytics, which is discussed in Chapter 9, "Analyzing Ecommerce Customers," applies to marketing and advertising analytics.

To do marketing analysis effectively, the ecommerce analyst needs to understand the demographics of customers, the social forces guiding consumer behavior, the economic forces at play within an industry, the competitive landscape, and the technology that supports marketing execution and, more increasingly, marketing automation. The analyst must use technique to segment behavior, audiences, customers, and advertising channels and units into similar groups and categories.

By conducting and compiling new analysis within a company, the analyst is said to be conducting *primary analysis*. When an analysis uses existing data and repurposes to prove or disprove a hypothesis, the analyst is conducting *secondary analysis*. For example, if an analyst is attempting to understand whether a particular shopping cart flow is effective for conversion, the analyst is doing primary analysis. If the analyst is examining research conducted by others to make recommendations influencing the redesign of a shopping cart, she is doing secondary analysis.

The type of analysis companies will demand of their ecommerce analysts will vary over time, with secondary analytics helping to inform early-stage product development and design, and primary analytics guiding the evolution of the ecommerce experience after a site is launched. It's feasible and possible for an ecommerce company to do primary research to prove out an idea before launching a site—and subsequently prove out the hypothesis learned with more primary research and/or secondary research. As an ecommerce company grows and evolves, both primary and secondary analysis will function together to guide development and understand the effectiveness of operations.

Marketing and advertising analytics can be further categorized beyond primary and secondary analysis into *quantitative analytics* and *qualitative analytics*, which may be combined in an analytical deliverable. For example, an advertising analysis may indicate how much was generated in sales (quantitative) and also describe the attributes of the customer who bought via the advertisement (qualitative). As you've probably figured out, quantitative analysis uses numerical methods in which the data can be summed, analyzed, and modeled using mathematics and statistics (data science!), whereas qualitative analysis makes use of non-numerical methods and techniques derived from traditional research methods where text, verbatims, and categorical data are perhaps more common than numerical data. The analyst is the person who will make the decision about what analytical approach to use for research. The decision on which approach to use (or both) can be based on whether the data can be quantified via data collection or acquisition, or whether unquantifiable or abstracted ideas are needed for the analysis.

Ecommerce marketing analytics includes activities such as campaign analysis, search engine optimization (SEO), search engine marketing (SEM), e-mail analytics, social media analytics, affiliate and reseller analytics, and marketing mix modeling. Marketing analytics requires interpreting data about the brand and messages that impact the brand. Advertising for an ecommerce site requires assessing the impact of advertising on sales and requires knowledge of the advertising lifecycle and the types of advertising available. Advertising analytics can include audience and demographic analysis, unit analysis, and reach and frequency analysis. It can also include analysis of the customer's journey across advertising channels from a temporal perspective as well as from the perspective of the advertising's impact on the other advertisements seen over that time (i.e., attribution). In this chapter we will explore these concepts, describe these types of analyses, and explain how to take the next steps for executing them at your company. Please note that I covered "competitive intelligence" in my book *Building a Digital Analytics Organization*. Additionally, ecommerce companies don't typically have a sales force, so this book doesn't cover the analysis of the sales team. In some companies, sales analytics may be part of or separate from marketing analytics.

Understanding the Shared Goals of Marketing and Advertising Analysis

The goal of most analysis is to uncover meaningful information that can be used as knowledge to guide business decisions that reduce cost or increase revenue. Marketing and advertising analysis in ecommerce companies is no different. The highest ideal goal for marketing and advertising analytics is to help a company drive financial performance based on the data collected. Because marketing can be a large cost center, analysis that can help improve how marketing spend is allocated and how a marketing campaign performs can help a company's bottom line.

Marketing analytics, of course, is the larger concept in which advertising analysis occurs. Marketing buys advertising. Advertising is a marketing tactic. Thus, we can consider that the same goals for marketing analytics can, in many cases, apply to advertising analytics. It could be argued that in this book I don't need to make the distinction between marketing analytics and advertising analytics, but I think it's helpful to make a distinction such that, although the two disciplines are closely related, there's enough investment and capital being allocated both in general ecommerce marketing and in ecommerce advertising that it makes sense to discuss them individually. Marketing and advertising analytics can be categorized into the following types of analysis:

- **Exploratory analysis** investigates an assumption about a particular topic. For example, you may come up with a hypothesis about a particular marketing channel, such as social media, based on particular beliefs shared by employees at your company. The hypothesis might be that the profile of the social media audience skews toward conversation being dominated by young females and that males are marginalized in conversations about the brand. As a result, the analytics team may choose to index the text of comments in social media, perform sentiment analysis, map names to gender, and then determine whether the assumption is true.

- **Descriptive analysis** relates to the act of making the subject of an analysis clear, lucid, and understandable. As the phrase suggests, descriptive analytics focuses on answering the question "What is this?" This type of analysis identifies what is happening and what has happened so that it can be comprehended and communicated. You might notice that every Friday your ecommerce sales increase to their highest point all week. A descriptive analysis would seek to describe how much revenue increased, in what products or categories, what events occurred around the revenue increase, what segments have increased revenue, and so on.

- **Predictive analysis** is a popular topic in 2016. It references analytics that are executed to predict what may happen in the future. Given certain inputs, predictive analytics will generate an output that represents a prediction of what might happen. Methods for predictive analytics can include regression analysis, survival analysis, various types of simulations, and more. For example, you may want to predict what might happen if the marketing spend for a particular channel is increased at the same time a new line of products is introduced. Predictive analysis, given the appropriate data, can be used to find out the possible answer to what might happen.

- **Conclusive analytics** attempts to derive a conclusion based on the available data and the relationships between the variables in the data. For example, an analyst might notice that certain products sell when there is a local marketing event, but the data collection doesn't support directly linking product sales to the event; yet the analyst has seen the causality enough to conclude that there must be a correlation between the event and sales. The analyst would then build a model to explore the relationships between the variables related to sales and the variables related to the event to see whether a mathematically valid conclusion about the relationships can be derived.

- **Prescriptive analytics** involves determining the right course of action to take given a number of variables and potential outcomes. The idea of determining the right action to take is referred to as prescriptive analytics and is an evolution of predictive analytics. It is one thing to predict what could happen, but it is more powerful to tell people what action to take and the impact a particular set of predictions and actions would have on the rest of the business. As such, prescriptive analytics suggests the best possible beneficial action to take after knowing the predictions, and it identifies the implications of each prediction so that the stakeholder is guided. For example, a predictive model in ecommerce may predict the certain set of products to show to a customer. A prescriptive model will identify the best set of those products to maximize gross profit.

When marketing analytics and advertising analytics are being performed, both qualitative and quantitative analytical methods will be applied. Qualitative analytics are research-based methods that involve collected data from people via focus groups, interviews, and approaches that collect human responses that are not expressed using numbers. Qualitative methods for analytics include these:

- **Focus groups** in which people are asked directly about their perceptions, opinions, beliefs, and attitudes related to an ecommerce brand or product.

- **Interviews** in which questions are posed by an interviewer directly to people in the form of conversation. Responses are captured and analyzed.

- **Projective approaches** in which a person responds to stimuli to help the ecommerce site understand how people are thinking about what has been presented. For example, new media may be shown, a home page design may be addressed, promotional offers may be reviewed, or creative text may be read. The goal is to uncover opinions and emotions that otherwise are difficult or impossible to measure online.

- **Panels** consisting of a group of individuals whose behaviors, thoughts, beliefs, and actions are sampled and inflated to project to an entire audience or population.

- **Surveys** with specific questions related to an area of interest sent to audiences to collect primary data based on the responses; or research about prospects and customers purchased as secondary data from research companies.

Reviewing the Marketing Lifecycle

Analyzing marketing and advertising requires knowledge of the marketing lifecycle. The marketing lifecycle can be expressed as a set of linear phases around which marketing programs are executed. The ecommerce analyst must strive to analyze the data collected during each of the following phases:

Phase 1: Activation. Activation is measured qualitatively via surveys and voice of the customer (VoC) data. Activation in analytics refers to the "awakening" of need in the customer. Activation can be acute (occurring suddenly) or realized (a result of long-term influences). Marketing activities across TV, print, or radio can influence ecommerce. Think of William Shatner or the trivago guy.

Phase 2: Exposure. In a state of activation, the potential customer (the lead) sees and perceives the brand and its associated physical and psychological properties and qualities through paid, owned, or earned media. Marketing activities such as online advertising can generate exposure for ecommerce companies.

Phase 3: Awareness. In an activated and exposed state, the lead who is exposed to the brand becomes cognitively aware of the exposure. Similar to when your mother told you, "You might hear me, but you aren't listening," you can understand how awareness results from exposure, but not all exposure creates awareness. Another case in point is the online advertising industries emphasis on a "viewable impression," which suggests a similar relationship between exposure and awareness. Search engine marketing (SEM) can generate awareness.

Phase 4: Differentiation. This is the process of evaluating a brand and its product or service qualities against competitors and substitutes. A lead compares attributes against each other to determine how to work through the infoglut of advertising. During this phase, the narrative of the advertising and exposure is accepted, viewed as aberrant, or resisted by the lead. Content marketing can help differentiate an ecommerce brand.

Phase 5: Consideration. A lead considers the brand against competitors and substitutes based on a judgment of the fit of the brand's perceived qualities against the customer's perceived needs. Consideration is where the many are slimmed to the few—and where it is most likely a customer will seek and be exposed to brand messages from multiple channels. Search engine optimization can drive consideration.

Phase 6: Acquisition. This phase involves accounting for the many paid, owned, and earned media across which your leads may have been exposed. For an ecommerce site these channels may have been used for earlier phases in the lifecycle. What drives acquisition is the fundamental question that attribution analysis tries to solve.

Phase 7: Conversion. Having transitioned from acquisition source and attributable marketing channel, the customer buys online, and a conversion occurs. The customer searches for products, adds them to a shopping cart, buys them, and generates a profitable conversion. Factors that influence conversion include the overall ecommerce experience and specific flows like the checkout process.

Phase 8: Retention. Although customer conversion, and thus the transition from "engagement time" to "revenue dollars," is an impressive achievement, it is even more impressive and profitable when the customer comes back to buy again. The business activities of nurturing and having a "customer relationship" are crucial to measure. Incentives, promotions, and discounts sent over e-mail and promotions offered via social media can drive retention.

Phase 9: Loyalty. A customer can be considered loyal after a second purchase. Loyalty analysis involves understanding why and how the customer purchased again from your company. Even more critical is how—post purchase—the customer again became activated and moved through phases 1 to 5. In both Retention and Loyalty, customer churn and lifetime value analysis are important. Customer reward programs, periodic events (like seasonal sales), and newsletters can help create loyalty.

If you are an advocate of the linear funnel, such a theory for linking advertising to conversion in ecommerce might read something like this:

1. Creates awareness through differentiation.
2. Positions the brand and buying experience such that it evokes favorability.
3. Reaches enough people so the advertising strengthens the brand and supports or maintains brand equity.
4. Informs and compels a person's purchasing behavior via a certain frequency of exposures.
5. Leads to a person visiting an ecommerce site or mobile app via an advertisement directly or indirectly through brand exposure.
6. Creates a frictionless buying experience that enables a person to easily find the product for which they are looking and buy it.
7. Generates or sustains loyalty and reactivation during the next cycle of realization of the intent to purchase by using targeted, customer-specific marketing and advertising.

The analyst's job is to ensure that business questions can be answered about the activities within the marketing lifecycle. To do so, the analyst must collect data within and across all of these phases, coordinating with the marketing team, IT, and supporting teams and ensuring data collection and availability for future analytical projects. Then the analysts must, of course, analyze the data.

Understanding Types of Ecommerce Marketing

Ecommerce marketing tactics are used in the marketing lifecycle to move people through each phase. The ecommerce analyst will measure the performance and outcomes of the advertising and campaigns of different marketing types such as these:

- **Activation marketing** can include programs that try to activate the brand in the mind of consumers by putting advertisements wherever they can be bought. But as Angela D. Nalica, professor of statistics at the University of the Philippines, says, "Marketing activation usually entails a universal blast of information to all consumers. Often, only a small proportion of the consumers react positively to such activation, resulting in waste in marketing expenses. If a circle of influencers can be identified for certain events or phenomena, then such activities can be focused into a group of factors or individuals, thus optimizing the outcomes."

- **Exposure and awareness marketing** can include public relations releases and communications; advertising on television, on the radio, and in print; online advertising; e-mail; and paid and organic search. The goal of awareness marketing is to drive home the message of activation marketing (if done). Its primary purpose is to get the brand or product recognized in the minds of potential customers.

- **Consideration marketing** appeals to consumers who are nearing readiness to buy. They are aware of the brands and products and are actively considering alternatives and options. Content, social reviews, events, and promotional offers sent by ecommerce companies can help to promote consideration. Social ads, social reviews, blogs, user-generated content (sponsored or unsponsored), and media such as webinars, videos, and other multimedia content are used in consideration marketing.

- **Acquisition marketing** focuses on driving traffic to an ecommerce site. Depending on the goal of the program, the acquisition may be broad to appeal to all possible consumers who are in the target market, or narrow to focus only on consumers who have certain attributes or are within a particular phase of the customer journey. Targeting and retargeting, online media, e-mails, promotions, direct mail, and focused advertising are used to bring prospective customers to the site.

- **Conversion marketing** drives addressable audiences toward the completion of a conversion activity, such as the purchase of a product. Conversion optimization, discussed in Chapter 8, "Optimizing for Ecommerce Conversion and User Experience," is a type of conversion marketing. Conversion marketing also includes paid search, targeted display ads with direct offers, onsite merchandising, and promotions.

- **Retention and loyalty marketing** focuses on the critical need of companies to sell more to customers who have purchased in the past. Promotional programs, loyalty programs, and targeted marketing across different channels can help to promote customer retention and loyalty. Community forums, user groups, social networks, blogs, newsletters, special promotions, targeted incentives, and offers to repurchase are all part of retention and loyalty marketing.

Analyzing Marketing and Advertising for Ecommerce

Marketing uses tactics and techniques for creating a brand, driving brand awareness, targeting customers, and then compelling and guiding them through a customer journey that results in a purchase. The phases of the marketing lifecycle can be thought of as supporting a potential customer as he moves through a journey from not having bought to buying. To analyze marketing and advertising, it's important, as always, to consider the business goal of the analysis, the type of the analysis you are going to do, the customer journey, and the types of marketing within phases of the journey. By considering all of this information, you can create and execute a plan for ecommerce marketing analytics, such as these fundamental types of analysis:

- **Campaign analysis** uses the campaign code as the primary dimension for understanding performance. Campaign codes are human-readable or encoded parameters in a query string. These parameters are name/value pairs that are meaningful to people, and usually understood by machines. Campaign codes typically specify the campaign name, the type of marketing campaign (i.e., paid search, display, e-mail, and so on), and other information, such as the placement, the version, the variation of the campaign, or the creative in it. It is a good idea to standardize on a specific set of naming conventions and valid names and values for campaign codes. These conventions should also fit the requirements necessary for automatically processing campaign data using campaign codes.

- **Search engine marketing** (SEM) traditionally refers to the business and technical processes and work required for bidding on paid search keywords and managing them to maximize performance. The work can include keyword research in which analysis is done into the words and phrases most likely to be used by people to search for the ecommerce site or its products. Ads are created, including the creative text that appears in the ads and is displayed in the search engine. The content in the ad is controlled. Most important, search engine marketing allows for the ranking of the ads to be specified (up to the cap or the available budget). SEM enables detailed and specific targeting of the keyword to specific devices, browsers, geographies, time periods, and more.

- **Search engine optimization** (SEO) describes the process for ensuring that the content on an ecommerce site is displayed in organic search results in the desired ranking for a specific keyword. Like SEM, SEO involves keyword research to identify important and relevant phrases for the ecommerce site and its products. But it also involves onsite technical work to determine whether the site's content is indexable by search engines and contains the specific keywords and relevant content to rank in search results. SEO also requires backlinking from other sites to the ecommerce site and an assessment of how sufficiently search engines are crawling and indexing site content. Other tools for SEO assist an analyst with understanding the factors that influence search rankings, the keywords used to find the site, the performance of organic search keywords toward KPIs, and other helpful information.

- **Affiliate analytics** is a way of analyzing the effectiveness of affiliates and affiliate networks in teams of conversion, revenue, and profitability. Affiliates are, of course, sites that send traffic or, optimally, customers who engage in transactions of buying products. In exchange for the revenue-generating customer or the traffic, the ecommerce site will pay for performance at an agreed-on rate. Analysts must set up the right tracking, measurement, and reporting to be able to analyze the performance of affiliates in order to assist with decision making. Affiliate tracking involves the customer and the ecommerce site, but also the affiliate (publisher) and the affiliate network in which they are a part. When tracking affiliates, you must use campaign codes specific to each campaign per affiliate, per affiliate network, and per offer—and you must be able to track these dimensions through behavior that leads to conversion.

- **Social media analytics** is about listening, engaging, and participating in social media through conversation, commentary, marketing, advertising, and other forms of multimedia-based social engagement (video, audio, and rich experiences). The goal of social media can be to build brand awareness, strengthen and inform customer relationships, influence prospective customers during the customer journey, create word-of-mouth virality, and drive consumer engagement and direct response. Text analysis, such as sentiment analysis, concept extraction, and classification, and text mining are useful when analyzing text-based social media data.

- **E-mail analytics** measures the effectiveness of e-mail as a marketing channel for causing purchases directly as a result of the e-mail or indirectly from latent visits and buying after exposure to e-mail. E-mail analysis includes understanding the customer data in order to create relevant segmented e-mail lists based on known behaviors and/or past purchasing history or other attributes. Analysis of the actual e-mail distribution includes deliverability metrics, opt-outs, bounces, open rates, click-throughs, and e-mail–specific attribution. Links, buttons, images, and other hot spots in e-mail creative can be campaign-coded and linked to specific landing pages, such as individual product pages, and their impact on conversion can be measured and reported.

- **Marketing-mix modeling** is the term used to describe the application of data science and statistical analysis to sales and marketing data in order to understand the impact of marketing on sales, and then to forecast, estimate, or predict future sales based on maintaining or modifying the mix of marketing. A marketing-mix model estimates sales in two ways. First, base sales are identified, which are the sales that result from natural demand. Second, incremental sales are estimated based on demand generated from marketing. Factors in a media-mix model include the price, promotions, the distribution strategy, competitor impact, and the different types and channels of marketing and advertising. These factors are all analyzed to suggest an optimal marketing and advertising mix and tactics that achieve the desired revenue or profit goals. Media-mix modeling can help determine the return on investment, as well as the contribution of, and effectiveness of, marketing tactics. This information can be used to better allocate marketing budgets, spend marketing investments more wisely, and guide promotional offers and advertising strategies.

- **Attribution** involves understanding the impact of marketing channels on revenue, engagement, or another quantitative indicator in rank order of their impact. See Chapter 11, "Attribution in Ecommerce Analytics," for more information.

- **Audience analysis** is about understanding the attributes of the audience from available data. This data can include age, gender, demographic, psychographic, propensity, mind-set, neurometric, psychological, transactional, behavioral, and other data. This information is used to create narratives describing and identifying the customer. Whether via personas or "buyer legends" or simply segments, clusters, and cohorts, marketing requires the ability to understand the audience across these dimensions in order to maximize lifetime value or reduce the cost of customer acquisition.

- **Online display ad unit analysis** informs the creative conceptualizing, building, trafficking, and placing of ad units on external sites by an ad server. This type of analysis involves describing and comparing how well ad units contribute toward the desired goals. Some ad units may be for branding; others, for direct response. The impact of exposure of these ads to awareness, favorability, consideration, and acquisition can be studied. In addition, fraud can be detected, investigated, and remediated.

- **Customer journey analysis** refers to an analysis that tracks prospects and customers as they move through different phases of the customer journey specific to the ecommerce site. Specific metrics can be measured, reported, and analyzed to inform about the count and behavior of prospects and customers with marketing and advertisements targeted to each phase in the customer journey.

What Marketing Data Could You Begin to Analyze?

One of the simplest marketing analyses is also the most complex and hardest to realize. The Customer Origin report shows the source of customers acquired from the different marketing channels; for example, direct, referral, paid search, organic search, social, and the various types of online advertising. It's a simple report because many tools will deliver it as a capability "out of the box." It is complex because it requires the ecommerce company to define how the traffic should be allocated to the various marketing channels and to practice and adhere to those definitions when adding campaign codes and metadata available for reporting. It also requires a specific attribution model to be used. For each traffic source or marketing channel, consider collecting data such as the number of visits by channel (including both prospects and customers), conversion rate, revenue, the number of orders, the number of customers (i.e., visitors who bought), repeat customers, repeat customer rate, average order value, and revenue per customer. From these core metrics and KPIs, you can begin to understand what marketing channels are contributing to performance, conversion, and revenue—and then direct your subsequent marketing and advertising analysis activities toward exploring, describing, concluding, predicting, and prescribing what you have uncovered.

7

Analyzing Behavioral Data

The analysis of digital behavior is a frequently discussed topic in ecommerce analytics due to the availability of free and lower-cost, powerful, and fairly easy-to-use analytics tools, like Google Analytics. Behavior in ecommerce refers to the ordered and unordered digital interactions a person has with the ecommerce experience. Digital behavior is commonly represented by the concept of a clickstream, which is a sequenced group or set of clicks on an ecommerce interface. Traditionally, clickstreams were associated with onsite behavior where clicks occurred. Not all digital behavior in 2016 is represented through clicks (and the underlying implicit server call used to capture the behavior). In fact, with the rise of rich media, the term "clickstream" has lost some of its meaning. Mobile apps may have clicks, and they also have other methods for interactions, such as haptic features of swipes, hard (peep) and soft (poke) touches (in Apple's 3D Touch), and scrolls. With the rise of asynchronous JavaScript, HTML 5, and other rich Internet experiences in which features are embedded within other features (such as a shipping calculator), it may not make sense or even be technically feasible to capture every click. Server calls may not be generated to collect data, so more complex data collection may be necessary. For example, to capture offline behavior in a mobile app, the data collection is cached and transmitted later. For data collection in contemporary ecommerce experiences, concepts like event-tracking and goal-tracking have been developed to augment and extend the clickstream in order to provide more detail about interactions and behavior. Events are specific interactions; goals are desired results. Adding to the shopping cart is an event. A purchase is a goal. Events and goals can sometimes be the same. Events, goals, and clickstreams can be analyzed discretely in KPIs and continuously in flows and paths. Go beyond simple click-based ecommerce behavioral analysis by collecting business-relevant behavioral event and goal data.

When you are analyzing ecommerce behavior, each business stakeholder will want to know something different about user and customer behavior. Segmentation and clustering can be helpful, as discussed in Chapter 9, "Analyzing Ecommerce Customers." The marketing team will want to understand behavior by channel. The product team will want to understand behavior about browsing, shopping, and checking out. The CRM team will want to understand behaviors that indicate loyalty and retention. The merchandising team will want to understand behavior around categories, brands, products, bundles, and promotions. Although the goals of each stakeholder will be different, the behavior you analyze will be expressed with the same concepts: clicks, events, screen views, page views, durations, financial measures, rates and ratios, and so on. See Chapter 3, "Methods and Techniques for Ecommerce Analysis" for tips on analyzing data.

Behavioral analytics in ecommerce benefits from having a consistent framework for understanding behavior. The following framework can provide a structure to start analyzing behavioral data:

- **Segment, cohort, cluster analysis.** While different, the analyses assign a grouping to which a behavior is identified and associated. At the most macro level, a segment could be a new or returning visitor. A cohort could be people who purchased in the past 12 weeks. In this case the grouping is based on assigning behavior to an identifiable customer (or a proxy thereof, like a cookie or ID). On the other hand, behaviors can be associated with other behaviors, with products, and with transactions, so the cluster and/or segment assigned to the behavior need not be related to only people. For more information, see Chapter 9, "Analyzing Ecommerce Customers."

- **Acquisition channel** is the marketing channel from which the customer was acquired as dictated by the attribution model used. The marketing channels include organic search, paid search, direct/unknown, social media, online media (such as display ads, retargeting), e-mail, and so on. See Chapter 6, "Marketing and Advertising Analytics in Ecommerce," for more information.

- **Time** is the progress of the sessions (visits by customers or prospects/leads) as measured in standardized increments of second, minute, hour, and day. The existence of virtual interactions, clicks, actions, events, and goals are measured on a temporal scale. As a result, recency, frequency, and time-based measurements of behavior become possible.

- **Sessions** are the interactions by prospects and customers occurring within your ecommerce experience within a given time. During a session, a user generates page views, engages in behavior measured over time, completes events and goals, and generates ecommerce transactions.

- **Pages or screens** are the unique renderings of user experiences within an ecommerce experience. Page views and screen views are the measurement of the instance when content fully loads on your screen—for example, a product page.

- **Events** are user interactions on pages and screens independent of the page or screen view. An event occurs when a person takes an action and does something within an ecommerce experience. An event occurs when a visitor clicks on a button or link, or touches a screen or browser. Important events to track in ecommerce include "add to cart," "start checkout," and "completed checkout."

- **Transactions** are financial interactions between a buyer and an ecommerce experience in which something of value is exchanged for something else. In ecommerce the purchase is the transaction when marketed and merchandised products are bought. See Chapter 10, "Analyzing Products and Orders in Ecommerce."

- **Goals** are specific interactions that represent the desired result of predefined behavior; for example, the goal of selling an item, or registering a new member, or engaging in another meaningful and measurable behavior, such as an advertising click.

- **Outcomes** are the consequences related to the behaviors, transactions, goals, and events that occur during the ecommerce experience. Most commonly the outcomes measured from behavior are financial in nature, such as revenue per visitor or revenue per customer and other "revenue per" measures, average order value, and cost per visitor and customer.

Let's apply this framework in an ecommerce narrative: A customer from a segment visits from an acquisition channel, generates a clickstream of clicks and events on the site, completes a goal such as a transaction, and thus generates a financial outcome for the business. For example, a new customer comes directly to the site, searches and finds shoes, adds them to the cart, registers a new account, purchases the shoes, and generates $325 in new revenue for the company. Or an existing customer visits the site, clicks through the product catalog, adds items to her cart, and abandons it; then, the following day, she clicks through a recapture e-mail directly to the cart, logs in, buys the items abandoned the preceding day, and increases her customer lifetime value. Both of these customer journeys can be understood and thus analyzed with the concepts in this framework.

In these customer journeys, the behavior analyzed is sequential in nature, such that it is ordered as a logical progression. X happens, and then Y happens, and then Z happens, and so on. This type of behavioral analysis is called *ordered behavioral analytics*. The pathing of clickstreams is ordered behavioral analytics. The opposite of ordered behavior is, of course, unordered behavior. *Unordered behavioral analytics* looks beyond the behavioral sequence and into commonalities or differences in independent behaviors—for example, analyzing the impact of an acquisition channel on detailed product views by answering the question "Do particular marketing channels generate more usage of zoom features and video product previews?" Asking "What happened before or after a product was added to the shopping cart?" is ordered analysis. Thus, you want to consider whether ordered or unordered analysis of behavior will guide your approach to fulfilling business goals with ecommerce analytics.

Behavior occurs around any concept in ecommerce analytics. Customers have behavior, so you can associate behavioral data with known customer attributes, like geography or propensities.

Answering Business Questions with Behavioral Analytics

I always advise that it is a smart idea to begin analytical activities by defining the business questions you want to answer before you start to do analysis. When you're doing behavioral analysis, it can help to start with a general question and then layer in more specific questions that relate to the topic and help the creation of value. These questions will guide the data you want to examine or, perhaps, will need to collect. They also provide the context for using the framework presented previously about the segment, channel, events, goals, transactions, and outcomes. Here are some business questions about ecommerce behavioral analytics that you may find helpful to consider to begin analyzing your data:

- What specific pages or screens do people who purchase always view?
  - On those specific pages what actions do people take?
  - Is there a relationship between certain actions on the page and transactions?
  - What are the most viewed product pages? Are those products the most purchased?
- What marketing channels drive the most time spent within the ecommerce experience?
  - What is the conversion rate by marketing channel?
  - Do people who come from particular marketing channels abandon carts at a higher rate?
- What promotional codes and coupons are most frequently used by people who spend the least amount of time onsite but engage in a transaction?
  - Are specific categories, brands, or products purchased by the low-duration, high-transaction-generating customers?
- What do people do after they search?
  - What keywords generate the most revenue—onsite and offsite?

- What keywords have the highest conversion?
- What pages do people who search most frequently abandon after viewing?

Understanding Metrics and Key Performance Indicators for Behavioral Analysis

Behavioral analysis is measured by KPIs and other metrics related to segments, channels, sessions, pages, events, goals, transactions, time, and outcomes. Keep in mind a metric is a number, whereas a KPI is a metric that is meaningful to your business and helps you achieve business objectives. Here are some common ways behavior is measured and expressed in quantitative terms. (For more information, see Chapters 3 and 4.)

- **Average session or visit duration** measures the length in time, the duration, from when a visitor views the first page to when he visits the second-from-last page. The last-page duration is not measured in most tools. When there is only a single page visit, the duration may not be measured.
- **Time between X** is known as "frequency." If a visitor visits the site every day, that visitor has a daily frequency. Other ecommerce goals, such as adding to a shopping cart or leaving product feedback, can be measured in terms of frequency. The goal of understanding frequency is to ensure that it meets expectations and to impact it positively through actions.
- **Time since X** is known as "recency." If a visitor hasn't been to the site in 90 days, that visitor's recency is 90 days since the last visit. Recency and frequency are related but different. Recency lets you know whether you are achieving the desired frequency when looking at an instance of behavior. If recency is decreasing, an action should be taken to bring the person back.
- **Number of X** before purchase is widely applicable. In this case X is any type of meaningful event or goal in the ecommerce experience. You can track the number of days, events, marketing touches, e-mail opens, or other important behavioral

events. The goal, again, is to take action to move the metric in the desired direction.

- **Time to purchase after acquisition** measures the duration in time it takes a customer to make a purchase after engaging through a marketing channel. This allows you to see which marketing channels occur closer in time to a purchase, and is related to attribution, discussed in Chapter 11, "Attribution in Ecommerce Analytics."

- **Sessions to purchase after acquisition** measures the number of sessions it takes a customer before he makes a purchase after being acquired through a marketing channel.

- **Conversion rate** by channel, by category, by brand, by product measures the percentage of sessions or of visitors who make a purchase. The way you define conversion is important. It's more common to measure conversion by the number of orders per session, and less common to measure it by visitor. The rationale is that every visit to a site is an opportunity for a conversion. Customers may also buy more than once in the measured period. As a result, conversion rate by session tends to be the most conservative measure. Segmenting the conversion rate measurement you choose to use by product, brand, category, and channel will identify areas to improve.

- **Average site searches before transaction** measures how many internal searches have been entered before the transaction. This metric helps you understand the performance of your internal search and how it helps to drive purchase. It also enables you to segment customers who have used search versus those who have not, to compare their behavior.

- **Abandonment rate by products (and thus channel, by category, by brand)** measures, in terms of percentage, how often products are left unbought in a shopping cart. Although the core concept is the product being abandoned, it is possible to roll up all abandoned products into measures that identify the abandonment rates by channel, category, and brand.

- **Checkout abandonment rate** is a simple measure that quantifies the percentage of shopping carts that aren't bought or completed to purchase. In the case of a shopping cart that contains items that aren't bought, while some are, then you can measure the related metric: *percentage of abandoned products of total products in carts that are purchased.*

- **Percentage of customers who repurchase** by channel, by category, by brand, by product measures the percentage of customers who come back and rebuy.

- **Correlation** between clicks, events, goals, and transactions is an analysis that provides a measure that explains the tendency of one click, or event, or transaction to occur when another occurs. Correlations do not mean one variable caused another but can indicate an association and dependence. For more information, see Chapter 3.

Make sure to distinguish between three types of KPIs and metrics: Business Outcomes, Activity, and Vanity. Business Outcome KPIs and metrics are usually revenue-based and released monthly when costs and finances are reconciled. Activity KPIs often focus on data about people, like prospects and customers; data about products, like supply and demand, elasticity, and carts; data about marketing, like campaigns, conversions, and flows; and data about infrastructure, such as operational KPIs about site reliability and site response time. Vanity KPIs are mostly useless, like the number of Twitter followers or Facebook "Likes." Segment KPIs by category, geography, time, and demographics, and seek to determine the drivers of change in those KPIs important to you.

Reviewing Types of Ecommerce Behavioral Analysis

Analyzing behavior requires deconstructing the ecommerce experience into a framework as suggested previously. First you have to define the goals of the ecommerce experience and the events that a customer and prospect would engage in. Buying requires the customer to look at and engage with one or more pages or screens to buy something, so each important event within the flow would be measured. Form completions and form fields could be measured to determine which ones are completed regularly or frequently incomplete. You can instrument and track events, whether Eisenbergian and Kaushi-kian "micro-conversion" and "micro-events" or larger common events and "macro" conversion, when analyzing behavior. What's important is that you look for outliers, anomalies, patterns, and commonalities using the techniques and tools you have available on the data. In many cases, to do behavioral analysis, ecommerce analysts will use digital analytics tools (such as Google Analytics, Jirafe, Adobe, Webtrends, and IBM), data from other sources both internal and external, Excel, a data visualization technology like Tableau or Qlik, and perhaps a data science tool or a language like R or Python. Regardless of the tool stack, there are several helpful approaches to examining and inter-rogating behavioral data, which is described in the remainder of this chapter.

Behavioral Flow Analysis

Flow analysis visually and numerically depicts the sequence of behavior across an ecommerce experience. A flow can begin based on the marketing channel in which a customer enters a site and then show the sequence of events until the customer leaves the site. Another flow may show the first onsite event in which the user engaged after acquisition and the subsequent events until site exit. Other flows may show the sequence of pages, screens, and related events based on a dimension. For example, a flow may show only the users who purchased a product and came from paid search. A standard flow is the shopping cart flow or the steps to engage in a transaction and buy a product after adding it to the shopping cart. The standard marketing funnel or order funnel is a flow in which behavior can be analyzed.

A helpful type of flow analysis is called the event flow. A simple customer journey could be the act of seeking a new product, shopping for a product, and then, after purchase, sharing information on social media about the product.

- **Seeking events** occur when the behavior is about finding products and site content, taking action to opt-in to communi-cations, and creating a profile to use:
    - *Site search events* can be captured when someone enters a query and receives a results list. Other search events can

be collected, such as the number of results returned, the searches with zero results returned, the search query and frequency entered, and the queries that had click-throughs.

— *E-mail signups* can be tracked to identify the volume of subscribers who opt-in to receive e-mail. Commonly, the signup is augmented with information about the name of the e-mail for which the user signed up.

— *Account creations* are measured to identify the number of users who provide some level of personally identifiable information (minimally an e-mail address). Commonly, credit card, name, address, and shipping information are provided during account creation.

— *Category, brand, and product views* measure the total number of category, brand, and product views that occurred. Often measured using screen-view or page-view totals, these views also can be measured as events—for example, knowing how many of these events occur before a purchase can be informative.

• **Shopping events** occur when the behavior is about interacting with the ecommerce experience in a way that relates to beginning, continuing, or completing the shopping process:

— *Add to cart events* occur when a user adds an item to a cart in order to consider it for purchase later.

— *Cart view events* occur when a user selects to view a cart to see a list of items within it.

— *Continue shopping events* are the conversions that occur when a user selects to leave a cart or checkout flow to continue engaging with content in the ecommerce experience.

— *Begin checkout events* occur when a user selects to transition from the cart to begin the checkout process.

— *Promotional usage events* occur when a user clicks on a promotion to use or enters and applies it as part of the checkout process.

— *Payment method events* occur when a user selects to use a credit card, a money order, or any of the myriad of ways to pay for products, such as Bitcoin, PayPal, Apple Pay/ID, and so on (Campbell 2014).

- *Complete purchase events* are the conversions that occur at the end of the purchase process after the transactions have been completed.

- *Abandonment events* occur when a user decides to leave the ecommerce experience without buying. Abandonment can be divided into cart abandonment, when items are left in the cart without being purchased, and checkout abandonment, when items are not bought during the checkout process because the user has left the ecommerce experience.

• **Sharing events** are when users share information and opinions about the ecommerce experience. Social functionality for sharing content on Facebook, Twitter, Pinterest, Instagram, Snapchat, and other social networks is common in 2016. These types of sharing events occur at any time during an ecommerce experience. They can be prompted at the end of a transaction, sometimes with an incentive. Or they may exist on certain page types. Sharing events include the following:

- *Social media events* are when explicit functionality for social sharing is embedded directly within the ecommerce experience.

- *E-mail events* are when a user sends an e-mail about the content of the ecommerce experience.

- *Feedback events* can be measured when a user provides feedback. The feedback may be in the form of customer service e-mail, contact, or form completion. It may be in the form of a social review or a star rating or another qualitative feedback mechanism (like Net Promoter Score).

It is also helpful to capture error events like these:

• **Cart errors** are errors that result before a product is added to the cart. These errors may result from selecting a certain option, feature, style, size, or other product attribute that prevents items from being added to the cart.

• **Checkout errors and related form errors** are errors that occur during the checkout process. These can result from promotional codes being applied, changing quantities, or problems with incorrect information being entered into forms, including name, address, zip code, country, shipping, billing, payment, 404 page not found errors, system and server errors, and other errors related to the ecommerce experience.

Shopping Behavior Analysis

Although the flow analysis of events is helpful, it may be necessary to analyze specific scenarios that are important to your ecommerce site. Using the behavioral framework and the events presented in this chapter, you can construct an analytical approach to the following:

- **Browsing behavior analysis** requires measuring search events, category, brand, product views, and the related functionality and specific content seen when browsing for items to buy.

- **Promotional behavior analysis** necessitates the measurement of activity related to promotions. Promotions may be merchandised on specific landing pages or category pages, or within inbound and outbound marketing. Codes and promotions will be used in checkout flows. Thus, promotional analysis focuses on understanding if the promotion was effective or not and why or why not.

- **Cart, behavior, and transactional analysis** requires measuring cart add and view events, checkout start and complete events, and other events specific to the shopping cart, checkout, and transactions.

- **Abandonment behavior analysis** involves analyzing behavior that results in people leaving the site. From looking at bounce rates and exit rates, to understanding cart abandonment events and checkout abandonment events, you can recapture significant revenue or keep it from being lost in the first place by studying, testing, and fixing abandonment.

A helpful cart abandonment analysis includes data that identifies the scope and financial impact of the problem. This data could include the Total Abandoned Revenue, which is the amount of aggregate revenue of all items left in carts, the Total Revenue sold on the site (to compare against abandoned revenue), and the Number of Abandoned Carts and the Abandonment Rate (i.e., abandoned carts divided by total carts). When the site is successful in recapturing revenue from abandonment, it is useful to measure the Total Recaptured Revenue and the Recapture Rate (total recaptured revenue divided by total abandoned revenue). These KPIs and metrics should be reported overall for the site and broken down by brands, categories, and products.

Content Analysis

The content on an ecommerce site can be understood when behavior occurring with the content is quantified. The common dimensions for analyzing content include **landing page, page, and exit page analysis.** Landing pages are the pages users start their sessions on. It's the first page in the visit. Landing pages can be measured to understand which ones result in the highest conversion, result in the lowest bounce, and contribute to sessions that have the most engagement with the user. Each page can be understood in terms of whether it contains the top-performing or worst-performing content as measured by how often that page is seen during visits in which people buy a product. Exit pages are the last pages in the visit, where a user leaves the site and ends the session. Exit pages can be identified and analyzed so that the behaviors occurring before the exit can be understood. In addition, **onsite search behavior analysis** can inform how the search experience is contributing to improving conversion and other goals. Queries can be evaluated to determine which ones lead to product views, cart adds, and conversion. The quality of results lists can be understood by measurement of click-throughs. Conversions when site search was used can be segmented out from overall conversion data. These types of pages and screens can be analyzed as content objects that are part of a customer journey or within a user flow. You could do a cluster analysis on internal search queries and topics in order to improve a function, like fuzzy matching, and thus increase the relevancy of search results; for example, clustering data to determine if the site should show "blue" when the customer enters "bleu," "navy," or "aqua."

In-Page or On-Screen Behavior Analysis

The links, the clicks, touches, and other possible interactions with content on the page or screen of an ecommerce experience can be measured, quantified, and visualized:

- **Clickmaps and page overlays** show the counts of clicks and other related metrics on a specific click. The question implicit is "How has this click influenced conversion or engagement within the site?"

- **Heat maps are clickmaps** that show a color gradient over areas of a page or screen where more interactivity occurred. For example, a heat map may show red in hotter areas where there were more clicks and blue in cooler areas with fewer clicks.

Identifying, defining, collecting, measuring, and analyzing behavioral data is a focus for many analysts and analytics teams. The data about behavior can be used in conversion optimization, discussed in Chapter 8, "Optimizing for Ecommerce Conversion and User Experience," and attribution analysis discussed in Chapter 11, "Attribution in Ecommerce Analytics." Behaviors are also analyzed in marketing analysis, the analysis of orders and products, and customer analytics. Behavioral data is used in many different types of ecommerce analysis, and the ecommerce analyst should strive to understand behavior relevant to ecommerce value creation.

8

Optimizing for Ecommerce Conversion and User Experience

Conversion optimization is a phrase used in the ecommerce industry to describe the process and application of methods that improve the ecommerce conversion rate. Conversion optimization attempts to unify methods and techniques from diverse disciplines, such as behavioral psychology, user experience, web development, copyediting, and neuromarketing by combining them with data collection and analytics. The goal of conversion optimization is to use controlled experimentation and the right experimental design to improve the conversion rate—that is, to increase the number and/or frequency of buyers within an ecommerce experience, or the number of people who create business value by transitioning from one state to another. For example, successful optimization may not just be a purchase; it could also be a newsletter sign-up or other user action relevant to the business. Traditionally, the application of conversion optimization is to landing pages for marketing campaigns, shopping cart flows and pages that lead directly to a purchase, and, even more generally, the key flows that lead to the shopping cart, such as the product pages.

The work of conversion optimizers focuses around a hypothesis to test. Selecting the best possible hypothesis is key to successful conversion optimization. Most typically, the hypotheses tested include the graphics, icons, buttons, colors, format, text, offer, and functionality on a page. For example, a simple hypothesis to test could be the text on a "call to action" such as a button to buy a product. An optimizer may suggest that the current color of the button be changed to another color (such as blue to red) or the text be changed (perhaps from "Add to Cart" to "Buy Now"). Although such a sample test is very basic, the best conversion optimizers test much more complex hypotheses. For example, it is common for a conversion optimizer to redesign an entire shopping cart flow or a specific landing page in such a way that tests the existing control against entirely new and different user experiences. Users may not know that they've entered a conversion test unless explicitly informed or unless they recognize a change in a familiar experience.

Conversion optimization is most frequently applied digitally to the following concepts:

- **User experience.** When a person engages with your experience, a number of behavioral interactions occur. A visit starts, time is counted, clicks are made, and events occur. People see a user experience rendered in a browser or displayed on the mobile application, including elements such as the colors, images, text, offers, links, fields, toggles, buttons, designs, layouts, formats, style sheets, and so on. These elements can all be tested. In addition, the underlying functionality that user may not be exposed to, such as site speed for downloading the pages or for the assessment of relevancy of the user's query, may also be tested.

- **E-mail.** AB testing was derived from offline marketing in direct mail. The content and format of emails can also be tested. Commonly, email subject lines are tested. The calls to action, fonts, colors, offers, prices, and everything that can be altered and rotated with a different option in an e-mail is fit for testing.

- **Mobile.** The importance of today's mobile landscape has never been clearer. Lots of ecommerce browsing and shopping is done on mobile devices. Billions of people worldwide use mobile phones and many of them are Internet-enabled through mobile browsers. Smart devices have a set of mobile applications available for download. Testing on mobile occurs both in apps and on the mobile web as well as in the device experience itself proctored by the companies that create the handheld devices. Developers who create mobile apps also test their applications, using approaches similar to web analytics testing.

- **Online advertising.** A profitable area that can benefit greatly is the testing of content, creative, size, and rich-media functionality in online ads. The different ad creative and persuasive copy in the ad as well as the promotional offers can be tested against different customer segments.

- **Social features.** With the abundant number of social options available to the creators of ecommerce experiences, each can be tested to determine whether the social feature was used by the audience, and if so, what the impact is on the business. For example, it might make a lot of sense to put a set of outgoing links to other sites in a prime area of your media site. The traffic arbitrage might be worth it. But then again, will people use the feature or will it cannibalize existing page views? These hypotheses and impacts can be adequately tested.

- **Content.** Whatever your company calls content can be alternated out and tested with other content. Pictures, text, form fields, video content, and so on and the features and functions that enable users to interact with content can be tested using multivariate testing.

- **Promotions.** Although some people may consider promotional testing to be advertising testing, it's worth calling out on its own. Promotions are offers, coupons, discounts, and other incentives that can be altered based on audience profiles, events, and behaviors, to provide different prices and options to identifiable customer segments.

- **Flows.** The screens, sequences, workflows, and persuasive architectures that create the experience and narrative within a digital experience are the flows. You may have heard of "conversion flows" and are familiar with the shopping cart flow. In this sense, each page or screen within a sequence of steps to complete an action can be rotated and tested.

Conversion optimizers use various tools. Most interesting, the majority of tools used for conversion optimization are analytical in nature and contain functionality dependent on analytics—from clickstream and pathing reports to heat maps to systems that collect, process, and report the specific test results using statistical methods. Heuristic methods derived from the data in digital analytics tools are often leveraged and employed by optimizers. These tools, their data, and the proprietary methodologies optimizers use may not be tailored to your unique needs in all cases. In these cases you may want to use conversion heuristics to move the effort forward. For example, a heuristic approach to conversion might be to simply look at the placement and click-through rates for specific calls to actions (such as "buy" buttons) and test those. Or a heuristic approach may be more elaborate and use a tool to provide deep segmentation based on personas to determine where and why the site is losing or not converting visitors. Voice-of-the-customer data and other qualitative data from user surveys and research, as well as secondary research studies about customers, the audience, or the brand, could be employed by a conversion optimizer applying a heuristic approach.

The mind-set of a conversion optimizer is one of stalwart belief that the right recipe to maximize conversion can be found. Optimizers are not conservative, and, in fact, approach optimization with ultimate liberality about what could possibly be tested. By starting the optimization process using data to identify breakpoints, bottlenecks, and points of friction and abandonment, a conversion optimizer can understand the user experience and hypothesize what should be tested. By focusing on discovery and learning, while not shying away from the sometimes complex and often simple mathematics of conversion optimization, conversion optimizers seek incremental improvement in conversion. Conversion optimizers understand the structure and flow of a site, but believe that no one size fits all audiences. They are ardent believers in the power of personalization or, at the very least, believe that mass customization is a way to improve the effectiveness of a digital experience. Conversion optimizers are relentless in their search for the best possible combination of elements of the user experience. In so doing, they must possess and use solid design skills. They also must be able to profile and understand a site's audience and the cohort of buyers and their segments. Optimizers deduce, from data, the impact of the user experience on the audience and gallantly try to improve it.

Optimizers have the brains of a scientist and a web developer and the design ability of an artist. They have the research skills of a market researcher, an understanding of user experience, and the capability to combine different information from different disciplines to ideate hypotheses. Then they know how to use technology to test hypotheses and identify, from those experiments and learnings, how to increase conversion and thus grow revenue.

This mind-set is not necessarily new; conversion optimization has descended from a lineage of offline testing, with its roots grown firmly in the soil of direct mail testing. The first conversion optimizers weren't testing web sites; they were testing snail mail and the design and layout of envelopes, fonts and typography, text, copy, images, colors, and calls to actions within direct mail campaigns. What was once called a "champion/challenger" test by direct mail optimizers is now called an AB test. It's important to realize that, even in the brave new world of digital electronic commerce, the precedents for work activities may have been first applied long ago in other lines of business. Understanding history and previous techniques will make you a better conversion optimizer and ecommerce analyst.

The remainder of this chapter reviews helpful knowledge and ideas about conversion optimization, including the importance of understanding your company's value proposition and the core concepts and constructs in analytics that guide conversion. Also reviewed is the conversion optimization process, the data from conversion optimization, and a review of the types of conversion optimization techniques.

The Importance of the Value Proposition in Conversion Optimization

A value proposition identifies why a person should purchase something from a company. Product companies whose products are sold on an ecommerce site have a different value proposition than the ecommerce site itself. An ecommerce site's value proposition may be based on best price, free shipping, the curation of inventory, exclusive availability, and so on. Or a product's value proposition may be the reason people fulfill their purchases on an ecommerce site regardless of the ecommerce brand. According to conversion expert, Peep Laja, the best conversion optimizers for ecommerce can maximize and improve on how the company's value proposition is communicated, understood, and acted on by a person within a user experience. They do this by testing different user experiences based on hypotheses about how customers will respond to digital stimuli, such as colors, buttons, copy, graphics, images, and so on.

Take, for example, a fashion ecommerce site that exposes users to the latest fashion brands. The value proposition is exclusivity and the uniqueness of inventory. For the users to find inventory, it has to be exposed, perhaps on landing pages, via search functionality on site pages, via cross-sells and recommendations as people browse, via promotional offers, and via creative copy. The conversion optimizers would work to develop landing pages and test them to find the best recipe of functionality, copy, and promotional offers to drive the most revenue. They might evolve and enhance existing product pages to emphasize uniqueness. Or they might help to suggest, test, and refine the user experience for personalization. The goal of all these optimizations would be to use the value proposition to appeal to the person by testing what works best and using it (while eliminating what doesn't work as effectively). The concept of optimization based on an understanding and exploitation of an ecommerce site's value proposition is not new, but it is essential.

The Basics of Conversion Optimization: Persuasion, Psychology, Information Architecture, and Copywriting

Conversion optimization is a process built on the art of persuasion guided and framed by the application of psychology within a digital user experience. The psychological cues necessary for persuasion are guided by the information architecture and enforced by the copywriting and design with the ecommerce experience. As an analyst, you will be asked to participate in, influence, guide, or even ideate and execute conversion optimization projects. The basics of conversion optimization are not necessarily analytical in nature; they are cross-functional and multidimensional basics, but basics nonetheless:

- **Persuasion** is the art and science of getting people to do what you want them to do. In the case of an ecommerce site, the goal is conversion by buying a product. The forefathers of conversion optimization, Bryan and Jeffrey Eisenberg, ideated

Persuasion Architecture, which is a seven-step process for improving conversion. Although I recommend you read the details of their thought leadership, the key takeaways involve the different personas and goals people have on the site. Some personas are more methodological than spontaneous, whereas others are more competitive than humanistic. Each type of persona has a different modality, whether they are just browsing, know approximately what they want to buy, or know exactly what they want to buy. Persuasion involves triggering different cues that lead to the desired behavior based on the modality of that persona.

- **User experience (UX)** is key to conversion optimization because it is the user experience that you are optimizing. Simply put, you are changing the look and feel of the site to the user. Jesse James Garrett's design of the Elements of User Experience is still a relevant framework that is applied today in contemporary UX design, and is thus relevant to conversion optimization. Garrett divides UX into the surface, skeleton, structure, scope, and strategy that bring together a user interface linked by textual and visual elements. The surface is the actual visual design. The skeleton is the design of the navigation, interface, and information. The structure is the interaction design and the information architecture. The scope and strategy are the business, functional, and content requirements that frame the user experience. A conversion optimizer works within the boundaries of these different layers of the user experience to persuade people to do something of value, such as buy that product.

- **Psychology** of the conversion optimizer and the buyer is important. Human psychology should never be underestimated as the powerful control mechanism that influences and frames conversion optimization. Psychology is the study of the human mind. In this complex subject, especially in experimental psychology, risk versus reward, and positive and negative reinforcement play a role in compelling a person to do something or complete a predefined outcome. In conversion optimization, the psychologies of the optimizer and the buyer influence each other. The optimizer's psychology is one of paced, incremental, deliberate change to influence perception and catalyze motivation. The buyer's psychology is one of fast, iterative, often comparative decision making in order to make purchases that meet their needs. The optimizer attempts to understand the perception and cognition of the prospect and of the repeat buyer in order to experiment with their psychology by testing. Bart Schultz's "toe in the door" technique and Peep Laja's "conversion anchoring" technique are two relevant examples.

- **Information architecture** is a major influence on **persuasion.** In Garrett's model of user experience, information architecture is part of the structure. Conversion optimizers test and change the structure of digital experience in order to find what works best for achieving conversion goals. The structural design of an ecommerce site and the art and science of defining, organizing, and labeling pages in order to ensure that they are viewed and usable are all part of conversion optimization. It is common for an optimizer to create an existing model or concept of information that is used within an ecommerce experience, and then alter and tune that model via testing to come up with the optimal information architecture.

- **Conversion copywriting** is the phrase used to describe the complete and total rewriting and redaction of textual content within a digital experience. The page headlines, the calls to action, the creative text in banners, the names of sections, the text on buttons, the words in your navigation bar, the text on error and alert modals, and any text within a digital experience can be optimized. Optimizers have realized substantial lift on pages, sometimes by rewriting them partially, sometimes by reworking just the headlines, or sometimes even by rewriting all of the copy and text in full.

- **Measurement and analytics** are absolutely critical and necessary to any conversion optimization project. Existing analytics need to be analyzed in order to describe, inform, and enumerate customer behavior relevant and applicable to conversion. Data and analysis also helps to pinpoint breakpoints, abandonment, pathing and flows, top pages, and much more behavior. The analytics not only guide you in identifying and pinpointing what to test, but guide the optimizer during and after testing to show current performance and the test results. From descriptive analysis, to statistical analytics, to the abstractions and visualizations of conversion funnels and ring charts, measurement and analytics for conversion optimization is a top priority. You simply can't be successful with conversion optimization without accurate data.

The Conversion Optimization Process: Ideation to Hypothesis to Post-Optimization Analysis

Every conversion optimization company and individual conversion optimizer has a process for optimization. You will hear the words *lift, increase, heuristics, intelligence, customer, survey, research, experiment, design,* and *test* in most conversations about the process of conversion optimization. The different approaches to conversion optimization advocated by the leading firms are similar to each other. All are generalized processes and approaches that can be used across any types of site, including ecommerce. Central to these processes is identifying whether the company has accurate data to measure conversion and identifying where are the critical, high-impact areas to test and experiment on.

The goal of these processes is to abstract an approach that can be applied and reapplied to whatever conversion event your company deems important—from shopping cart conversion to purchase, to product page addition to shopping cart, to newsletter sign-up on a landing page. The goal of a conversion optimization process is general applicability to a number of conversion goals across an ecommerce experience.

Listed here is a process for conversion optimization, which I created over the past several years based on my experience and immersion into the world of optimization, starting in 2005:

1. **Ensure that your analytics are accurate and sufficient.** To assess correctness and fit, you must compare business requirements to your analytics tool's currently implemented capabilities. Most simply, if the goal is to increase performance, then

you need to have clear definition of performance and ensure that the data is available during testing. For example, the goal may be to simply increase the conversion rate. Great. What are the denominator and numerator and what are the accurate measurement and data? Or is the goal to increase the average order value, the number of products in the shopping cart, the creation of a wish list, the creation of a user account, or the usage of a promotional code? Whatever it is, the data must fit the purpose and be accurate.

2. **Do heuristic analysis.** My friend Peep Laja likes to say this all the time, and, for good reason, because it makes a lot of sense. By heuristic I mean (and I think Peep also means) that you explore the data set to find unusual data. You may explore the data using filters, using segments, drilling up, drilling down, crossing dimensions, and building data visualizations. Of course, it's also possible to be more analytical and apply business statistics to determine the characteristics of the data. A heuristic-based approach would include the following:

   a. *Determining your conversion rate for different device types (mobile versus browser).* A helpful place to start is to determine whether the conversion rate for orders is different by device.

   b. *Segmenting your critical conversion rates by key dimensions to understand differences, such as by marketing channel.* You may segment conversion rate by paid search on the mobile versus paid search on the desktop.

   c. *Identifying the bounce rate on your landing pages.* Product pages, category pages, brand pages, and the home page can be landing pages for e-mail, search, and display advertising campaigns. Ensuring that these pages perform as effectively as possible by testing the creative is important.

   d. *Identifying the exit rate on important pages.* The exit rate is the percentage of people who leave the site on that page. If you notice large exit rates on certain pages, such as login pages, purchasing pages, shipping pages, and order summary pages, then you can consider testing them.

3. **Perform qualitative analysis.** A common tactic employed by conversion optimizers is primary research via the user survey to elicit voice-of-customer data. Different surveys can be rendered in an ecommerce experience upon login, after a certain user action, or as the visitor is exiting the site. It's possible to ask a visitor to select from a set of programmed responses or enter free text. If the data has indicated that a particular page has a high bounce rate, you may prompt a survey to ask the user how the page could be improved. Other online surveys may be provided by research vendors to help you understand customer satisfaction, net promoter score, and other opinions and preferences.

4. **Use market research to frame a conversion hypothesis.** Contextualize the data, analytics, and user research with available market research about customers, competitors, and overall market needs. The optimizer who consults market research can learn about how competitors differentiate, message, and sell their products. Understanding the customers and their needs influences testing.

5. **Understand your internal assets.** Most companies have creative copy, images, videos, and other collateral about marketing, sales, and the product that may be helpful in the conversion optimization process. In addition, people throughout the company may have ideas on what to test based on their experiences and perspectives; these internal human assets should not be overlooked.

6. **Create a hypothesis to use for ideating and framing different experiments to test.** After analyzing the data both directly and heuristically, and considering how existing primary or secondary research can help inform the design of tests, now is the time to create a hypothesis. A hypothesis is the starting point for your experimentation. It is a statement that you think to be true or false (which you can use as the null hypothesis). For example, "conversion rate would increase if we reduce the number of form fields" might be a hypothesis to test.

7. **Design a testing and experimentation plan and deploy necessary technology.** After identifying the hypothesis or set of hypotheses to test on the site, you need to create a testing plan that identifies the scope, requirements, technology, resources, goals, and schedule for deploying, monitoring, and concluding tests. In some cases, conversion rate optimization technology may need implementation or configuration.

8. **Deploy and monitor tests.** Regularly reviewing the in-flight tests and making judicious decisions about when to end tests and make a conclusion ensures that you don't waste time and resources. Tests should continue for as long as necessary to provide the organization with the belief in the test results. You don't simply stop testing because you see an increase in the short term. Regression to the mean can occur the longer you test, which is a positive outcome meaning that the test doesn't work despite any earlier indications that it does. Run conversion tests across at least one business cycle. Identify your business cycle by finding fluctuations in customer behavior and sales across a time period, such as the peaks and valleys that appear in ecommerce data from "seasonality."

9. **Roll out and document successful tests.** After you have determined that a test is successful over the control, you deploy it through your company's standard processes. Although some optimizers will leave tests running in whatever tool they used to execute the experiment, it is a better strategy to deploy the test within the actual experience. You want to avoid outsourcing site functionality to third-party conversion optimization companies as much as possible in order to control your customer experience. Also maintain documentation of your tests and their results. You can use Excel and simply capture simple metadata such as the test name, description, timing, results, and decision made based on the test. Or you can develop a more elaborate archive of testing information, including creative and more.

10. **Repeat what works and keep testing.** For tests that are successful and have applicability outside of the hypothesis tested, you can test these successes in other areas. For example, if you

have determined that a type of creative conversion copywriting has increased conversion in one area, then apply the same tone and diction to another area. Whatever you do, don't stop testing. Test, don't guess, about ecommerce user experiences.

The Data for Conversion Optimization: Analytics, Visualization, Research, Usability, Customer, and Technical Data

Data is at the heart of conversion optimization. In the conversion optimization process outlined in this chapter, ensuring the accuracy and sufficiency of your analytics is essential to successful hypothesizing, measurement, and the evaluation of success. In addition, the process suggests consulting other forms of data, such as primary and secondary research and other qualitative data, to influence your testing plan. Here are the types of data most frequently used in testing and experimentation:

- **Digital analytics data** is generated by the behavior of visitors or users of an ecommerce experience, including site, social, and mobile. Also included is data related to marketing campaign performance, technical data about the digital experience, and concepts such as visitors, visits, sessions, users, referrers, conversion rates, download times, and so on.

- **Business intelligence data** is first-party data generated by operational and transaction systems within a company. Some of the data in BI systems may have been sourced from systems and sources external to the company. This data may, however, be stored in the cloud. Or it may exist in both internal and external systems and sources. BI data can include order, transaction, product, sales, and customer data.

- **Voice-of-customer research and surveys** involve qualitative data derived from methods for surveying and understanding populations, demographics, propensities, and preferences. This data could include ethnographies, persona data, and other research related to consumer preferences, actions, and opinions.

- **Funnel and flowcharts** are a form of data visualization most typically rendered in digital analytics tools. Funnel and flowcharts show sequences of pages, screens, actions, and events that lead to a specific conversion event, such as an account registration or a purchase. These visualizations show the exit, entrance, and abandonment rates for each step in a progressive sequence.

- **Heat maps are visualizations** in which a color is associated with a numeric value. The most common heat map is an infrared diagram in which red may indicate the highest numeric temperature. In ecommerce heat maps can be used to visualize dwell time on a screen or the amount of time spent hovering with the mouse, and the rate of clicks on specific sections of the screen.

- **Mouse, finger, and eye tracking** is software that tracks and visualizes where the digital users move their mouse, direct their eyes, or touch their screen during the usage of an ecommerce site.

- **Neuromarketing data** is derived from testing the cognitive and psychological response to stimuli within an ecommerce experience. The data could include heart rate, respiration rate, and other physiological measurements.

- **Human psychological research** derived from a long academic history can be applied to conversion rate optimization. Concepts such as loss aversion, self-efficacy, anchoring, visual cuing, dual process theory, incentivizing, and positive reinforcement can all play into optimization (Smale 2014).

- **Technical and network data** collected from the servers running and technology creating the ecommerce experience are a good source of data to learn about technical externalities that impact users beyond what can be seen. Data such as latency, site speed, error rates, and server response can be useful to examine.

The Science Behind Conversion Optimization

The data science powering conversion optimization and testing software generates the testing results. Not all tools use the same underlying approach to processing the data collected. Regardless, the data generated by conversion optimization tools may be automatically analyzed such that statistical significance is reported by default. In other cases, the optimizer may have to apply basic (or complex) statistics to understand the data output and form a conclusion. Regardless, it is helpful for an optimizer to understand statistical concepts such as mean, variance, sample size, confidence intervals and margin, and the basics of hypothesis testing (like z-tables and p-values) and regression. Conversion optimizers may refer to Frequentist or Bayesian methodologies when discussing conversion testing and the science in testing tools. The differences in these approaches really don't matter too much, as long as the approach chosen is consistent; however, understanding the difference between them may be useful. Bayesian techniques, discussed in Chapter 3, "Methods and Techniques for Ecommerce Analysis," use data from other experiments that occurred in the past as part of the calculation for the current experiment. Parameter estimates are stochastic (random) in Bayesian models. Probabilities are assigned to values for parameter estimates based on a probability distribution. Frequentist techniques use only the data from the current test; they just use the data in the current experiment to calculate the conversion conclusion. In Frequentist models, parameters are static or fixed based on the values in the known data set and frequencies are estimated based on that sample. Frequentist approaches use a sampling distribution from the current data set. Fortunately, if you are using the same technique and the results are positive, then one need not be too concerned about which is right. Mix results derived from both methods, and confusion can occur. What follows is a list of the most commonly embedded experimental design techniques in vendor software for conversion optimization regardless of Frequentist or Bayesian notions:

- **Taguchi method.** Genichi Taguchi was an engineer and statistician who developed revolutionary concepts related to improving the quality of manufacturing processes. His methods have been employed by and influenced many digital optimization engineers and innovators. Taguchi looks at the concept of "loss"—in multiple dimensions—in order to improve process by understanding parameters and tolerances. Using complex math to fine-tune the parameters and understand the influence of multiple factors, Taguchi was able to demonstrate that his mathematical and statistical methods could effectively reduce or maximize the output of one or more variables in the manufacturing process. His work is widely employed in multiple scientific disciplines.

- **Choice modeling (or choice design).** This is a method by which the optimization is considered a function that can be maximized by choice. The notion of choice as something that can be modeled using math was a theory derived from modern psychology, where it is considered that choice must have a behavioral basis. As such, the theory is that these behaviors can be identified and applied to estimate the likelihood of a particular person, or customer segment, making a certain decision. One way to understand choice modeling is that concepts like brand affinity and known demographics and behaviors of customer segments can be modeled against previous purchasing patterns to estimate what type of advertising stimuli may elicit the desired response.

Different Frequentist or Bayesian approaches to experimental design include the following types of testing:

- **Multivariate testing.** According to Wikipedia, this type of testing is also called "multi variable testing." This more descriptive name communicates excellently that two or more variables are tested to determine the impact of one against another.

- **Univariate testing.** This occurs when only one variable is tested. For example, the color of button may change and the impact of that change against the original color (i.e., the control) is measured. For example, the color of a "download button" (red versus blue) can be tested to determine which button color results in more orders.

- **Fractional (or partial) factorial testing.** This is a way to describe the type of testing that will be done. "Partial" means that only a certain set of the possible combinations of all the factors will be tested. In other words, if you have 10 elements to test, you have 10 to the 10th power possible combinations. Testing 10 to the 10th takes a lot of time, and many of the possible combinations of elements likely will make no sense (for example, testing a white button on a white background); thus, partial factorial testing is a way to accommodate for this fact. The number of combinations is reduced to the most critical set of combinations (which still can be a large number) and then tested for however long it takes to reach statistical significance.

  Tim Ash, CEO of Site Tuners and author of *Landing Page Optimization*, cited the following about fractional factorial testing in the context of Taguchi, in which he claimed that his experience in applying this testing construct to landing pages across sites in multiple industries was problematic. Tim cites the following concerns:

  - *Very small test sizes.* Testing has to be performed to a statistical significance level. The sample size will depend on the population and types of sessions, so don't risk your reputation by putting forward analysis based on invalid samples of very small sample sets.

  - *Restrictive and inflexible test designs.* The underlying digital technologies that render the user experiences across web sites and other Internet-connected devices limit testing. As a result, tests can be slightly nuanced based on different sets of features, flows, creative, offers, and experiences, reducing comparability.

  - *Less accurate estimation of individual variable contributions.* Statistical rigor is necessary when one is analyzing the results of testing. Measures such as covariance and various statistical matrices that express the relationships between variables need to be accounted for testing.

  - *Drawing the wrong conclusions.* Just because analysis for testing software reports that a given variation outperforms another variation or even the control, the result does not necessarily mean that that performance is guaranteed to continue over a long term or to the entire customer audience.

- *Inability to consider context and variable interactions.* I've often heard it said in analytics that we know what we know and we don't know what we don't know. In the same sense, the tests are only as smart or as dumb as we program them to be. It is difficult to collect every possible interaction on a digital experience, and the risk of not doing so is that in testing you may miss other contexts and the interactions between other variables that are important to consider (Ash 2008).

- **Full factorial testing.** This is when all possible combinations are tested against the control in order to identify the resulting increase or decrease in utility of what is being tested. It is more common to find full factorial testing used in applications in which the customer doesn't directly interact with the test; however, that restriction is not always necessary. Full factorial testing is often used in machine learning processes and statistical data mining/controlled experimentation.

- **Optimal design.** This is a pattern in optimization that involves rapidly cycling through sets of iterations of tests to identify, as quickly as possible, the combination of test elements that "wins" against parameters for the testing. Optimal design takes into account the relationships between the elements being tested. That way, odd combinations are not tested (such as white buttons on white backgrounds, which a full-factorial approach would test).

The inner workings of the AB and multivariate tools and professional services are likely going to be less important to stakeholders and the team as long as they produce desired results. Some people may question how statistical models developed for scientific fields, like operations management, or for use within factories and supply chains, are relevant to the behavior of digital customers. Although in some cases these criticisms could be accurate, the available options for controlled experimentation and optimization testing enable this science of testing to be applied widely across ecommerce experiences.

Succeeding with Conversion Optimization

For ecommerce companies new to conversion optimization or stuck in a rut trying to be successful with optimization, or that want to evolve and expand past successes, here are some tips I've learned over the years that can help:

- **Democratize the testing process.** Ecommerce companies that have embedded testing and optimization within their business process have succeeded, in part, because they involve different groups and align people to support testing. When projects around testing are executed, they are planned and coordinated with supporting groups and not run in isolation by a testing team.

- **Appoint a leader for conversion optimization.** This leader should make the decision on what to test. Testing at its best will drive revenue, so it's important to appoint a business leader who connects business to the customer experience to the testing program. This leader may manage a testing team and represent conversion optimization in meetings. One person or a leader of a group or optimization steering committee may decide on what to test, but any employee is encouraged to submit testing ideas.

- **Invest in conversion optimization software.** Although some notable ecommerce companies, like Amazon, have invested capital to build their own testing software, most companies can't support and execute the development of custom software for internal conversion testing. Vendors offer significant functionality and differentiated products for conversion optimization. Companies that can't build their own testing software invest in testing software, usually after testing out free software and proving a potential return.

- **Allocate sufficient technical resources.** Testing and conversion optimization has an element of overhead associated with it. If you are going to test three versions of an experience, you have to do three times as much work—and only one version will ultimately be rolled out as the winner. To pull off the creative and technical work to ideate, deploy, and monitor conversion optimization work, companies need the necessary allocation of employees to support. That allocation is not typically part-time.

- **Don't let the executive team get too involved.** Testing is detailed work that is based on data analysis, customer observation, and experimentation. Although opinion can come into play during the testing process, the work of conversion optimization is not necessarily defined or prioritized by executives who parachute into a room and make assertions about their preferences. Although this managerial involvement can happen, the team needs to temper the positional power with facts resulting from data and research gathered during the testing process.

- **Test small changes, not total redesigns.** When you are testing, the idea to complete radical overhauls and partial or total redesigns to site functionality will inevitably come up for discussion. You want to resist the urge to change too much at once. Instead test small changes to functionality and flow in order to understand their impact for incrementally improving the conversion rate. The last thing you want to do is spend money to create a new version of your experience that doesn't perform to existing expectations and benchmarks.

- **Don't end tests too soon.** All too often I've seen companies desire to end their tests as soon as positive results are shown. This rush to judgment is a mistake because tests need time to smooth out. In other words, tests that are successful in week two may end up falling back a bit or even inverting in later weeks. If you roll out a test to the live site too early, the long-term results may not meet expectations. Thus, it is appropriate to roll out tests when you are certain that the trend in data will continue—and the only way to be certain is to give sufficient time (often at least one business cycle) before judging testing success.

- **Double down on successes.** Improvement in one area of your ecommerce experience may have applicability to other areas. For example, the length of forms, the tone of the creative copy, the types of offers, the images, and the functionality in the purchase funnel may make sense to test in the registration funnel. Test the broad applicability of what has worked across your experience.

- **Formally socialize and announce testing results.** When you win with testing, let people know by socializing the results. Whether you hold a meeting, send an e-mail, do a webinar, or put up a poster, what's important is that you broadcast the business effectiveness of your conversion optimization efforts. Publishing and communicating your results will not only help you gain credibility for your efforts, but also help you marshal resources to support your efforts.

- **Reward failure and also success with testing.** Optimization leaders should offer incentives and provide rewards as testing is executed. Activities like "testing parties" and contests to help ideate suggested tests can help put attention on testing. In companies that crowdsource suggested tests or that have multiple people working on testing, managers can give rewards to the person or team who suggested the idea that generated the highest lift. Celebrate failure too—because it is learning.

The field of conversion optimization is evolving quickly in ecommerce analytics. It combines multiple perspectives to give context to data and analysis and offers tools to action on data and test hypotheses in real time. The resulting lift in conversion and performance can be quantified in terms of behavior (engagement) and value (revenue). Expect conversion testing and other forms of controlled experimentation to increase in popularity going forward.

9

Analyzing Ecommerce Customers

Customer analytics refers to the process of executing analysis on data about the people or businesses that visit and transact in an ecommerce experience. Customer analytics includes any type of analysis that uses individual-level data about a customer to describe, predict, or prescribe something about them or their past, current, or future behavior, attributes, or propensities. The Wharton Customer Analytics Initiative defines customer data to be inherently granular, forward looking, broadly applicable, longitudinal, behavioral, multiplatform, and rapidly emerging. Customer data can be analyzed to answer business questions about how to generate new or incremental revenue, reduce cost, or boost profitability of existing, new, or potential customers. In most ecommerce companies, customer data is stored in customer relationship management systems, enterprise databases and data warehouses, and in external systems in the cloud. This data can be brought together or analyzed in silos, and the resulting insights from these customer analyses can be applied throughout an ecommerce company, from strategy and planning, to merchandising, to customer service, to marketing, to finance.

Customer analytics involves segmenting and clustering customers in order to describe them. Different types of customer analysis, such as cohort analysis, can help to better understand customer behavior across time. Customer data can be used to calculate financially significant customer metrics and related data, such as cost of customer acquisition and customer lifetime value. Data science and machine learning on customer data can enable personalization, predictive, and prescriptive experiences. Data about customer satisfaction, retention, churn, and loyalty can be analyzed.

Customer analytics has material financial results when done well. Companies successfully using customer analytics are 2.6 times more likely to have a significantly higher ROI than competitors, according to a study by McKinsey (Bokman et al 2014). With such positive data, one would think most ecommerce companies would engage in customer analytics. After all, the customer is the most important part of ecommerce. People and businesses are the core objects around which commerce revolves. Without ecommerce customers, there would be no ecommerce businesses. Yet ecommerce companies don't do customer analytics as much as you might expect. According to MECLABS, only 37% of ecommerce businesses were using historical customer data to improve performance (Marketing Sherpa 2014).

Customer analysis is challenging to execute. Like all analysis, data is required. And customer data is highly scrutinized data. It is likely to be some of the most secure data in a company subject to legal requirements. Thus getting access to historical data to analyze about customers can be harder than expected. First, customer-level detail is often in the domain of business intelligence. Internal BI systems can be gated by data governors and privacy teams that don't enable customer data to be widely used. More generally available tools that can be used on ecommerce sites, whether free or paid, may not have features for collecting record-level customer data. In the case of Google Analytics, customer-level data can be obfuscated intentionally and only recently made available as a user ID. The volume of customer-level data for larger ecommerce companies can certainly be described as "big data," which requires specialized tools, technology, resources, and commitment from IT to work with it. Additionally, there are legal requirements related to privacy in certain jurisdictions and countries about working with a customer's data with both an opt-in and an opt-out. Nevertheless, customer analytics is an important business activity from which successful ecommerce companies generate value every day.

What Does a Customer Record Look Like in Ecommerce?

Customer record is a phrase used to describe the customer's data. It may be represented as one more dimensional data models across one or more database tables, with each field being an attribute of the customer. Because many systems touch a customer and collect customer data, customer records in ecommerce companies can exist as multiple data sets in disparate systems. Alternatively, ecommerce companies that have a data warehousing or CRM strategy and/or apply master data management principles to customer data may have a master customer record containing their master customer data. Even in such controlled data environments, it is entirely possible that analysts may be enhancing that customer record with data that isn't in the master file or part of data governance or stewardship activities (though it should be). Regardless of how many sources there are, where the customer data resides, and the way you master customer data, the customer record contains personally identifiable information (PII) about the customer and also important business information. The data in a customer record includes the customer's identifier (as a primary key), customer's first and last names, shipping and billing address(es), city, data, region, country, zip code, and other PII such as birthdate, gender, email address, phone number, and credit card number/expiry/3 digit code. Other business information can be included, such as the segment and cohort to which the customer was assigned, their first and last purchase dates, the attribution source, preferences, opt-ins/outs, and the sales total and predicted customer lifetime value. The customer ID is the key that can be used to join customer data with order data, product data, and so on. By using keys in your customer record, you can bring together data that isn't currently part of the customer record. For example, you could view the products a customer purchased and do clustering and segmentation based on both product and customer data.

What Customer Data Could I Start to Analyze?

A **basic customer analysis** could include the total number of active customers (however defined by your company), the total new customers, and the percentage of new versus existing customers during that time period. Additional helpful data to report include the cohort, segment, attribution, lifetime value, cost of acquisition, and other customer-specific data you collect and deem important. A good starting point could be to create a data table that has rows identifying each customer and columns for the customer segment, first-order attribution, first-order date, first-order amount, the last-order date, last-order amount, and predicted lifetime value. From this data set, you can start to rank customers by lifetime value, assess recency and frequency, identify top channels for attribution, count and cluster by customer type, and more.

Questioning Customer Data with Analytical Thought

Thinking about the customers and their data helps to humanize the analytical process. Instead of dealing with products, channels, pages, clicks, events, transactions, and other business data, customer analytics puts the customer at the center of the data and analysis. Successful ecommerce customer analytics answers business questions that stakeholders have about the impact of their program, projects, campaigns, and initiatives on the customer, and thus the business. Questions about customers and their behavior can be asked by stakeholders with specificity or with frustrating generality. In fact, one of the signs of a good analyst is the ability to help stakeholders—at all levels—ask the best possible question given available, relevant, and timely data. Here are some good questions about customers that you may want to use to guide your customer analysis:

- What customers are most valuable?
- When is it the best time to contact a customer?
- What channel or channels are the most effective for reaching customers?
- Why did the customer respond to X in Y way, and what can we do about it now for the future?
- How can I use customer data to help us do X?
- What recommendation about products can I make to customer X?
- How much does it cost us to acquire a customer?

- How much do we earn from a customer, and what is our customer lifetime value?

- How are customers who buy again different from those who buy only once?

- How do discounts and promotions impact customer behavior?

- How are the characteristics and attributes of customers changing over time?

As you can see from the themes in the questions, the best customer analytics programs can answer what has happened in the past, what's happening now, what may happen in the future, and what the possible actions and best action to take for achieving a business goal are.

Understanding the Ecommerce Customer Analytics Lifecycle

Customer analysis is best understood within a customer lifecycle. Simply defined, the customer lifecycle is the stages a person goes through prior to, during, and after buying a product using ecommerce. The events, behaviors, transactions, customer-provided data, machine-generated data, and associated metadata collected during the customer lifecycle are the data to be analyzed in customer analysis. This data about the customer isn't applicable to only marketing and sales, where customer analytics is frequently applied; it's valuable data for informing ecommerce operations from planning and merchandising to user experience to optimization and testing to fulfillment and customer service. A simple way to think of customer lifecycle is a three-phase model: Seeking > Shopping > Sharing. I call these three-phases the "Tumbler." Customers tumble around, move in and out, across and around these three phases:

1. **Seeking.** A person determines a need for something, such as a product (or service). Then marketing and advertising, both online and offline, such as TV, radio, word of mouth, and billboards help a person gain awareness of a brand or product. And then various media, marketing, and advertising amplify

the awareness through messages that differentiate the brand or product such that people determine what is favorable to them and preferred. Sometimes, however, people just stumble upon a brand or product, and then they search for more information. In the Seeking phase, different media, marketing, and messaging amplify and assist the customer in becoming aware, considering, favoring, and then being acquired to begin the next phase: Shopping.

In the phase of seeking, marketing activities and higher-order customer thought such as activation, awareness, consideration, favorability, and acquisition occur. The data collected during seeking can be mostly anonymous data and it is used primarily by the marketing team.

2. **Shopping.** After a person has been acquired and is now a prospect or a lead, he or she is shopping within an ecommerce experience and generating data. Behavioral data and machine-generated data collected from all the tagging and BI systems measure and track events, interactions, profiles, orders, and the other data elements in your ecommerce data model. This is the data to be analyzed and used across the entire ecommerce organization: product management, IT, marketing, merchandising, planning, customer service, and more.

3. **Sharing.** Sharing is the digital or manual process of a customer communicating about his experience, usually through social channels or via word of mouth. This data is helpful for marketing, customer service, merchandising, and product management.

The Tumbler customer lifecycle described previously as a construct for understanding customer behavior is unique because the customer lifecycle has traditionally been thought of as pathing on a linear flow of acquisition to conversion to loyalty. The Seeking > Shopping > Sharing lifecycle doesn't have to be linear. People can jump in and out and across these phases as they engage with an ecommerce experience. There can be many different customer touches in an ecommerce customer lifecycle. As a result, it's usually necessary to integrate data from different data sets and then analyze those combined data sets to answer questions about customers. For example, integrating data from the web site, television (set-top boxes), mobile apps, social media, and qualitative research (VoC and surveys) into a holistic, full view of the customer at various stages in the lifecycle can provide unified data that may be useful for informing strategy and guiding tactics for ecommerce companies.

Other approaches to the customer lifecycle, beyond the Tumbler model I reviewed previously, include the *customer funnel*, the *customer journey*, and the *customer path to purchase* models. The *customer funnel* is a way to describe the specific, predefined series of steps that a prospective customer takes on the way to buying something on an ecommerce site. The "top of the funnel" is the entire pool of qualified prospects who are aware or would consider buying. These prospects drop off or abandon the funnel as they progress across each step. In the best case, prospects who have reached the final step have bought the product and converted. The *customer journey* can be thought of as having elements of the customer funnel, but it doesn't require a specific sequence of steps. Instead, the notion of a customer journey can start in the qualitative world of data collected from voice-of-customer research to understand awareness, top-of-mind recall, and favorability. The journey can enter acquisition, behavior, conversion retention, and loyalty. *Path to purchase analysis* is like a customer journey analysis except that it is less concerned with the cognitive states of prospective customers and the steps they take to buy a product. The path to purchase instead considers the customer as being exposed to all sorts of media, advertising, and other commercial and social influences that compel the person to eventually decide to buy or not to buy a product. Thus, the path of purchase involves understanding not necessarily the customer's action, but the influence of many different things (i.e., the variables) on the eventual purchase. Customer journey and path to purchase analysis are interrelated in the sense that the customer's journey is a path that leads to a purchase where the customer's cognition and actions are measured (the journey) and the influences (the path to purchase) are also measured.

Defining the Types of Customers

Not all customers are known equally. Companies know more about some customers than other customers. Customers have all sorts of attributes, attitudes, opinions, and perceptions, and similarly there are customer records, however standardized, with many different values for each field in them. There is a lot to analyze in the different data compositions that compose customers. In ecommerce, customers are usually known individuals because to buy something they provide their information. In the best case, their customer record contains the name, address, and other personally identifiable information (PII). In the worst case, it may only have an e-mail address and some bitcoins.

Some customers can be anonymous (when someone is buying from them as a proxy, such as a buyer's agent or even via an online auction). Thus, in ecommerce there are **anonymous buyers**. There are also **mostly** or **partially anonymous buyers**—those who have provided very little information, perhaps their IP address, an e-mail address, and some bitcoins. There are **mostly known customers** who have provided payment information that can be traced back or looked up. This data can be enhanced with other consumer data to round out a picture of the mostly known customer.

And finally, there are **fully known customers** who provide personally identifiable information that can be enhanced and/or joined with other data to create rich customer profiles. In ecommerce, the idea of incremental registration helps to create customer data by collecting small amounts of information. These small data points collected about or given by the customer can be stored and analyzed to build out a larger customer profile. Thus, incremental collection of customer data can be an approach for ecommerce sites to round out the information given by the customer and move them over time from an anonymous state into a fully known state.

Reviewing Types of Customer Analytics

There are many ways to analyze customer data. What's common across all of them is that there is customer data available to support each type of analysis in a customer record. Although you could use personally identifiable information in customer analysis, you may be limited by your company and law in doing so. Thus, it is a good idea to encode PII or anonymize it if necessary to support certain customer analyses. It's important to always be cognizant of privacy, data security, and the impact that even the perception of mishandling customer data could have on an ecommerce business. Ecommerce sites that can't secure their customer data don't stay in business for long because they don't maintain customers. Would you return to an ecommerce site that lost your personal information or credit card number to a hacker or other bad actor?

Customer analysis is meant to help customers by giving them reasons to create more value, to spend more money, to buy more things. In many ecommerce companies the CRM system acts as the master customer data repository. In other ecommerce companies, customer data may exist in pieces across disparate systems that are not connected. Use customer data to describe customers, segment them, understand their lifetime value, ascertain their behavior within your ecommerce experience, and determine what marketing is most effective for creating new or repeat customers.

Segment your customer data. Identify and analyze cohorts. Calculate and compare lifetime value to the cost of customer acquisition. Analyze what people say about your ecommerce site versus the positioning of the messages about your brand. Analyze the behavior of customers in terms of how frequently they shop or how long they pause between purchases. Score customers based on their actions. Personalize experiences based on customer profiles. Measure customer attrition and customer churn, understand why it happens, and learn how to predict it.

Segmenting Customers

Customer segmentation refers to subdividing customers into groups based on the known attributes that are shared by other customers. For example, you may choose to segment simply based on a single data point like geography; or you can segment across multiple data points, such as customers in major U.S. cities who have bought in the past month and have a lifetime value of above $500. The goal of customer segmentation is to discover new relationships and insights about the members of a segment, and then, based on that discovery and learning, to find the best ways to improve their value. Because segmentation helps in understanding a customer, it is frequently used as a way to identify and prioritize high-value customers. Marketing messages and other content can be targeted to the segment to drive response and action to drive the highest value. Although it is common to segment customers based on easily available metrics, such as demographics, revenue, or products purchased, I suggest segmenting based on lifetime value into deciles or quartiles. Armed with this information about lifetime value or even profitability, the ecommerce company can ideate programs to drive demand and retention. You may even target segments based on where they are in the customer lifecycle.

To execute a customer segmentation analysis, the analyst must do the following:

1. Determine the customer data available to segment.

2. Divide customers based on available data put into a business context. That is, you must estimate which customers generate the most profit.

3. Identify specific segments that are performing below or above expected levels.

4. Target advertising, marketing, communication, and brand communication to the segment.

5. Create new programs, services, offerings, and even products that align with the needs of the segment.

6. Measure the segments over time to see how they change in terms of key metrics, like profit. If you've segmented effectively and targeted your offerings and communications in a compelling way, you should see more customers generating more value and profit over time.

Segmentation can be a very effective method for finding insights that can be used to generate ideas for improving performance. You may realize that certain segments aren't satisfied with the current product mix, so merchandising activities can be adjusted. Some customers may not be connecting with your company due to marketing programs or distribution not reaching them. The features of your ecommerce experience that are engaged in by high-value segments can be identified and tested. Prices can be adjusted based on segmentation (Bain and Company 2015).

Performing Cohort Analysis

Cohort analysis is a way to segment ecommerce customers and prospective customers based on their behavior as they move through time. It's different from segmentation in that instead of dividing people up based on known attributes, it groups people together based on shared behaviors and measures across time. Time is the main difference between cohort analysis and segmentation, such that cohort analysis enables you to look at a small population over time separate from the large population, whereas segmentation provides a snapshot in time.

Cohort analysis enables an analyst to mine entire populations and discover behaviors about audiences and ask questions about those behaviors based on metrics. For example, a cohort may be created of all people who buy over the course of a month, and a question asked of that cohort might be how much did they spend or what marketing channel did they engage with prior to purchase. Another example of cohort analysis would be to determine when the prospective customer first visited the ecommerce site, and then build cohorts of the customers who convert on day 0, day 1, day 2, and so on.

The powerful thing about cohort analysis is that, like the analytics process, the best cohort analyses start with business questions and layer in metrics specific to the cohort that inform the business question. Because cohort analysis is aligned with time, such concepts as the customer lifecycle, the customer journey, and the path to purchase can be evaluated. For example, who bought products during the last sale, when did they first visit the site, and what promotions did they use and what margin was contributed can all be evaluated.

Analysts can examine cohorts over time to see how their performance changes day by day, week by week, month by month, and so on—and the impact of recent merchandising, pricing, and marketing activities can be understood. Because cohorts can be built to answer specific needs, you can see trends in cohort behavior, understand retention and loyalty, apply metrics that show engagement, or analyze the cohorts for consistency, decay, and change over time. To execute a cohort analysis, do the following:

1. Identify your business question.
2. Determine the goals and metrics to measure to set those goals.
3. Segment your audience into cohorts, starting with a specific time period.
4. Analyze the changes in cohort behavior over time.

Calculating Customer Lifetime Value

It could be argued that measuring, calculating, and understanding customer lifetime value (CLTV or CLV) is the most important type of customer analysis. Wikipedia defines customer lifetime value as "a prediction of the net profit attributed to the entire future relationship with a customer. The prediction model can have varying levels of sophistication and accuracy, ranging from a crude heuristic to the use of complex predictive analytics techniques." CLTV is a powerful metric that can be used in segmentation, cohort analysis, and many other types of ecommerce analysis. It is highly meaningful for ranking customers and to use as a proxy for estimating the impact of marketing, advertising, promotions, and changes to the user experience.

As the words mean, this type of analysis pinpoints the exact financial value of a customer. Customer lifetime value is a prediction of future value by using past purchasing to predict future revenue and then discounting it using some cost of capital to identify a predicted lifetime value for the customer. CLTV isn't customer profitability analysis, which is descriptive in nature based on past purchases. It is easier and more straightforward to calculate value in terms of discounted future value because a profit calculation requires understanding the cost, discount, and revenue of all items that customer ever purchased. Customer lifetime value must be a prediction based on the future because otherwise you only have "current life" value with no emphasis on the customer's future value (discounted to profit in today's dollars). I have, however, seen analysts calculate lifetime value based on all revenue generated by the customer; this measurement isn't wrong per se. It's just the current value of the customer; it doesn't try to infer or predict future value from customer retention, repurchasing, and loyalty.

Executives like lifetime value because it is a long-term, strategic measure that indicates the current performance and may predict the future performance of the business. Predictive customer lifetime value is a leading indicator of future performance. The roots of CLTV are in financial analysis and, more specifically, capital budgeting, in which an investment is understood over time in relation to the revenue it generates, discounted by the cost of capital to identify the present value in today's dollars or future revenue. CLTV analysis turns a customer into another financial asset that can be quantified and modeled. In that sense, CLTV represents what a customer is worth and provides guidance on the amount of investment that should be allocated to retain the customer or acquire similar customers.

One of the major uses of CLTV is customer segmentation, which starts with the understanding that not all customers are equally important. The CLTV-based segmentation model allows the company to predict the most profitable group of customers, understand those customers' common characteristics, and focus more on them rather than on less profitable customers. CLTV-based segmentation can be combined with a share of wallet (SOW) model. This combined analysis can identify "high CLTV but low SOW" customers—with the assumption that the company's profit could be maximized by investing marketing resources in those customers.

To do a customer lifetime value analysis, you have choices because there are no industry standards. Common to most formulas are the time period, the retention rate, the churn rate, and the cost of capital, as well as margin (either gross or contribution margin). A formula for calculating CLTV can be as follows:

(Gross Revenue per Customer * Margin per Customer) / Churn Rate

This is another formula:

Gross Revenue / Margin per Customer * (Retention Rate / 1 + Cost of Capital – Retention Rate)

A complex formula cited in the *Journal of Interactive Marketing* by Berger and Nasr (1998) is as follows:

$$\text{CLV} = \text{GC} \cdot \sum_{i=1}^{n} \frac{r^i}{(1+d)^i} - M \cdot \sum_{i=1}^{n} \frac{r^{i-1}}{(1+d)^{i-0.5}}$$

Determining the Cost of Customer Acquisition

Another extremely powerful and meaningful customer analysis is called **cost of customer acquisition analysis**. Simply put, this analysis determines how much money it costs to acquire a customer. This financial metric indicates the effectiveness and, potentially, the health of your acquisition efforts. It is the yin to the yang of customer lifetime value. The best ecommerce companies constantly measure and know from rote organizational memory the cost of customer acquisition and customer lifetime value.

By comparing the cost of customer acquisition against customer lifetime value, the analyst can identify the profitability of customers and the effectiveness of marketing in terms of financial performance and return on investment. A ratio of 1:1 between cost of customer acquisition and customer lifetime value means the company is breaking even over time, and likely losing money in the short term. A 2:1 ratio means the company is spending way too much money to acquire a customer because the revenue doesn't exceed the cost. The business is not healthy! However, a ratio of 1:3 means that for every dollar spent on acquisition, three dollars are generated in lifetime value. This measure points to a healthy, growing business that is retaining customers and growing them. As the revenue multiples versus cost of acquisition increase to 1:5 and beyond, the business may be growing so fast that it could have problems scaling up to meet demand (Hughes 2015). The inventory is just flying off the shelves. It's a good problem to have, but only if cash flow can cover the inventory turns since customers keep buying. As you can see, a simple analysis of the ratio of cost of customer acquisition to customer lifetime value can be informative.

The cost of customer acquisition can be calculated at an overall company level, involving all costs—fixed and variable—that are part of customer acquisition efforts. Or the analysis can be performed on specific marketing channels, such that the company knows the cost of acquisition for paid search versus display ads versus retargeting versus offline events and so on.

Again, there are no standards for calculating the cost of customer analysis. A simple way to do so is to determine how many new customers were acquired during a time period. Then you would total all the expenses associated with acquiring customers. You would tally costs such as campaign costs, software costs, hardware costs, operational costs (electricity and real estate), and headcount costs, and then simply divide the number of new customers by the acquisition costs. For example, if 10,000 customers were acquired in a month and the company spent $40,000 to acquire these customers, then the cost of customer acquisition is $4 per customer.

Analyzing Customer Churn

Churn is a way to describe customers who don't buy. Traditionally, this metric is applied in subscription-based businesses, of which ecommerce can be one. In more typical forms of ecommerce, in which the customer initiates a transaction, the definition of what is customer churn needs to be identified. The end of a customer relationship could be based on recency such that when a customer hasn't rebought within one year, that customer is considered to have churned. Churn must be understood within business cycles and against seasonality. It is most common to analyze churn in two contexts. The first context is whether the churn was voluntary. Sometimes customers don't come back for expected reasons. A kids' ecommerce site loses customers as those customers' kids grow. Involuntary churn is a way to describe this type of churn, in which circumstances beyond control of the company cause customer attrition.

On the other hand, voluntary churn is when customers actively decide to disengage and not buy again. The most costly churn to the business is voluntary churn. The analysis of churn first begins by looking at the number of customers across a time period, such as the number of customers this month compared to the number in the preceding month. The count of the loss of customers month over month is the churn. From that data calculate the churn rate by dividing the loss of customers during that period by the total customers in the previous period. If a site had 5,000 customers in June and 4,000 in July, the churn rate is 20%. This rate is considered the gross churn rate. There is also a concept known as net churn rate, which factors in both the growth of new customers and the loss of existing customers. If a site had 5,000 customers last month, lost 1,000 customers, but added

500 new customers, for a total net count of 4,500 customers, the net churn rate would be 10%.

Churn rate can be analyzed against customer lifetime value. By subtracting the customers' past purchases against their expected future purchases (based on CLTV), you can begin to understand the financial impact of customer churn. If the customer lifetime value was on average $5,000 and the customer who churned had spent $1,000, the site lost $4,000 in expected lifetime revenue. Although it is nice to replace this revenue with customers who are new (and quantified using the cost of customer acquisition), losing customers is not good. Measuring net churn rate must be understood against gross churn rate to tell the whole story.

From the measurement of churn, there are several types of analysis to reduce customer churn. Many of these programs involve sending targeted marketing communications and using advertising channels to convince lapsed customers to repurchase. Promotional discounts and other incentives may be offered. Qualitative surveys may be employed to ask the churned customer to explain the rationale and reasons for churn. An ecommerce site can study the customer behavior to see whether site problems or issues, such as errors or out-of-stocks or changes in the category or brand types may be the reason. Measuring churn is necessary for ecommerce sites, and this analysis helps to keep an ecommerce business healthy.

Understanding Voice-of-the-Customer Analytics

Voice-of-the-customer (VoC) analysis is a type of customer research in which an ecommerce brand analyzes qualitative data to better understand the customer. The methods for generating qualitative data could be surveys, ethnographies, diaries, social media, customer feedback forms, focus groups, digital customer feedback tools, and transcripts from customer service phone calls or chats. The many diverse sources of voice-of-the-customer data have one thing in common: They capture data directly from customers. This data can be about preferences, opinions, complaints, ideas, stories, and other communication about the ecommerce brand. The data is organized hierarchically and prioritized based on business value. For example, an ecommerce site analyzes social media and qualitative data and figures out their current promotion is being negatively impacted by stock-outs in popular sizes of a sale item. The business, now aware of the issues, can respond. Text mining, concept extraction, and concept classification can be performed on VoC data. It's data rich and ready for data science.

Doing Recency, Frequency, and Monetary Analysis

Recency, frequency, and monetary analysis, or RFM analysis, is a type of ecommerce analysis that identifies the best customers by comparing how much time has passed since a purchase (the recency), to how often they purchase (the frequency), and to the amount of money spent (the monetary). It is related to lifetime value analysis in the sense that it contextualizes lifetime value in terms of customer activity and engagement. The idea is that people who buy the most and visit the most are likely your best customers. By tracking these customers against their own behavior, you can ensure that they remain so. In other words, if you know that a customer has high monetary value and usually purchases every week, and then you notice he hasn't purchased in two weeks, you want to identify that behavior to address it (by contacting the customer in some way).

RFM analysis, of course, requires collecting the data about recency, frequency, and monetary. Many ecommerce tools enable this type of data collection. After you have the data, do the following:

1. **Analyze the customer data and sort your customers.** Figure out those customers who have spent the most, visited most recently, and had the largest number of sales. These are your best customers.

2. **Benchmark the RFM data to create a segment of these customers.** You must determine what measurements indicate that a customer has spent a lot of money and that the customer has visited and revisited the ecommerce experience. To do so, you want to understand customer distributions in terms of average order value, lifetime value, and measures of recency or frequency.

3. **Score these customers by assigning a value to these behaviors and segment the scored customers into tiers.** For example, you may assign a score of 10 to those customers who spend more than $100 a week, every week, and visit once every seven days. Other customers may receive lower scores based on the RFM thresholds you set. The customers with the 10 score are segmented and labeled as "best customers."

4. **Set up alerting and behavioral tracking against the customer RFM score.** In this way, you can recognize when customers move in and out of the segments.

5. **Provide merchandising and marketing with these scored lists.** This way, they can merchandise and market uniquely to these valuable customers and can try to improve the performance of lower-RFM-scored customers (Novo 2015).

Determining Share of Wallet

A share-of-wallet analysis is used to estimate what percentage of a customer's money is being spent on your ecommerce site compared to those of your competitors. It can be a helpful analysis for ecommerce sites that are highly competitive or that offer a selection of products that complement each other. For example, if a customer is buying a table, you may also want to sell him chairs, a tablecloth, plates, and so on. Another way to think of it is that a customer may spend $1,000 a year on clothes. He spends this across three ecommerce sites, but only $100 on your site. That means you have 10% share of wallet, and an opportunity to earn that other 90% of $900, correct? Sort of. Unfortunately, R. Y. Du (University of Georgia), W. A. Kamakura (Duke University), and C. F. Mela (Duke University) have shown that "there is no correlation between the volume of sales a customer has with your company, and the volume of sales they have with your competitors."

Enter the "wallet allocation rule" developed by Timothy L. Keiningham, Lerzan Aksoy, Alexander Buoye, and Bruce Cooil. They state that a brand rank in the minds of the customer is most important in driving a larger share of wallet (McCarl 2013). Thus, they propose that if you can identify the rank of your brand against the total number of brands used, you can estimate the customer's share of wallet. They suggest doing the following:

1. Identify the total brands a customer uses in the product category.
2. Survey customers to provide the rank.
3. Use their "wallet allocation rule" formula: (1-(Rank/(Number of Brands+1)))° (2/Number of Brands).

For example, assume that the customer ranks your brand #1 out of four total brands. But this customer still spends only $100 on your site (of $1000 in total spend across all competing brands). The wallet allocation rule would be applied as (1-(1)/(4+1))°(2/4) or 40. Thus, your share of wallet is 40%, so you could only expect the customer, in the best case, to spend another $300 with you on top of the $100 already spent. Your ecommerce company would earn $400 or 40% of the customer's "wallet."

Scoring Customers

Scoring is a way to enumerate customers or the behavior of customers in a way that allows for common sizing and understanding of the customers and their behavior. Enumeration is a fancy way of saying "assign a numerical value" to something, which in this case is customer data itself, such as transactions, behaviors, segments, or other business-meaningful data. Most typically, a numerical value is applied to a behavior, such as what I described in RFM analysis. However, Bryan Brown from Silverpop, an IBM company, identifies several additional types of ecommerce-related scoring:

- **Engagement scoring**, where behaviors, events, and interactions that are considered proxies for interest are scored. For example, viewing a product page, adding an item to a shopping cart, or clicking-through from a newsletter to the site.
- **Loyalty scoring**, where behaviors, events, and interactions that indicate loyalty or the propensity to become loyal are evaluated. For example, customers who sign up for a newsletter, register for a VIP program, make frequency use of discounts, or regularly review or score products.

- **Profile completeness scoring**, involving scoring customer profiles based on their level of completeness overall or for a certain purpose. For example, a profile with an e-mail address would be scored lower than one with a name and address.

- **Inactivity scoring**, enumerating recency and frequency against expected patterns in the customer lifecycle in order to pinpoint customer inactivity and fix it. For example, if a customer who bought once a month stopped buying for several months.

- **Game scoring**, representing customers' behaviors as scores that are compared against each other. Certain customer activities and events are enumerated and summed, and those with the highest score are winning the game. For example, two customers who looked at the same pages, but only one added a product to the cart. The customer with the cart add would be scored higher.

Predicting Customer Behavior

Entire books have been written about predictive analytics. Although some analyses discussed in this book require forecasting, not all require prediction. However, prediction can be applied to most types of analysis. If RFM analysis tells you what is happening, then can you predict what will happen? If a share-of-wallet analysis identifies what has happened, can you predict future share of wallet? You know your churn rate, so can you predict what it would be next year? In all of these cases, given the appropriate data, skill set, and tools, you can predict many things. That doesn't mean that the prediction will be precise or accurate—you won't know that until you compare predictions to actuals. But it does mean that prediction can help put parameters around what could happen. The types of predictions about customers come from these types:

- **Clustering based on customer behavior and attributes.** For example, clustering customers based on geography and lifetime value.

- **Predicting what will happen based on propensities or tendencies or behavioral triggers.** For example, if a customer visits three times per day and looks at the same product page each time, can that behavior be predictive of a future purchase? Or would that customer be open to a marketing offer, such as a limited-time promotion on that product?

- **Recommending based on collaborative filtering.** This is where data about overall customer behavior and other customer data such as preferences, rankings, satisfaction, and transactions are modeled such that recommendations are generated to customers based on universal preferences and likelihoods to prefer.

Clustering Customers

Clustering is an analytical technique that uses data mining. In clustering analysis, customer attributes are evaluated and compared to one another and grouped together based on similarity. Clustering has its roots in graph theory, if you want to read more about it. Basically a clustering coefficient is calculated for both the group (i.e., all customers) and the local node (i.e., the specific customer). This coefficient is used to assess the degree and tendency to which the nodes can be grouped together into clusters. Clustering is applicable to customer and to products. See the discussion in Chapter 10, "Analyzing Products and Orders in Ecommerce," for a discussion about clustering products. Clustering and segmentation are related since a clustering algorithm segments the audience; the difference is that the clustering occurs automatically and across many more variables that a human could easily or timely calculate. Clusters may be built based on hundreds of attributes, whereas human-built segments have only a few. As you can deduce, clustering is a machine-generated analysis that can fall into the world of "data science."

Clustering is most commonly done on behavioral data, like those generated from digital analytics tools. The behaviors measured and applied in behavioral clustering can include data about recency, frequency, conversion, clicks made, features used, marketing campaigns touched, and other data generated by people within an ecommerce experience. A clustering algorithm would group these behaviors into clusters of people who exhibited them or didn't exhibit them—and from that data conclusions and inferences can be drawn about what behaviors might drive other behaviors. For example, if it was noted that viewing videos and reviewing social feedback was a behavior correlated with purchases, then it could suggest targeting people who viewed videos with campaigns that included social feedback in a test to drive conversion. And vice versa.

Another approach to clustering involves product attributes, such as the category or brand. You may choose to cluster all customers based on the categories they purchase and/or the brands they buy. Previous unrealized relationships may be found: Customers buy only a certain brand; or customers who buy one brand also buy this brand; or people who buy combinations of brands and categories don't buy these brands or categories but other people do. In this way, it becomes possible to find new combinations of ways of thinking about what people buy and in relation to what other attributes, which can then be used to fuel merchandising, buying, or marketing ideas.

Predicting Customer Propensities

Propensity is a fancy word that means "a tendency toward." It's these tendencies toward something a customer will do, such as buying or no longer buying, that matter in ecommerce. Data scientists can use predictive analytics to create statistically rigorous and valid models related to ecommerce business issues, such as these:

- **Predicted lifetime value.** CLTV was discussed in this chapter. It requires a forecast of lifetime value from all available purchase data, but that forecast does not necessarily have to be automated, ongoing, and available instantaneously; however, it can be. Predicted lifetime value often is automated and the prediction made available after the first purchase. That is, from the first purchase a prediction of that customer's CLTV is generated. Typically, the first purchase is compared to those of other customers who have the same first purchase to generate the estimate.

- **Predicted share of wallet.** Share-of-wallet analysis was discussed earlier in this chapter. It tells you how much of the total customer budget you have converted to sales. By corollary it also tells you how much competitors are earning. To make it predictive, you must answer the question "How much of what the customer could spend will she spend with me?" The answer isn't simply the total she spends on others; it's how much she has left still to spend with you. For example, if a customer buys an item four times per year, once per quarter, but has bought only once from you in July, it's likely she will purchase only two more times in the year, not three. It's a simple example, of course, but the idea should be clear. A predictive share of wallet analysis factors in other relevant information, including the "wallet allocation rule" discussed earlier in this chapter.

- **Propensity to buy.** This predictive analysis indicates which customers are ready to make a purchase so that you can respond, communicate, and even target them in relevant ways. This type of analysis may identify how many visits are made on average before a purchase is made; or it may factor in other behavioral triggers, such as viewing the same item over and over again over time, or adding items to wish lists or shopping carts but not choosing to buy them. All of this information would be used to detect when a person enters into the buying mode in order to market or engage with them.

- **Propensity to churn.** This predictive analysis refers to predictive models that classify customers to identify those likely to stop being customers, or churn. Customers are ranked from least likely to churn or most likely to churn, usually in a quadrant analysis. The data used to identify churn may be recency, frequency, monetary, and engagement data.

- **Propensity to use.** This predictive analysis relates to modeling whether or not your customers will use a promotional offer or discount. This type of modeling is important when you are sending promotions and coupons because you want to target people who will not only use the promotion, but use it in optimal ways. For example, you may not want to make an offer of "30% off $100 or more" to a low-value customer who doesn't respond or engage with the site, nor might you want to send the same offer to your highest-value customers who will buy anyway. Instead, you may want to send the offer to low-value customers who have bought more than $100 in a single purchase.

- **Propensity to engage/disengage.** It is possible to predict other digital behaviors related to ecommerce, such as if the customer will click on an e-mail link or how frequently communications should be sent to reduce disengagement (like newsletter unsubscribes). As with many other predictive models, a hypothesis can be drawn about engagement and disengagement by comparing behavior that occurred in the past near engagement or disengagement. These behavioral triggers then become the variables in your predictive model.

Personalizing Customer Experiences

The highest art and science in ecommerce today is personalization. The idea is that, given a data set related to a customer, an ecommerce experience can be created that is perfectly suited to the customer's intent, wants and needs such that it creates the highest possible levels of engagement and revenue. In personalized experiences, the experience is so compelling that it drives higher lifetime value. Doing and applying many of the analyses described in this chapter is how insights about personalization can be realized and the relevant data used to power algorithms and models that create personalized ecommerce experiences. Segmenting and clustering customers, and understanding how customer attributes and behavioral triggers influence predictions of lifetime value and churn, enable the analyst to frame the challenge of personalization. From the learnings and conclusions derived from other analyses, the rules and recipes for personalized experiences can be tested using off-the-shelf conversion optimization software and marketing automation software. Other companies may build personalization engines, using collaborative filtering or recommender systems that are based on using customer data to render personalized shopping experiences. The goal of personalization is of course to create higher lifetime values for customers.

Customer analytics in ecommerce can take many different forms. The different methods and techniques discussed in this chapter review and explain techniques that are widely used, in some cases, across the best-in-class ecommerce companies today.

10

Analyzing Products and Orders in Ecommerce

Orders are the financial core of ecommerce and represent, at a macro level, the interaction between a buyer and an ecommerce site when value, usually money, is exchanged in a transaction. Products are bought within orders. Ecommerce order data, thus, represents the attributes and properties of the order itself (such as the total sales price, discounts used, and margin), the individual products in the order (such as their sales prices and margin), and the customer behavior that occurs before and after the order. At a technical level, ecommerce orders are transactions defined as a logical operation on data and are said to have atomicity, consistency, isolation, and durability (ACID) within databases (Wikipedia 2015). For the purpose of this chapter and in general within analytics, the transactions that we want to analyze are ecommerce orders for products (or services) that are captured, stored, and processed in ecommerce and analytical systems. It is useful for an analyst to have an understanding of technical details related to ecommerce transactional processing systems and related systems for order analysis. But business stakeholders don't care very much about the database or the atomic-level detail captured about customer orders—that is, until the database doesn't function as expected, doesn't contain desired data, or can't be used to provide data for answering a business question. In these cases, business stakeholders will want answers about why they can't get the data they need. But for the most part business stakeholders will be more concerned about the financial impact and monetary measures of orders and the products. The analyst must help stakeholders ensure data is collected about products and orders via a data pipeline and governance/stewardship that results in clean and curated data that can be used for analysis. Analysts will explore and develop an understanding and perspective of the facts and dimensions about orders and products. They will apply this understanding to answering business questions, making recommendations, and describing insights derived from business questions about ecommerce orders and products.

The analysis of products and orders requires the analyst to think of the order as a transactional record in which detailed data is stored about not only the products in the order but also about the order itself. For example, an order has revenue generated in total, and that revenue can be broken down by product. The marketing channel that contributed to the transaction can be attributed. Promotions used, tax applied, and shipping charged can be analyzed within the boundaries of ecommerce order analysis. The customer can be tied back to the order, which may contain information about the gender, size, style, brand, and season of the product purchased. This rich transactional data set of order and product data and metadata can be mined and analyzed. By digging and mining the order-level detail in relation to the customer, marketing and advertising, and conversion, you can find and understand the data to answer business questions. You may want to look for trends, patterns, outliers, and anomalies in order data. Keep in mind that ecommerce order and product analytics also include data that you may not expect and that isn't commonly considered for capture and usage. This data could include information about the privacy policy applied to the order, such as details or its version. Flags indicate whether the order was an outlier in some way, perhaps by the revenue amount, number of items ordered, possible fraudulent IP address, unusual device type, and more. The data model corresponding to an ecommerce order contains the data to analyze for different business purposes:

- Orders are important to analyze for all business stakeholders. Depending on the goals, questions, and seniority of the stakeholders, an analyst has a wealth of information to provide for answering each question.
- Senior leaders want to review summary information at the aggregate about orders and the products sold within them, such as changes in the number, pacing, revenue, trends in the

purchase categories, and the impact of promotions and discounts on the revenue and profit.

- Marketing staff want to understand orders overall and the performance of products, categories, and brands as they relate to different marketing channels, campaigns, and promotions; high-value customers and cohorts; device types; and more.

- Technical staff want to understand the sufficiency of the data captured within existing systems and current data models to help define the road map and how the data is being used as it relates to scaling technologies and ensuring technical alignment in terms of resources and systems against business requirements.

- Buyer and merchandising staff want to understand analysis about the specific products purchased, the revenue and margins of specific products, brands and categories, as well as the impact of discounting and promotions on price and profit. Additionally, the merchandiser will want to understand (and test) the impact of visual merchandising in the ecommerce experience on the volume, size, and financial return on orders and products (Cutroni 2013).

What Are Ecommerce Orders?

An ecommerce order, from a business analytics perspective, represents a transaction for one or more product (or service) items. As with all data in analytics, creating, socializing, and approving definitions for order data requires data stewardship and governance. Order data will be represented by a data model that will have metadata that may not be properties of the transaction, but rather properties of the ecommerce site—such as total transaction time or measures of server load or latency, which can be helpful to include in order analysis.

At the summary level, an order could have these data elements in a conceptual data model:

- **Order ID** is the unique identifier associated with the order event however it is defined at your company.

- **Revenue** is the amount of money spent on buying the items in the order.
- **Shipping** is the cost of shipping the items bought in the order.
- **Tax** is the taxation on the cost of the items bought in the order.
- **Promotion** is the name of the promotional discount or code, if any, applied to the order.
- **Affiliate** is the source of the order if different from the core ecommerce experience.
- **Channel** is the marketing source, if any, that resulted in the order as identified from the attribution model applied to orders.
- **Device** is the type of machine used when the order occurred, such as a desktop, tablet, or mobile device.
- **Customer ID** is the unique identifier for the customer who bought the items in the order.
- **Time** is the time stamp at the time when the order occurred.
- **Geography** is the physical location of the customer who purchased the items—as semantically correct for your business. This location could be self-entered, derived from the shipping information, or assigned by resolving the IP address to a geography.
- **Technical information** is the IP address, various device or hardware IDs, and information available about the order in HTTP headers or via other data collection.

Related to and necessary for detailed order analysis are the individual products or items that are part of each transaction (notice how the transaction ID is the key to join the transactional data with the product data, and transaction ID can be joined with a customer ID):

- **Transaction ID** is the unique identifier associated with the order however it is defined at your company.
- **Product ID** is the unique identifier associated with a unique product in the shopping cart.
- **Product name** is the human-readable name for the product purchased.

- **SKU** is the "stock keeping unit" represented by a unique alpha-numeric code for the product.
- **Price** is the price paid for the product excluding tax and shipping.
- **Quantity** is the number of units of the product purchased.
- **Category** is the qualitative descriptor that separates one item from another, often derived from a taxonomy.
- **Brand** is the name of the manufacturer or marketing label for the product.
- **Style** is a qualitative descriptor that indicates product distinctness in terms of fashion.
- **Size** summarizes the physical dimensions of the product along a set of known labels, such as small, medium, and large.
- **Season** describes the time of the year for companies selling goods specific to calendar activities and weather patterns.

From this order-level data and the product-level data, many different variables are available for analysis and visualization. An analyst can aggregate order and specific product revenue over time. The most popular products and SKUs can be derived. Assumptions and hypotheses about the customer base can be drawn based on the brand preference or style preference. Information on shipping, tax, and discounts, as well as marketing channel and affiliate data, can help with planning and operations. Models can be built from order and product variables to predict revenue and create recommendations. The best data model and facts and dimensions to use for orders and products will be custom to your business but will likely consist of at least some of the data we just reviewed.

What Order Data Should I Begin to Analyze?

You might be wondering what type of order data the analyst should analyze. In my experience, there is overall data you want to report and understand about all the orders on your site and data about the individual orders. Thus, measuring, tracking, reporting, and analyzing the following overall, aggregate data about all orders can be helpful: the number of total orders, units sold, total ordered revenue, total discounted revenue, average discount percentage, average order value, and average gross margin. Also, the analyst should analyze data about the specific, individual orders, including the order number, the order date, the products in the order, discounts used, discount percentage, the subtotal, the shipping cost, the tax cost, the total price, the gross margin, and net profit.

What Metrics and Key Performance Indicators Are Relevant for Ecommerce Orders?

Key performance indicators (KPIs) are metrics and ratios that are measured and tracked over time against business goals and benchmarks in order to understand performance. KPIs provide a numeric indication of the positive and negative trends in important business data. They are used by ecommerce workers to make decisions about what has worked or not worked so they can make the right decisions about how to do their job. KPIs help to drive business planning, set goals, and when analyzed can help the company derive understanding of the business in a way that informs decision-making. Many metrics and KPIs can be created for understanding what's happening with your ecommerce transactions and products. What follow are several KPIs that can be helpful for understanding orders. By analyzing the trends and movements in these KPIs over time and across periods, and by drilling-down and up and segmenting KPIs by dimensions, you may find insights. Here are some helpful KPIs for ecommerce orders:

- **Total Revenue Versus Total Profit** is a KPI that shows the top line and bottom line of the order. It can be drilled up or drilled down, segmented to infinity.
- **Margin** usually represents the contribution margin, gross margin, or net profit margin—all powerful KPIs to work with at the aggregate and in the detail of transactions.
- **Median and Average Revenue per Order** are KPIs that result from application of business statistics to revenue data. These KPIs can become benchmarks to calculate upper and lower control limits to find outliers.

- **Orders per Customer** is a KPI that when assessed across the customer universe enables segmentation to find the potentially highest-value customers based on their volume of orders.

- **Visits to Order** for an ecommerce digital experience is a KPI that begins to elucidate the customer journey. By finding out what the customer did in prior transactions or what influenced the prior visits, the ecommerce company can better respond to the customer and use the information to help other customers buy more quickly.

- **Days to Order** is like Visits to Order but instead denotes the number of calendar days between the first measurable and identifiable behavior by the customer and the date of the order. Again like Visits to Order, this KPI suggests that a customer journey occurs over a time period, and that some customers convert and place orders sooner than other customers. Thus, the period of time between when a customer first visits and places the first order can be determined—and effort can be placed in marketing and persuading customers to convert sooner.

- **Revenue by Category** is a helpful KPI for buyers, merchandisers, and planners because the distribution of revenue when mapped against business goals makes performance clear.

- **Orders and Products Bought by Marketing Channel** is a KPI that requires attribution to be made about the exposure of the customer to a marketing channel before the order.

- **Events/Pages/Steps until Order** are KPIs that can be used to denote a flow of events before an order. In ecommerce, the sequence of pages in the shopping cart flow leading to purchase or the steps to fill out a form can be tracked and measured to understand the impact on revenue.

- **Top Shipping Methods** is a list that helps an ecommerce company eliminate waste from offering fulfillment methods that are infrequently used.

- **Top Promotions** is a list that helps marketers understand current effective discounts in order to manage them and plan for future promotions.

- **Top Products** is a list that guides merchandisers on what products are most sold and/or have the best sell-through.

Approaches to Analyzing Orders and Products

Order and product analysis for the ecommerce analyst can take many forms. As with all analytical activities, the work is most successful when done to answer a business question that can drive a decision that results in an action that achieves a business goal. With orders and products, there are many ways to analyze them:

- **Financial analysis** on revenue, cost, tax, shipping, and so on.
- **Item analysis** of specific products and their attributes.
- **Promotional analysis** about the impact of different promotions on revenue, profitability, and customer engagement.
- **Category and brand analysis** to understand the financial measures, customer behavior, and purchasing volumes of categories and brands of merchandise.
- **Event and goal analysis** to understand the specific actions and pre-identified goals that customers engage in within the ecommerce experience before purchase.
- **Checkout path analysis** to identify what's working and not working during the checkout process, or across the path of linear steps within a digital ecommerce experience leading to a purchase.
- **Funnel analysis** to identify points of friction, abandonment, and fluidity in multistep processes that result in a user taking an action.
- **Cluster analysis** as a method for grouping orders and products together with similar characteristics to understand them as a group.
- **Up-sell and cross-sell analytics** to utilize recommendations to suggest items that are related in some way to the product being browsed.

- **Next-best-product analysis** from data science models that suggest products frequently purchased when other products are added to a cart or purchased.

In the next sections of this chapter, we'll explore each of these types of order analysis in more detail.

Doing Financial Analysis on Orders

Financial analysis concentrates on the monetary metrics related to an order. Measures and derivative calculations based on revenue, cost, taxes, margin, and shipping can be analyzed. The business questions to answer by doing financial analysis include the following:

- What orders have the highest value?
- What orders result in the lowest shipping cost?
- Do tax rates impact the quantity or amount of revenue in purchases?
- What might my future costs be for orders of this type?
- What will my margin be next month?

Doing Product and Item Analysis on Orders

An order includes one or more products or items, which have attributes such as product name, promotions applied, size, style, brand, category, department, cost, revenue, margin, and more. Digging into the details of products that have been purchased can help you answer questions like these:

- What products are most frequently included and bought in orders?
- Do certain items provide a larger or smaller contribution to margin?
- What brands are bought when other brands are bought at the same time?
- What sizes should I reorder or order next season?
- What categories should receive more attention from merchandising?

Doing Promotional Analysis on Orders

Discounts and promotions in which something is offered as an incentive to purchase are very common in ecommerce environments. Promo-code aggregators, coupon sites, and sites that track discounts and promotional offers exist across the Web. These promotions are typically selected by marketing and merchandising, which base predicted financial return of these incentives using ecommerce data. Thus the analysts should help merchandising with promotional analysis in order to answer questions such as the following:

- What promotions generate the highest and lowest margins?
- Are promotions causing adverse user behavior, such that categories or brands aren't being bought without promotional discounts?
- What promotion should I offer to drive the highest revenue, the most number of products in an order, or the highest margin?
- Do promotions have a net positive or a net negative impact on the overall business?
- What promotions should I always offer or never offer?

Doing Category and Brand Analysis on Orders

Orders include, of course, the purchase of products. These products are associated with a category and/or department, and they are manufactured or marketed by a particular brand. Taxonomies (and ontologies) are often used to define categories. For example, the brand Nike sells athletic apparel and shoes. The department into which a Nike brand may fall may be the men's department, the footwear category, and the athletic shoe subcategory. This information becomes valuable to describe and predict orders when it is captured over time and analyzed to answer business questions like the following:

- What categories generate the highest revenue?
- What brands have the lowest cost?
- What brands and categories will be popular next year?
- What brands and categories are most and least popular?

- What brands and categories have the highest inventory turnover?
- What brands and categories have the most days in inventory?

Doing Event and Goal Analysis on Orders

Customers complete various actions when engaged in an ecommerce experience. They may search for a product, browse a category, examine a lookbook, add items to a cart, register for a newsletter, sign up for an account, buy products, and more. It is possible to measure and track user and customer events and user goals such as those just listed. These events and goals can be tracked against the customers who buy and the people who do not buy in order to understand which events and goals assist in generating orders and creating value. Some of the questions you can answer with event and goal analysis include these:

- What specific events did customers complete compared to noncustomers?
- How many instances of a specific event occurred?
- What events are likely to occur in the path to purchase?
- What events occur when people report positive or negative experiences?
- Do certain customer segments complete certain events?

Doing Path-to-Purchase Analysis on Orders

The path to purchase describes the sequence of touchpoints that a customer has before buying. This approach to understanding what influences a person to buy examines all the touchpoints where a prospect could have been influenced before a purchase. For example, paid search clicks would be captured, but so would visits to product review sites and social conversation. Less concerned with collecting data about exposure and interaction with specific channels or ads, path-to-purchase analysis looks to explain the impact of all interactions before a purchase. That way, instead of prioritizing one way to interact with a customer, the ecommerce site could figure out how to maximize all interactions in the path to purchase (Kimelfeld 2013). Path-to-purchase analysis on transactions can reveal these details:

- What marketing channels are my customers engaging with before purchase?
- What sources outside of my control tend to influence customers who buy?
- What interactions do customers have with my brand or the products I sell before purchase?
- Are there common touchpoints within all purchases?

Doing Funnel Analysis on Orders

Funnel analysis is among the most common types of analysis that can be done on orders. If you consider a funnel, like the type used to capture water, the transaction point is where the consolidated water exits the funnel and enters the container. In this metaphor, the water is the customer and his money and the exit of the funnel is the conversion event when money changes hands between the customer and the ecommerce site. Funnels are composed of pre-identified steps that, when performed in a sequence, lead to a transaction. In ecommerce the series of steps, events, interactions, or pages required to buy a product after it is added to a shopping cart is the "funnel." Each step that a prospective customer takes in your predefined funnel is measured to understand whether people proceed to the next step or drop off. Your ecommerce funnel will be specific to your company but will likely include the Add to Cart > View Cart > Start Checkout > Checkout Steps > End Checkout with a Conversion. Many of you understand this funnel metaphor innately; you know that a conversion rate is calculated by measuring the ratio of how many people start the funnel compared to how many complete it. A macro-conversion may begin with the first page in the session and end with an order (i.e., conversion as the ratio or orders to sessions). Or the conversion may be considered a "micro-conversion," in which the starting point in the funnel begins within the site (such as when the product is added to the cart). Funnel analysis helps to answer business questions about transactions, including these:

- Do people start the sequence of steps on my ecommerce site in the order expected and where we expect?
- Do any of the pages or events in my funnel work well to propel people to the next step—or do not work well and cause people to abandon the funnel?
- What is my baseline in terms of total conversion, abandonment by step, and step-jumping for understanding how the steps in the funnel impact conversion?
- Are there particular points in the funnel that need to be addressed because they cause abandonment or aren't working as expected?

A basic funnel analysis could include four simple steps and related KPIs:

1. **Visits (or Sessions).** The total number of people who visited the site.
   - *Conversion Rate.* The percentage of orders from all visits.
2. **Shoppers.** The total number of people who viewed one or more products.
   - *Product View Rate.* The percentage of visitors who viewed a product page.
3. **Add to Cart.** The total number of cart adds.
   - *Cart Add Rate.* The percentage of people who added one or more products to their cart.
4. **Orders.** The total number of orders.
   - *Purchase Completion Rate.* The percentage of people who completed the purchasing process and ordered.

Doing Cluster Analysis on Orders

Cluster analysis is a method for analyzing data by automatically categorizing or sorting it into groups based on similarities in the data. Data with the maximum similarity are clustered together separately from clusters with weaker or no similarity. Based on the attributes listed at the top of the chapter, cluster analysis is suitable to be performed on orders and their product data and metadata. Clustering isn't a specific approach to analysis as much as it is a set of methods for grouping together like data. To do a cluster analysis, you need to prepare the data to support the approach chosen. For example, you might assign a value (vector) to a transaction to do a centroid-based clustering, or you may cluster based on the distributions of the data or values in your data using a clustering coefficient. The approach that's best for you, of course, depends on your business questions and your analyst and the level of data science they want to apply. Clustering orders and product data from orders is often a start to investigating customer or marketing data. Cluster analysis can answer questions like these:

- What orders are similar to each other and how are they similar?
- What are the unusual orders that aren't similar to other orders, and how?
- Are there relationships between the data about orders that I haven't seen before?
- Are there particular aspects of high-value orders that can be better understood?

Doing Up-Sell and Cross-Sell Analysis on Orders

Selling another item to someone who purchased is called a cross-sell. Convincing someone to spend more money when he is buying a product is called an up-sell. Since every order is associated with one or more products or items purchased, it is possible to determine what else people who bought that product also bought. If you are capturing what products other people purchased when they didn't purchase the product the current person is buying, then you have the data to up-sell. For example, if people buy shoes, you may be able to cross-sell them socks, or leather protector, or shoelaces. If people are buying one brand of boot and another more expensive brand of similar boot has been bought or looked at by other people, then the more expensive boot may be suggested as an up-sell. Use data about products in transactions to power analytically driven recommendations for up-selling and cross-selling.

Doing Next-Best-Action Analysis on Orders

After a transaction, people do something related. They may fill out a registration or warranty card, check for shipping tracker identification, check on shipping status, search for related items, buy more things, return items, come back to the site and browse, and more. By associating the after-purchase behavior with the previous order, you can do analysis to answer the following questions:

- What actions do people take after completing an order with these products?
- What actions should be suggested to the customer based on this order?
- Are there common or uncommon actions people take after ordering?

Analyzing Products in Ecommerce

Many different approaches to product analysis are useful for ecommerce. Each type of product analysis answers different business questions for different business groups and stakeholders. For example product analysis for merchandising focuses on understanding inventory, creative design, offer detail, the optimal price, sales impact, suppliers, and promotional markdowns/discounts. A product analysis for marketing would be more concerned with marketing channels, the user experience within the ordering flow or purchase funnel, and what products caused customer frequency, retention, and loyalty.

Understanding Useful Types of Product Analysis for Ecommerce

From an analytical perspective, it is helpful to consider the buyer lifecycle to frame product analytics. The buyer lifecycle implicitly, if not directly, involves a person using an ecommerce experience where they are doing the following:

1. Starting with the selection of a product category or brand
2. Narrowing to a specific brand or category

3. Selecting a product and adding it to a cart

4. Completing the steps in the funnel to order the product

5. Optionally, having contact with customer service

6. Optionally, returning the purchased product

7. Optionally, providing feedback about the product

8. Using the product (if it is not returned)

9. Communicating socially about the product

Each step of the product within the buyer lifecycle presented here can be understood by product analysis. Use the buyer lifecycle to help merchandisers, buyers, planners, and other business owners better understand how products are found and ordered as part of the overall ecommerce customer experience.

Product Brand Analysis

Ecommerce experiences contain catalogs of products from brands. It's important for a merchandiser and manager to understand which brands drive desired performance. I have seen cases in which less than 10% of brands drove 90% of the revenue. A Zipf distribution or power-law curve applies. You could hypothesize that 80% of an ecommerce site's revenue is driven by 20% of its brands. Understanding the financial performance of the brands offered on ecommerce sites means measuring and calculating the revenue, margins, and turnover of brands. Brand analysis goes beyond finance into behavioral analysis to understand the influence of certain brands on purchasing patterns—for example, showcasing premium brands while also offering lower-cost alternatives. Consumer perceptions of brand values and attributes reflect onto the ecommerce brand, so it is important to research qualitative aspects about brands. Market research such as brand awareness, top-of-mind recall, and customer sentiment are part of brand analysis. Analyzing the brand requires an understanding of the qualitative descriptors, lifestyle, and feelings people have about brands and products, while aligning with quantitative research about prospect and customer acquisition, behavior, and conversion. Product brand analysis answers questions such as these:

- What brands are most popular and drive the largest share of revenue versus margins?
- How do the attributes signified by particular brands influence the perception of my own ecommerce site?
- Am I applying the right merchandising and resources to support brand partnerships?
- What products within brands are value drivers?

Product Category Analysis

For ecommerce companies that sell products against more than one category, it is extremely important to understand the financial, acquisition, behavioral, conversion, retention, and loyalty data for each of the categories. What is a category? It's the highest level in the ontology/taxonomy—or the hierarchy of terms and concepts—that appears on your site.

Categories are such things as shirts, jackets, pants, underwear, socks. When products are grouped under an often-complex categorization hierarchy, both employees and customers can more easily understand and find available products. Product categories may be defined by information and librarian scientists, based on the industry knowledge or expertise, or created to support merchandising conceptualization. Regardless of origin, the only way to really know whether your ecommerce site's categorization scheme is optimal is to measure and benchmark performance and test it. The metrics for analyzing category performance include measures of financial performance, such as revenue, margin, and profit, and metrics, such as conversion rate, cost of customer acquisition, and lifetime value. By understanding how your customers perform on a category basis—separate from yet related to products, orders, and brands—you can make decisions that reduce the cost of categories and maximize the value. Some of the questions that can be answered through product category analysis include the following:

- What categories are most profitable and drive the highest lifetime value?

- Do particular categories influence product orders for other categories or are particular categories of products frequently bought together?
- Are particular categories viewed at higher or lower rates for engagement and for conversion?
- Which drive the most orders? Which have the highest margins? Which are most discounted?
- What categories drive the most customer acquisition? Does that differ from retention?
- Should I eliminate or redefine categories?

Customer Service Analysis

Customers will inevitably need help with their site usage, purchasing, shipping, transactions, and product usage. Ecommerce sites fulfill these pre- and post-sale customer needs through service capabilities. Many ecommerce sites enable customers to self-service—whether through FAQs; or via online capabilities to chat with agents who can diagnose, communicate, and resolve issues. Some ecommerce sites may even use expert systems and artificial intelligence for customer service. Human or robotic assistants may be offered to guide customers in getting service. Analytics can let you know when you have good or bad customer service. Fortunately, poor online ecommerce experiences can be turned around and made positive through excellent customer service, whether that customer service is delivered by machines or humans. On the other hand, positive online customer experiences that lead to the need for customer service can be diminished and negatively impacted by poor customer service. Thus, ecommerce companies that provide online features and capabilities for self-service and offline features and capabilities benefit from analytics around customer service. Business questions to answer around customer service include these:

- Has my company developed metrics to measure customer service efficiency and satisfaction?
- What customer service capabilities are most used and effective?
- How are our customer service capabilities impacting customer satisfaction?

- When are customers reaching out to customer service and what are the most frequent reasons?
- What do customers contact our company about and how does this impact our top and bottom lines or inform our user experience?

Product Returns Analysis

Customers sometimes return products bought in orders. For all ecommerce providers, it is nearly impossible to stop returns. Customers have buyer's remorse, products don't fit, the products don't match the buyer's perception of what was described, or people change their minds. A business can't avoid returns unless they explicitly disallow them. And even then, there are manufacturer's defects, shipping damage, and other issues that can't be foreseen. Companies that care about retention and loyalty may not welcome returns, but they need to understand them. A company can determine problematic products and quality issues and also understand the revenue and marginal impact of product returns through analysis. Business questions that you should be able to answer for stakeholders include the following:

- What products, brands, and categories are returned most or least frequently over what rate and time period?
- How do returns impact profitability?
- Are there specific customer types or customers that return products?
- Are there identifiable behaviors that increase the likelihood of a return?
- What actions should we take to reduce the amount or frequency of returns?

Social Media Product Analysis

Social media analytics is far beyond the scope of this book, and not possible in the page limit. It's an important type of analysis highly resonant with most companies because it's trendy and buzzworthy; people and your colleagues engage in it. Social media is also important because it can direct revenue and, perhaps more important, it influences people's perceptions about your ecommerce brand. In that sense, it's important to analyze the ecommerce impact of social media on the ecommerce brand overall, the products sold, direct response that lead to conversion/purchase of products in transactions, and about customer service, and the overall customer experience. Jim Sterne's book, *Social Media Metrics*, is a good starting point. Business questions that are important to understand about social media by using social media analytics include these:

- Do people referred from social media behave differently and transact differently?
- What social channels are most effective for selling specific categories, brands, and products or building brand awareness?
- What's the cost of customer acquisition and lifetime value of social-media-referred customers, and does that differ from other channels?
- How does social media impact the customer journey on the path to purchase?

Analyzing Merchandising in Ecommerce

Merchandising for ecommerce has its roots offline in physical stores. It's the term used to describe work activities related to selling the products on the shelf, ensuring that those products are displayed effectively, and successfully offering promotional offers and discounts. To do so, merchandisers work closely with buyers, who purchase and manage the inventory, and finance, which helps to ensure that the monetary impact of merchandising decisions is net positive. Wikipedia describes merchandising as "any practice which contributes to the sale of products to a customer.... It refers to the variety of products available for sale and the display of those product in such a way that it stimulates interest and entices customers to buy."

Merchandising and merchandisers are, of course, important for ecommerce businesses. They perform the activities defined previously for online retail; instead of the store, there is the site, mobile, or connected experience. In online environments merchandisers will participate and even lead efforts to optimize the experience (see Chapter 8, "Optimizing for Ecommerce Conversion and User Experience"). Doing so requires online merchandisers to understand the elements of user experience and design, and also comprehend the data around the customer (see Chapter 9, "Analyzing Ecommerce Customers"). Approving and participating in designing user experiences around merchandising necessitates knowledge of the customer who is buying the products, so data analysis is important. Merchandisers use tools and technology that are part of, connected to, or ancillary to the ecommerce platform (see Chapter 12, "What Is an Ecommerce Platform?"), so merchandising teams can require not only business support interpreting and reporting data, but also technical support. In some ecommerce companies merchandising may buy and order inventory. In large companies, merchandisers will work with buyers who find and buy inventory that merchandising will work with to merchandise.

Some of the techniques, technologies, and tools ecommerce merchandisers will use include data visualization, AB and multivariate testing tools, digital analytics, search, and other research tools for competitive intelligence, product comparisons, and social feedback such as ratings and rankings, and product reviews (wherever they exist). These tools are used by merchandisers to fulfill their goals, which can be measured only through analytics. Goals related to prospect and customer behavior, such as recency and frequency of purchases, may be targeted. But more commonly, merchandisers are incentivized by improvement to conversion rates, increases in average order size, the number of products in a transaction, and the margins resulting from orders.

Because merchandisers actively make decisions and are often empowered to change the site, it is important for analysts to work closely with merchandisers. Otherwise, merchandisers will simply use available data and analytical systems without guidance. The best merchandisers can be tough customers for ecommerce analytics teams because they have to act based on the data—and depending on ecommerce business, merchandising decisions can be made multiple times a day or even thousands of times a day in larger ecommerce sites. Setting up suitable analytics environments for merchandisers, which are self-service based, is necessary. Merchandisers can then come to the analytics team when they have larger concerns not satisfied through self-service systems, which require deeper analysis.

Testing Merchandising Creative

Creative testing and optimization is an activity that may be led, directed, or influenced heavily by the merchandising team. You can read about ecommerce optimization in Chapter 8. For merchandisers, the primary concern will be on category, brand, and product pages—and the home page. But other pages may also be in scope, such as shopping cart flow and purchasing pages. The testing that merchandising will need help with may be multivariate, but it is more common, in my experience, for merchandisers to want to perform AB testing. In other words, instead of testing multiple combinations of elements, such as creative text, font, offers, and images, it is preferred to test one thing against another (i.e., control versus test). In this way, the merchandisers can understand simply which test is working best to support goals, and worry less or get confused by trying to understand which elements that were tested were most important to the increase in performance. Some of the merchandising questions that can be answered with testing creative include the following:

- What creative text and conversion copywriting perform better for goals, such as conversion, repurchase, up-sell, cross-sell, and revenue per visitor?
- How should we rearrange or change the product search, product viewing, product selection, or product purchasing experience?
- Are there particular styles of typography, font, tone, and other stylistic design elements that when present or different improve performance?
- What impact do personalization features have on merchandising, discount usage, and promotions?

Performing Inventory Analysis

The analysis of inventory drives financial performance by controlling stock levels. The goal of inventory analysis is to ensure the appropriate amount of inventory, such that stock levels are minimized and overstocking is avoided. The idea is that by controlling inventory levels so that products are sold (i.e., they turn over), you maximize margin and profitability and also cash flows. As a result, inventory analysis can be largely driven by the finance team and, in companies that have a warehouse, also by the team that manages the warehouse. Finance will of course look at such concepts as revenue, margins, and profitability in relation to inventory—and also track metrics such as days inventory on hand, inventory turnover, and stock outs. The warehousing team will be responsible for managing and ensuring data collection about inventory, but doing so may require analytical and technical guidance. At the very least, inventory data needs to be governed so the data is synched such that stock availability on-site matches inventory availability. Merchandising will review the data and reports generated by these analytics and finance teams to curate and tune inventory items and levels. Again, the shared goals of analytics collaborating with merchandising and finance is to ensure the physical inventory, if any, for the ecommerce site supports business goals. Ecommerce inventory analysis helps to turn stock into cash while managing the inventory such that there are sell-throughs and turnovers, and so that there is a minimal amount of overstocking and sellouts.

Inventory analysis requires data not just about the inventory levels on hand or anticipated, but also about how that data is selling over time. As such, it's a ripe area for using key performance indicators to understand the inventory, such as these proposed by inventory control expert Jason Sentell:

- **Inventory Turnover,** which refers to the number of times the inventory sells a year (annually). The more times an ecommerce site has turnover, or sells out of inventory, the more revenue is generated. Thus, the more inventory turnover, the better, assuming that it isn't marked down below cost. Turnover can be a leading indicator for identifying how much inventory you need on hand to drive desired results. To calculate inventory turnover, you would divide the cost of goods sold from stock sales during the trailing 12 months by the total inventory investment during the same period. For those of you who studied accounting, the way you value inventory matters to this analysis.

FIFO (first in first out) and LIFO (last in first out) accounting will impact the turnover levels, and is also why alignment with finance is important. Because inventory turnover takes a snapshot in time, it can be tracked on the frequency most applicable to the ecommerce site and aligned with financial concepts and compliance.

When doing an inventory turnover analysis, you have to consider many things. First, you must set goals for turnover. For typical ecommerce sites, I have seen this goal range from four to six turns per year. The lower your margins, the more turnover you want in order to maximize the revenues and profits. Higher-margin ecommerce sites need to turn over less to make the same money—but any company, regardless of margin, wants to turn over as much as possible. Inventory turnover must be calculated for all products, not just overall across the entire set of inventory. That way, faster- or lower-selling products can be understood in the context of revenue, profitability, and lifetime value. With the right analytics environment in place, it is even possible to calculate inventory turnover for customers from marketing channels. Keep in mind that inventory turnover is generally applicable only to products sold by the site, not via drop shipping or direct shipping or sales of items not in stock.

- **Number of Stock Outs,** which is a KPI used to measure the number of occurrences of backorders and the average duration to fill stock. When stock is sold out and people are ordering it, they will have a poor customer experience because they can't buy what they want, and your revenue and margins will be negatively impacted; lifetime value may be at risk and stock outs could cause customer churn. To understand how to use this metric to guide merchandisers, consider that if you have many occurrences of out-of-stock items, you must spend money to correct stock levels. This can be due to underordering at the onset when the product is first bought, or it could be the result of suppliers taking too long to replenish you. In the first case, buy more. In the second case, find a new supplier or set appropriate customer expectations. If you are manufacturing your own items, you need to look at your supply chain and manufacturing operations to accelerate the availability of your products.

- **Customer Service Level (CSL),** which is a KPI that measures customer satisfaction based on meeting their demand and sending them what they have ordered on time to their expectations. To calculate CSL, you would divide the number of stocked products ordered by the number of those stocked products that you deliver by the date you said you would deliver them. CSL credits only transactions in which all the products are shipped and delivered. If products are only ordered (and not shipped/delivered), then no CSL credit is given to the order. As such, this customer-centric measure demonstrates how well you satisfy the customer. As with stock outs, you count only the inventory you stock on hand (and not drop shipments or direct-from-manufacturer orders for which the ecommerce site is the middleman). A perfect CSL score would be 100%, meaning that all orders shipped, with all products ordered were delivered on time (Sentell 2013). It's unlikely a business could meet the 100% level. Since this KPI will be distributed between 0 and 100, you can plot it on a graph, visualize it, and determine what the appropriate level for your business is. You want to tie CSL to customer satisfaction.

Analyzing Product Offers

Offer management is a type of merchandising analysis that speaks to the effectiveness of what was presented to prospects or customers, such that they accept or reject the offer. From this acceptance or rejection, the offer can be expanded or dialed down. An example of an offer might be "free shipping if you order more than $49" or "30% off on all orders over $200." Other offers might be for additional features (buy a shirt, get a free monogram) or might represent other attributes of a product. For example, an ecommerce site may offer a personalized stylist at an additional cost to work with the customer.

Offers are managed and analyzed over time, as part of marketing campaigns, within the site on particular page types, and within advertising and other marketing communications. Offers will have attributes such as the offer name, the offer description, the channel in which the offer is made, and the page on which the offer is to display. Offers can have different versions depending on the amount of mass customization or one-to-one personalization. These versions may all be based on one template or a number of templates that may be tested. Certain customers will be targeted with offers, so analysis requires understanding how the customer got the offer and why, and then figuring out whether that offer was effective and targeted correctly. The metrics and KPIs to measure and manage offers are standard, including total revenue by offer, profitability by offer, conversion rate of offer, and so on.

What's hard is not the task of defining the financial measures and other metrics for comparing offers to goals or against themselves, but rather the task of setting up the right data model, data collection, reporting, and visualization to analyze in order to provide guidance, insights, and recommendations. Offers will need to be coded with data collection so that they can be measured in the way required, and so that they can be tested in multivariate and AB testing tools.

Determining the Optimal Price via Pricing Analysis

Pricing analysis refers to the set of techniques that enable an ecommerce site to set the price that achieves the company's objectives. Often, pricing is set to maximize revenue at the lowest possible cost. Economists reading this book will recognize that the optimal price is set when marginal revenue equals marginal cost, which can be plotted and visualized. Pricing may be set based on a customer manually agreeing to buy at the identified cost due to demand for the product/service (Uber's surge pricing is an example) or dynamically based on a number of factors built into a statistical model and automated in real time (like normal Uber pricing, and of course surge pricing overall is dynamically suggested). Before doing pricing analysis, it is helpful to do the following:

1. **Identify the pricing objective.** An ecommerce site must determine why it wants to charge the money it charges. Maximizing shareholder value is a solid and common reason for public ecommerce sites. For private ecommerce business, pricing can be driven to maximize profitability or contribution margin, or to generate the highest possible revenue. When pricing is maximized for profitability, it is assumed that both demand and cost

are understood and relatively fixed over time. Pricing for profitability ensures short-term financial health, but may sacrifice long-term health because prices may be too high compared to those of competitors. Other reasons for charging the highest price may be to ensure the highest rate of return on investment. But ROI can be challenging to control via pricing because you don't know the amount of product returns you will have when you make the investment. Thus a better option may be to test prices over time and adjust them for estimated returns to maximize return. Many ecommerce sites do not generate profits, so in this case, pricing may be used to provide cash and ensure available cash flow so the company continues to exist (by providing money needed to pay bills). Survival may mean taking a loss on pricing, just to generate cash flow to survive and to continue operations in the short term as more capital is raised. Pricing may be used to take or improve market share by underpricing against competitors. The idea is to sell so much stock that it can be purchased less expensively (economies of scale) and generate higher future profits as more and more people buy from this company as opposed to competitors. Still other ecommerce sites may set pricing based on scarcity or even product quality. The more scarce the product, the higher the cost. The higher quality the product, the higher the price.

2. **Estimate demand.** Estimations are based on understanding the number of potential customers who want to buy the product, and also on how sensitive customers are to prices. Economic concepts like the Price Elasticity of Demand may be used to estimate the impact of the quantity of orders to changes in the price, by dividing the percentage change in demand by the percentage change in price. The resulting value will be between zero and infinity. Zero means that the price is perfectly inelastic, such that prices do impact demand. Between zero and one, the demand is said to inelastic, and demand changes by a smaller percentage than price. A value of one means that the demand changes at exactly the same percentage as the price changes (it's called unitary elastic). A result of one to infinity means that demand is elastic such that the demand changes

by a larger percentage than the price. Infinity means that the demand is perfectly elastic such that customers will buy at one price but not at the other (Banerjee 2015). Other methods for understanding demand may include statistical analysis to analyze past prices and demand and other factors. Some companies may test different prices with minimal statistical or economic rigor. Others may do customer research and ask consumers to identify or select what they want to pay, which is then used as a proxy to estimate demand at different price levels.

Demand estimation also involves understanding price sensitivity based on other cognitive or mind-set factors of the prospective customer set (Banerjee 2015). Demand can be impacted by the following:

- Shared cost, when the site is bearing some of the cost (like free shipping)
- Income levels, when the maximum price is set to some ratio of total income
- End benefit, which reflects that the customer may want to pay in increments, being concerned less with the total price and more with the monthly payment
- Sunk cost, when buyers may have more demand for products that complement existing products
- Comparison shopping, which causes sensitivity in the sense that some customers want the lowest possible price, but if they can't find it, then they buy at the cost available
- Unique value, which describes how demand may increase if the product has some level of distinction that can't be found elsewhere
- Substitution effect, in which, if there are not competing products or substitutes, demand may be higher
- Quality impact, when customers will pay more for items perceived to be of higher quality
- Inventory effect, in which the scarcity of inventory or places to purchase it impacts the sensitivity of the price charged

3. **Estimate costs.** Costs come in two forms: fixed costs and variable costs. Fixed costs don't change; they are your overhead and do not vary with the amount of money a company makes. Variable costs change based on different factors, such as the cost of materials or the quantity of items ordered. Total cost is the sum of fixed and variable costs. For an ecommerce site it is absolutely critical to understand costs to target a contribution margin that you must achieve on average to protect the financial health of the business.

4. **Do competitive intelligence.** The analytics team can help merchandisers set product prices by researching what competitors who offer identical or similar products are charging for them. Market research on customers is necessary to understand if the product's quality and function are superior to those of products in competitive offers. As a result, if the quality or function is identical, superior, or inferior, then the price should be set accordingly against competitors' prices. If the product is superior, the price should be modeled higher, or if inferior, then lower. Competitive intelligence is covered in detail in my book *Building a Digital Analytics Organization*; this information also applies to ecommerce.

5. **Choose a pricing method.** Analysts will want to calculate both the *floor* (or bottom price) and the *ceiling* (or highest price) for the product's price, and put that in the context of what competitors are charging. To do this work, the analyst must create or develop a cost function to set the floor and estimate demand to set the ceiling. A cost function requires creating a short-run or long-run average or total cost-curve using economic principles. The demand function could use an approach like the price elasticity discussed in step 2.

6. **Set the final price.** In ecommerce, the manufacturer may have recommended a sales price, which the pricing analyst may use without analyzing, or the company may follow the steps given previously to set the price. Small producers or entrepreneurs may prefer to use the methods described previously and test prices to understand demand and pricing sensitivities of their prospective customer base. In such cases, the final price

requires the analyst to analyze all costs against demand, and other consumer psychological and competitive influences and factors to set a price that will sell product against sales goals.

Understanding the Sales Impact of Merchandising

The goal of excellent ecommerce merchandising is to sell product and drive profitable revenue. Merchandisers can take many different approaches to repositioning and reframing merchandising to sell it. To do this type of analysis, you need a control group that is merchandised normally to use as a baseline. As an analyst, you can use several modalities to analyze, deconstruct, and categorize merchandising activities, to compare them against the control:

- **Function-based merchandising** refers to analyzing the product in terms of how effectively the merchandising communicates or places the product against its functional use. Product features and attributes will be used, along with visual merchandising cues to drive sales. Tools or household items are often merchandised based on function. Compare this treatment to the control.

- **Event-based merchandising** refers to analyzing the product in terms of how it was merchandised to support a specific event, such as the Super Bowl or World Cup. The control merchandising is compared to the event-based merchandising.

- **Holiday-based merchandising** refers to analyzing the product in the context of a specific holiday, like Christmas, to determine how the offer, messaging, and price helped to drive sales against the control.

- **Seasonality-based merchandising** refers to understanding the merchandising impact on sales by analyzing the control against a seasonal categorization or display related to the current season, such as winter or fall.

- **Popular culture–based merchandising** puts a product within a specific cultural context—for example, selling clothes based on the lifestyle of a rapper or a popular music artist. The analyst compares the product sales of the control against the new merchandising treatment to understand the financial impact of a celebrity endorsement.

Analyzing Suppliers and the Supply Chain

Entire books have been written about supply chain analysis in which systematic operations between producers, wholesalers, and third-party shipping and logistical providers are analyzed. The goal of supply chain analysis is to help the ecommerce company reduce the cost of the supply chain by being more efficient overall and in handling and transporting inventory—from producers to supplier to warehouse and delivery operations. Although it is beyond the scope of this book to cover the detail and intricacy of supply chain analysis, it is helpful for the ecommerce analyst to understand the supply chain and some of the analysis relevant to it, such as modeling product demand, tracking the delivery times to the warehouse or directly to customers, helping to improve inventory planning, and understanding warehouse delivery scheduling.

Determining Effective and Profitable Markdowns, Promotions, and Discounts

A key activity of merchandisers is creating sale events that mark down products, provide discounts, and communicate promotions in order to turn over and sell-through inventory. To analyze product promotions, do the following:

1. **Understand the promotional plan.** The analyst must learn the details of the promotion, such as when it will be rolled out, what products are impacted, what new treatments or experiences will be created on the site, and, of course, the suggested promotional discounts and pricing.

2. **Assist with the customer targeting.** The attributes of customers must be analyzed to understand, determine, and select which customers to target with the promotion. It may be that all customers see it, or only specific customers who log in or who respond to an e-mail, and so on. The point of targeting is to use the data to find the customers most open to the promotional offer.

3. **Help set the promotional price.** Based on analyzing past pricing and cost and demand models, the merchandising team may rely on the analysts to set or help to set the specific discount or promotional price.

4. **Implement and ensure data collection.** When new functionality, new user experiences, or new features are rolled out to support merchandising promotions, they must be tagged or instrumented to collect the relevant data. Campaigns related to the promotion need to be coded, and the discounts identified in a way that can be tracked to the purchase.

5. **Analyze the promotional pages against the controls.** You want to compare the key performance indicators you created for sales performance against those on the new promotional pages.

6. **Analyze the category performance.** Because products exist in categories, it is important to analyze how the financial performance of the category was impacted by the promotion of one or more products within it.

7. **Understand the impact of the media mix.** Analyzing the effectiveness of the marketing channels that were used to communicate the promotion and drive people to the site is important. Again, compare this performance to your baseline to assess it.

8. **Determine the return on investment (ROI).** Model and calculate the ROI by understanding cost, revenue, margin, and profit and/or loss so that you can communicate it to merchandising and management and explain the net financial impact of the promotional activity.

What Merchandising Data Should I Start Analyzing First?

A merchandising analysis should allow the merchandising stakeholder and other ecommerce stakeholders to understand data about the category, brand, product, and, if used, SKUs. As reviewed in the discussion on data modeling in Chapter 5, "Ecommerce Analytics

Data Model and Technology," merchandising analysis may require the creation of new data models, with custom facts, measures, and dimensions. Important dimensions for merchandising analysis include category, brand, and product. At the macro level, data for merchandising analysis should include financial measures such as Total Merchandising Revenue, Average Product Price, Average Order Price, Average Discount, Average Discount Percentage, Average Gross Margin, and even the Price Range for all products. Other customer and product-centric merchandising measures at the macro level can include Total Shipping Costs, Number of Total Products Sold, Number of Discounted Products Sold, Number of Total Orders, and the Number of Discounted Orders.

For each merchandising or product dimension you create, such as category, product, and SKU, consider collecting and analyzing data such as the merchandising revenue by category, by brand, and by product and the percentage change since the last comparable period. For each dimension, you may want to analyze the Number of Orders, Quantity of Products, Units in Inventory at the Start of the Period and End of Period, the Weeks Supply On-Hand, the Sell-Through Rate, and the Average Unit Cost. Every product category that is merchandised should use similar data as presented previously available for each subcategory. Helpful categories and subcategories to analyze include the total percent of category revenue represented by that subcategory, including the product name, brand, the number of visits, views, visitors, shoppers, and orders. At the SKU-level, if used, all of the metrics and data previously presented can be analyzed by SKU code or other metadata and attributes.

11

Attribution in Ecommerce Analytics

Attribution is the name marketers use for the process of identifying and ordering the customer interactions over time based on which are most important to particular business goals, such as revenue, engagement, and conversion. Ecommerce attribution involves collecting data in as near real time as possible about all customer interactions and touches a company has with a customer and then using the data to create a mathematical model that is refined and tested over time to best classify and identify which interactions and touches drove a particular KPI, such as conversion rate or revenue per user. The customer interactions modeled for attribution include behaviors, such as visits and events that occur online (and offline), and business concepts, such as the marketing channel, campaign, or advertisement.

Over the past several years, attribution has emerged as an important topic in ecommerce because companies want to understand the effectiveness of different marketing strategies delivered across different media types, formats, and devices. Attribution is widely considered to be a way to this understanding because it enables a company to determine important interactions and sources that influence KPIs and other data. For example, if paid search is thought of by an ecommerce company as contributing to or driving 40% of sales, then the company has attributed 40% of sales to paid search. Why were sales attributed to paid search? The answer is because a paid or free software tool calculated the attribution based on a custom-built mathematical model. This model is called an "attribution model." At the core of an attribution model is the assignment of credit to a variable (i.e., the interaction or customer touch) that drives measurable business outcomes. The variable is most often marketing or advertising and the business outcome is most often conversion or a purchase.

Attribution enables accountability because it indicates what business activities were financially important. As a result, an attribution model can be used to guide business investment into those important activities and away from less important ones.

Attribution, thus, is considered most relevant to understanding the effectiveness of the allocations of budgets related to the interactions and goals that are being attributed. These budgets most often impacted by attribution analysis are marketing and media spend because in many companies this type of spend is large and even a small improvement can generate large returns. It is fair to say that an appropriate and correct allocation of money can be a positive outcome of attribution analysis. It is also helpful in ecommerce for the merchandising teams to understand attribution in order to help guide where products are placed on the site—for example, showcasing products on a landing page for the top attributed source of revenue. User experience teams apply attribution data to better understand the creative design that was most effective in driving conversion and other desired behaviors. IT can use attribution data to inform technology strategy and capacity planning. Attribution is something discussed when planning business strategy.

Attribution is not be to be confused with marketing mix modeling or with media mix modeling. Both of these types of models are frequently used in marketing analysis, but these models are one-time snapshots in time that contain marketing information and other helpful data. In the case of marketing mix modeling, this information is used with the overall marketing planning process and the entire set of activities and events the marketing team will execute. In the case of media mix modeling, the model attempts to define the impact of specific media buys across different channels, not typically offline—and not to the level of totality as attribution aspires to attain. A media mix model allocates the impact of each media buy on marketing performance in order to understand the financial impact and tune the media mix to improve the monetary return. Attribution can use similar or the same data as media mix or marketing mix modeling, but an attribution analysis is continual and ongoing. Attribution technology can involve data collection and automatic evaluation of that to classify performance. Some attribution tools from vendors offer functionality in predicting future attribution and even prescribe the best possible business action to take to achieve the performance.

Attribution, pre-2007, was largely relegated to the digital domain and focused on what is widely known as the "last click" model. The most recent click immediately before the conversion or purchase was given all the credit for the conversion. It was an easy way to look at things, and it served the purpose of defining a simple baseline. In many ways, last-click attribution is still the way many people are first exposed to attribution because many free tools expose it to users. The last-click model is simple. The last click (usually an ad) gets the credit for the sale. This approach is similar to offline attribution based on "last interaction" so it's easily understood by offline retailers that do ecommerce. However, it's not a very accurate approach to attribution for a number of reasons:

- **People are exposed to many media and advertisements, online and offline.** Through inexpensive access to high-speed Internet and pervasive advertising in-home, out-of-home, digitally and offline, consumers can be exposed to hundreds of brand messages per day. The cumulative or incremental impact of all these media exposures must contribute, in some quantifiable way, to an eventual purchase of an advertised brand's products. By giving all the credit to the last advertisement seen, the last interaction with the product, or the source of the last click, then important exposures and latent impacts remain undiscovered and non-applicable in the last-click attribution model. These earlier exposures before the "last" exposure have some contribution, which is totally missed in last-click attribution.

- **There are many types of media and advertisements and methods for distributing them.** Similar to the way in which there are many more exposures to ads and touches by brands to potential and current customers, there are many new types of media. From mobile applications and in-app advertising, to augmented reality, to virtual reality, to advertising on "Things" and Internet-connected devices, to new technologies for rendering ads, whether holographic or via rich user experience, new forms of advertising continually emerge. The last-click model doesn't take into account the engagement or impact of these new types of ads, or the frequency, richness, canvas size, or interactivity of these new types of ads and ways to connect with consumers.

- **More and more advertising content is available.** Not only are there more kinds of ads, more formats and sizes, and more interactivity and engagement, but the content in advertising is also changing. In fact, advertorial content may merge traditional editorial approaches to journalism with advertising copy to create hybrid advertisements that influence customers in new ways. Last click also doesn't take into account the type and impact of the creative.

  The rise of big data and data science have made it more possible to employ alternative and powerful approaches to attribution. Since 2009 or so, the title of "data scientist" has emerged to define a person with a combination of statistical, mathematical, technical, programming, business, artistic, and communication skills that can almost single-handedly create value from data. Data science is at the heart of algorithmic approaches to attribution and even applies to less complicated, sampled attribution methods. Because companies believe in and are investing in data science teams and technology, accurate attribution analysis is technology ecommerce companies can choose to build instead of buy.

- **The cognitive rationale for purchasing something is not quantified in last click.** The click is not necessarily a deliberate expression of a human intention. It is an action that can be deliberate or trivial, or even accidental. Thus, making an attribution calculation based on only a click doesn't capture the influence of other influences and exposures that could lead to the action.

- **Looking at only the last click ignores intermediary touches and advertising that influence a purchase.** Taking into account only the last click ignores everything that preceded it. Logically, it makes sense to believe that when exposures are repeated, each exposure has a contribution to making a decision, which the last-click model neglects.

Given all those factors, newer methods to attribution have been developed. The full list is itemized later in the chapter, including first and last click or interaction attribution, linear attribution, weighted event-based attribution, time-decay attribution, position-based attribution, and custom attribution models.

As an ecommerce analyst, you will be called upon to answer business questions that can be responded to only by analyzing attribution. It can be helpful to understand the types of attribution modeling techniques, such as survival models and proportional hazard models, which are reviewed in this chapter. Most important, the understanding of attribution can be different because people mean different things when they talk about attribution. Agreeing on the business questions to answer with attribution reduces confusion, as does aligning on what your ecommerce companies define as "attribution." The business questions you may be asked that can be answered with attribution include these:

- What marketing channels are driving the most sales?
- What marketing campaigns are driving the largest average order size and conversion rate?
- What sources of customers have the lowest churn rate and highest retention rate?
- What combination of advertisements leads to the highest lifetime value or have the lowest cost of customer acquisition?
- What sources of traffic lead to the highest user engagement with product pages and other content pages?

Attributing Sources of Buyers, Conversion, Revenue, and Profit

Attribution can tell you how much revenue was generated on an ecommerce site from customer interactions, such as those that occur within different media and within marketing advertising channels. It can also be applied to specific advertisements within those channels. In addition, attribution can assist in understanding the origins of people who buy, and identify the interactions, touches, sources of traffic, and marketing channels that drive the highest conversion versus the highest revenue or profit. The metrics or KPIs to focus on with attribution analysis depend on the needs of your business. Some ecommerce sites may concentrate on member acquisition or retention for attribution, whereas others may look at cost of customer acquisition, lifetime value, and loyalty. Others may look at these and others such as average order value, conversion rate, highest gross margin, and more.

While attributed interactions and touches change by company, what isn't very different across companies are the sources of traffic attributed. Traffic sources for ecommerce sites are definable spaces. At the core of attribution are sources that generate traffic and customers from paid, owned, and earned media. Paid media is bought by a company, such as ads on television or paid search. Owned media is created using company resources, such as events or content pages. Think of the Red Bull Stratos event or a "lookbook." Earned media is generated externally by people outside of the company. Think of social networking and virality.

You will see paid, owned, and earned media reported, for the most part, in attribution and analytics tools. The media may be named differently, defined alternatively, or described or categorized in different ways. Regardless, paid, owned, and earned can be broken down into the following traffic sources:

- **Paid Media.** Paid media is just what it sounds like. You or your company pays to advertise for various consumer and shopping goals in the mind of the current or prospective customer.
  - *Display Advertising.* Banner ads and other ad units of all sizes served on Internet-enabled devices delivered through technology in some way, whether automated or manually, to buy, sell, match, target, or automate Internet-enabled advertising in some way, including exchanges and demand-side platforms (DSPs).
  - *Affiliate Marketing.* Marketing resulting from relationships in which some form of capital is exchanged, such as a revenue share; for example, purchases of your products sold on another site and fulfilled by you.
  - *Paid Search.* The purchases of keyword(s) on search engines in order to display a relevant link/offer to a current or new customer.

– *Retargeting.* The delivery of advertisements about a specific topic to a device or browser after an initial exposure.

• **Owned Media.** If you have ever "built it because they will come," you know about "owned media." It's what happens when you spend your capital to create something fully or partially owned by you in which you have some sort of stake—whether shares or salary.

– *Referral Traffic.* Traffic from other web sites, whether domains or subdomains.

– *Social Media.* Media controlled by the company.

– *E-mails.* E-mail communications driven by CRM programs sent to your customers with relevant offers derived from customer analysis.

• **Earned Media.** Earned media is the good or bad content, branding, perception, mind-set, awareness, and (un)favorability that results from your business activities, including your products, your PR, and even your marketing, both online and offline.

– *Organic Search (SEO).* Listings on search engine results pages. Although some people would argue that SEO is a paid activity, the ranking of your site and pages will happen whether or not you attempt to "game" the system. The best SEO is always "awesome, relevant" content—not simply complex magic and monitoring from an agency or SEO firm. That said, SEO is altogether something that can be gamed in a black-, grey-, and white-hat way. Analytics lets you know how you are doing—and even can tell you if you are black hat when you wear all white.

– *Social Networks.* Traffic from sources such as Facebook, Instagram, Twitter, Pinterest, YouTube, LinkedIn.

– *Blogs.* Another type of social media. I think, however, that it is important to call them out because blogs often exist outside of corporate product that provides an online user experience. It is also valid, of course, to call out other types of digital social media as necessary for your business goals.

- *Direct.* Traffic from an unknown source, which could be directly entered or bookmarked.
- *Other.* Visits from uncategorized sources lumped into a default category. Analysts should examine campaigns and traffic assigned to the "other" category to ensure appropriate categorization.

Attribution can be applied to understand the business performance of all sources in paid, owned, and earned media, over time, to determine the impact they have on causing people to take actions relevant to the business.

Understanding Engagement Mapping and the Types of Attribution

The concept of engagement mapping is relevant to attribution. An engagement map "maps" the different channels, as described in the preceding section, over time based on the sequence of their exposure. These exposures are then enumerated by scoring and weighting in a calculus that tells you what channels have the most impact for a specific business goal.

The concept of engagement mapping was developed in the early 2000s as a way to address many of the issues people had with last-click or last-interaction attribution. The focus of engagement mapping is to identify and measure all the different instances, or events, in which a person was exposed to some type of ad or media before taking an action, like buying a product. For each exposure a value is assigned and weighted against all other exposures to determine its importance in causing the person to act (Latham 2013).

The value for each exposure in the engagement map is determined based on the person's engagement with the ad or media, including the recency, frequency, format, size, device, and more. The exposures and different attributes of the media become variables in an attribution model that identifies what ad or media had the largest contribution toward the desired action, in real time. From this determination, the analyst can then suggest increasing or decreasing investment to drive business performance. Or a machine can automate the buying and selling of ads and media to adjust the mix to predicted performance.

Attribution approaches range from the complex, like engagement mapping, to the simple, like last interaction. It's important to pick one approach to guide decisioning, but also to look at the results of other models. Remain flexible enough in your analytical thinking to accommodate different interpretations of attributions. But don't get bogged down in trying to figure out differences. Act on what your core model is saying—and challenge your thinking with alternative models. Also be cautious of tools that overattribute success to specific channels in which they have financial interest—for example, the cart abandonment retargeter's estimate of attribution for recaptured revenue. Be cautious of self-supporting attribution from vendors and agencies.

The types of attribution are described here:

- **First interaction** attributes the source of the action to the initial interaction first experienced by the person.

- **Last interaction** attributes the source of the action to the initial interaction last experienced by the person.

- **Last nondirect interaction** is like last interaction but it excludes the Direct source of traffic. It can be helpful to eliminate Direct visits to your site as being relevant and applicable to attributing a goal or outcome because Direct traffic is a misnomer. It may include traffic from people typing in your URL, but it also includes any traffic that lacks a referrer and a campaign code; thus, Direct traffic is really traffic of an unknown source (Google 2015).

- **Linear** is a simple approach to weighting equally the contribution of each channel to the eventual action. A linear model weights all interactions the same and identically.

- **Time decay** is a weighted approach to evaluating the contribution of each channel in which events and interactions that happened first are given less weight than actions that happened closer to the action.

- **Position-based** is a weighted approach that allocates 40% of the credit to both the first and last interactions and apportions the last 20% across all interactions in the middle.

- **Starter-player-closer** is an attribution method, like position-based attribution, that allocates a given weight to the starting interaction, allocates a given weight to the closing interaction, and disperses the remaining credit across the player interactions. The difference between this method and position-based is that you custom-define your weightings for the different interactions.

- **Latency scoring** identifies a score for each interaction and allocates a weight to that score based on the days it occurred before the eventual action. In this case the credit is apportioned based on the days before the action, which means that interactions have different weights for the same interaction for different people due to latency windows (Halbrook 2012).

- **Logistic regression** is an advanced analytics approach that is used because it is helpful and easy to interpret. The dependent variable is binary, such as whether a conversion occurred, and can take only one of two values. The model estimates the probability of each outcome based on the independent variables.

- **Stacking** is an approach in which interaction data is calculated to identify how many interactions preceded the action; then, this number is used as the basis to test different channel mixes to understand which ones work most effectively for generating the action.

- **Pathing** is an attribution optimization approach that can be used with stacking. After the number and type of interactions are identified, the discrete sequence of steps across the different channels, the pathing, is evaluated to further inform the attribution—and to guide planning of communication sequences.

- **Custom-weighted attribution model** is a model derived by experimentation and empirical evidence to create weightings that apply to your specific business situation, or are used as experiments to test the output of other attribution models against a test budget.

- **Proportional hazard modeling including survival analysis** uses time to convert as the dependent variable and the customer interactions (like views and clicks) as the independent variables. From the data, covariates are identified and evaluated against an underlying hazard function. The hazard function denotes how the risk of the conversion event occurring changes over time (Pepelnjak-Chandler 2010). As Andrie de Vries, author of *R for Dummies*, claims about survival analysis: "The insight is that each event in a clickstream (the series of impressions and clicks) gives an indication of whether the clickstream is still alive. Only at the final click (or impression), when the user converts to purchase, does the clickstream 'die.'" Thus, these models allow you to model the effects of time, interactions, media formats, and traffic sources on conversion (de Vries 2013). A referenceable hazard model for attribution analysis is the Cox proportional hazard model, while a helpful survival model used for attribution is named the Kaplan-Meier Survival Function—both are available in data science technologies, such as the R language.

To understand how these types of attribution methods would yield different results, take an example in which a person's path to purchase took 25 days and involved exposure to five different touches during that time in this order: Display Ad > Paid Search > Organic Search > Retargeting > Social Media, which finally led to an order or conversion. In this case the different attribution models would indicate the following:

- **First interaction** would give all the credit to the display ad.
- **Last interaction** would give all the credit to social media.
- **Last nondirect interaction** would give all the credit to social media (there is no direct source in this example).
- **Linear** would give 20% of the credit to each interaction. In the case of $100 of revenue, each channel would get credit for generating $20.
- **Time decay** would give 30% of the credit to social media, 25% to retargeting, 20% to organic search, 15% to paid search, and 10% to the display ad. The weighting in time-decay attribution is defined by the analyst.
- **Position-based** would give 40% of the credit to the display ad and 40% to social media. The remainder 20% would be divided

equally across the paid search, organic search, and retargeting. Weighting can vary by model.

- **Starter/player/closer** would weigh the interactions similar to position-based (or possibly the same). The idea here is that a source was the "starter;" the other sources are "players;" and the final source before conversion is the "closer." The weightings to the designations of starter, player, and closer can be custom (Halbrook 2012).

- **Other approaches** such as regression, latency scoring, and stacking would require more data to elaborate due to the math and statistics required to apply to the data but are worth reading about in statistical detail beyond the scope of this book.

The Difference between Top-Down and Bottom-Up Approaches to Attribution

When learning about attribution, you will encounter the phrases "bottom up" and "top down" as approaches to attribution. These polarities are defined by the different granularity in the data used to determine the attribution. Top-down attribution, simply defined, is derived from sources that mostly do not contain user-level data. The audiences are quantified in counts, frequencies, and measures that are summarized and not detailed. Traditional formats for advertising, such as TV and radio, usually have only summary-level data that does not identify addressable audiences (Gross 2015). Top-down attribution starts by collecting summary data from sources with interactions. If possible, user-level data could be collected as might data sets from other, relevant sources. Other data collected can include the business activities during the attribution period, so changes in trends can be evaluated against those activities. Finally, a top-down approach would apply any business rules specific to data used for the attribution, so the analysis would be in the right business context. For example, if cookies expire in 30 days, having a 90-day attribution window would not work.

Bottom-up attribution is derived from user-level data that contains unique identifiers that can be tied back to sources and interactions with (mostly) known people and thus to "addressable audiences."

When you can define and target an audience with a communication or with marketing, it is said to be "addressable" (Emarketer 2013). Digital data, such as cookies, behavioral data, or mobile device identifiers, can be used to build a bottom-up attribution model. Other data sets that expand on and augment user data may be used. Business activities during the attribution period are captured and understood against changes in trends. Custom business rules specific to the ecommerce company, of course, would be included. For both top-down and bottom-up attribution, all the relevant data is brought together, a performance measure (the action) is calculated, and statistics are applied to understand the relationships among the data, sources, and interactions. A model is then created that attributes the credit for resulting actions, like conversions, based on the customer's interactions and source.

A Framework for Assessing Attribution Software

Numerous attribution vendors are selling software and services to help ecommerce companies understand attribution. Listed next are some important factors to consider when selecting attribution software. Some of these factors can even apply to selecting service-providers for attribution. You can customize this framework for evaluation to apply to your unique business situation, requirements, and needs:

- **Algorithmic.** Basing your ecommerce attribution on basic models that aren't tightly aligned to business requirements, but instead are more generalized, can be a good place to start. However, many companies grow to require a more elaborate and faceted view of attribution realized through the application of multiple algorithms applied to support the same attribution goal. For example, an algorithmic attribution model may be based on a logistic regression and/or a survival model.

- **Unsampled.** It's common for off-the-shelf or free attribution tools to operate on exclusively sampled data, whether from a single source or from multiple sources. Other tools require full, unsampled data. It has been claimed that unsampled data analysis will result in a better fit model to the data. Others will claim that using unsampled data is in fact a necessity for attribution. Fifty percent of the data is used to train the model, 30% to tune the model, and the remaining 20% to refine the model. Having larger sample sizes can yield better results.

- **Access to addressable and unaddressable audiences.** When people say "addressable" in attribution analysis, they mean that the data is available at the individual level. User-level data can be applied, at some level, to identify that user and "address" the user with some form and format of media. Unaddressable audiences, on the other hand, are those audiences that are not directly targetable by media on an individual level, such as TV audiences or audiences engaged offline or by mass communications; or, it relates to attributes of the audience that can be used effectively only when matched to addressable data, such as zip code purchasing propensities.

- **Multidevice and cross-channel.** Not all tools support assigning credit, weighting variables, and associating metadata with the data from all available channels or devices. As the customer journey becomes increasingly more complicated involving "omnichannels," it's helpful to have an attribution tool that can make attributions across channels and tie them together.

- **Ability to enhance data.** By joining external data sources, whether second- or third-party, to your first-party data, you create an enhanced data set on which segmentation, clustering, and even cohort analysis can be performed. By enhancing data, you provide more information to analyze for discovering insights.

- **Integration.** Attribution data can be integrated into business processes and decision making. Simply identifying order or conversion attribution and making decisions based on it is a useful business activity. Attribution data can also be integrated into automated processes. Automating the buying or selling decisions for media and marketing using attribution data is a common use case, or using attribution data to automatically allocate budgets could be done.

- **Prediction, simulation, and prescription.** Reporting data and showing the breakdown of attribution by channel is fundamental. To take reporting to the next level and speed the analytical process, some tools offer the capability to apply a predictive model or models to the data to help guide decision. Other tools allow for "what if" analysis and simulation to help project the impact of decisions made to the media mix. An emerging feature is the ability to use attribution data to prescribe what to do next to support an attributable goal (for example, the automated suggestion to dial down spend in social and increase spend on e-mail).

- **Offline and online.** To help ecommerce teams understand the full impact of business activities, an attribution approach must be able to support offline and online data. The more data, the more refined the attribution model can be. In addition, the ability to create an attribution model based on a bottom-up or a top-down approach requires offline and online data (Shao and Li 2011).

- **Time to insight.** The time it takes to get up and running with attribution must be considered. Some software requires set-up time before insights can be generated, whereas others require a longer wait time. Evaluate your requirements against execution time to insight (Lindauer 2014).

- **Scalability.** As with all software, the capability for the program to scale to meet your data needs will vary by vendor and service. Ensure that you identify data sources and volumes and assess them against the capability of the software to support.

- **Cloud or on-premises.** Another common decision point is whether the software and your data will live on your servers or someone else's. Given the user-level data required in many attribution models, the location of your data is an aspect to consider against data privacy and security (Pepelnjak-Chandler 2010).

Attribution is an important type of ecommerce analysis. It assists companies with understanding the sources, interactions, and touches that contribute most effectively to business goals. Ecommerce analysts should apply attribution to their data to realize new ways of thinking about the customer, their journeys, and how value is created in ecommerce.

12

What Is an Ecommerce Platform?

An ecommerce platform is a software solution used to create a storefront, administer back-end functions, and integrate with other systems (such as digital analytics, BI, databases, CRM, and marketing technology). One or more ecommerce experiences may be delivered from a single ecommerce platform. For example, a mobile site and web site would be served by one ecommerce platform used to create, deploy, and maintain both of them. Ecommerce platforms provide the technical foundation for building the digital experience and managing it—or connecting and integrating with the technologies to power it. You can think of an ecommerce platform as the central nervous system and/or circulatory system for an ecommerce business. The ecommerce platform enables the totality of functionality that creates the ecommerce experience, such as the product catalog and pages, other content pages (like the home page and landing pages, the shopping cart, and promotions).

Ecommerce platforms are available for businesses of all sizes. For smaller businesses, there are a number of software-as-a-service (SaaS) products that can provide the end-to-end functionality needed for running an ecommerce site. For example, these platforms may provide a template-driven, build-it-yourself set of features. Larger businesses and retail corporations may choose to build their own end-to-end ecommerce platform using technologies such as Java, .net, PHP, Ruby, and more (Adams 2015). Still other companies choose to buy a software product that may be hosted (in the cloud) or run by the company within their data center. Whether to choose an on-demand or on-premises solution or a custom, licensed, or managed SaaS will entirely depend on the company. Other companies may choose to integrate open source ecommerce technology or an assortment of pre-integrated ecommerce products used for specific functions that work together based on shared technology protocols. Typically a company will hire a systems integrator to implement and customize a commercial ecommerce platform. Other companies choose to do their own integration.

An ecommerce platform, at the most fundamental level, contains a consumer layer (the storefront), a data integration layer, an analytics layer, a data layer, and an operations and monitoring layer:

- The **consumer layer** represents the channels for the user experience, which can be a web site, mobile, or other Internet-connected device (Internet of Things, Internet of Everything). The consumer layer will also contain the technology for the shopping cart, product catalog, product pages, and any other programmatic or API-based technology that must be integrated to render and fulfill the ecommerce experience to the end user.

- The **integration layer** is the set of technologies that bring together the services and technologies in the consumer layer so that the experience actually works and isn't just a set of non-functional screens that display in a browser or smartphone. The integration layer contains the rules and instructions for integrating user data at the session level with shopping, transaction, and service capabilities such that the ecommerce experience is enabled as one shared operational environment that unifies the ecommerce capability from the start of the visit to the purchase.

- The **analytics layer** is a set of analytics and data science technologies and tools used to analyze and work with data: from cleansing to preparation to modeling to analysis to visualization and so on.

- The **data layer** is where the data is stored, processed, and queried after being sourced from wherever it comes from. The data could be generated by the operational processing and system integration of services that support your ecommerce platform. Or the data could come from third parties, such as partners, resellers, or data vendors. The data layer contains the traditional relational database management systems, data warehouses, NoSQL technologies, and newer processing frameworks like Hadoop and Spark.

- The **operations and monitoring layer** contains tools for managing the platform and technologies and can include tools that enable ecommerce operations, such as CRM, inventory, merchandising, finance, customer service, and so on.

From the layers, different applications can be developed that provide for ecommerce site functionality and for the features that create the ecommerce experience. Applications and features in an ecommerce platform can be categorized as follows:

- **Content.** The content management system, including videos, images, and other publishing capabilities such as advertising, including external sources of content such as social media, partners, and resellers.

- **Search.** Search-based navigation, querying, and filtering to find products to buy and also to find other content.

- **Catalog.** The collection of attributes about products used to create the product catalog and content pages, like the product page. The catalog includes the product specifications and details, the pricing and discounts, promotions and offers, the product images (from content), the taxonomy and categories (nodes), the product bundles, and cross-sells.

- **Customers.** The customer management technologies, including the customer record and profiles that contain customer data, such as gender, name, addresses, e-mail, phone number, first order date, last order date, segment, and other relevant customer data to your business.

- **Shopping.** Order capture functionality, such as fast-buy (one-click) experiences, long-form checkout and shopping carts, quick-order and one-page shopping cart, and other checkout and buying features and functionality.

- **Ordering.** Order functionality, including order capture, order management, order verification, order tracking, and so on.

- **Payments.** Processing, security and fraud, and financial and tax management technologies are payment-related functions.

- **Inventory** and **merchandising.** Tools for inventory management, preorders, back orders, and allocation and inventory release to customers.

- **Fulfillment.** Functionality for shipping and address verification, warehouse management, delivery status, and order tracking.

- **Customer service.** Capabilities for online self-service, call center, order returns, product exchanges, and site credits.

- **Analytics and data science.** Capabilities for data collection, storage, processing, preparation, modeling, analysis, reporting, and visualization that enable ecommerce analysis. This includes descriptive, predictive, and prescriptive capabilities created using business intelligence and data science, such as data mining, machine learning, and artificial intelligence.

Understanding the Core Components of an Ecommerce Platform

Another way for the analyst to begin to understand how to think about analyzing the data in an ecommerce platform is to consider it as a set of components. Each component has related functionality and features for a business function that is provided by the underlying ecommerce platform and its many layers. These components are for marketing, user experience and interface, orders and transactions, customers, and data (Kumar 2015):

- **Marketing components.** In ecommerce the marketing team is concerned about making potential customers aware of the brand, acquiring them to come to the site, ensuring that they have a positive site experience that leads to an order. And then they are concerned with using marketing to retain that customer and make him loyal so he orders again and again. An ecommerce platform, thus, will have functionality that ensures that marketing activities can be executed and managed over time and the resulting data captured for analysis. Enterprise ecommerce platforms have specific marketing functionality already integrated, such as shopping cart abandonment identification and recapture, social media features, and functionality for personalization. Other platforms may provide integrations with ecommerce products that provide video, product photos and zoom, Facebook integration, product up-sell, product reviews, and more. It is important for the analyst to determine how an ecommerce platform supports the analytical needs of marketing to ensure appropriate measurement.

- **User experience (UX) and user interface (UI) components.** The UX and UI components are the look and feel of the site or mobile experience. The UX will generally be mapped out in what is called the "information architecture," which identifies the sitemap, the different categories for the site, how many templates will be needed, and what the content, elements, and calls to action will be on each page of the experience. To do this work, a designer will often work hand in hand with a technologist who understands the ecommerce platform. The designer will be responsible for determining the visual elements of the user experience, the font and typography, and the logos and branding, and for specifying the high-level layouts of pages, like the product page and landing pages. From this design work "wireframes" will be created that bring together the design decisions and create a two-dimensional view of what the experience should look like. These wireframes act as the blueprint for where the elements of the user experience, such as the images, content, links, and interactions, will go. From the wireframes interactive mock-ups are created that are "pixel-perfect," meaning they show the look and feel of the site as it should appear in a browser. The interactivity provided is generally based on hyperlinks that show how the experience flows when the links are clicked. The final mock-up will include each specific design element, define the actions that occur when interacted with by customers, and provide a set of design assets (jpegs and gifs and so on) that can be used by development to code the site. The final mock-up is usually a file, like a Photoshop file, that is then coded by a development team using the technology of their choice (for example, Java and CSS).

- **Transactional components.** The product catalog, content management system (CMS), shopping cart, payment processing, and order fulfillment systems are required for an ecommerce transaction to occur. The transactional components of an ecommerce platform include order management, payment processing, shipping and warehouse management, pricing and inventory management, and even fraud and risk management. All these transactional components can produce data for analysis. For example, the shopping cart experience can be tested for conversion optimization. The order process from warehouse to customer can be tracked and measured. You can analyze customer interactions with the product catalog. The impact of shipping and warehouse management on order fulfillment is another useful area for analysis.

- **Customer components.** In an ecommerce business, the customer relationship management (CRM) system often contains the master customer record—also known as the "golden" customer record—which contains personally identified information about the customer (such as the customer's name, address, preferences, products purchased, and so on). For more information about the customer record, please see Chapter 9, "Analyzing Ecommerce Customers." CRM systems may integrate with or stand alone as campaign management systems enabling the company to send communications, such as e-mails, that contain specific content relevant to the customer profile. CRM systems may provide an analytical layer and the capabilities to pass information to other systems for more complex integrations. For example, a CRM system may create a unique customer ID and pass it to a digital analytics system. CRM capabilities are also important for enabling customer-centric marketing automation.

- **Internal and external data components.** An ecommerce experience is dependent on being able to store data. The data could be about customers and their behavior, products, suppliers, transactions, and other events specific to the business. Traditionally, these data would be captured in a CRM database or back-end database with a custom data model. For this discussion, the data component is all the data and systems that house it. The data component will contain customer data, product data (SKU, description, picture, price, and so on), order data, promotional data (name, type, discount, code), inventory data, and so on. The platform can be configured to support data business logic applied to data. For example, when a product catalog for a specific brand is displayed, related products are shown. The product images, descriptions, text, and so on are stored in the database, and the logic for rendering the related products is also coded as business rules. For more information about the data model in ecommerce, see Chapter 5, "Ecommerce Analytics Data Model and Technology."

I have simplified the components in an ecommerce platform to fall under marketing data, user experience and interface data, transactional data, customer data, and internal/external data in order to help you understand what to analyze. As an analyst working on an ecommerce site, you will be asked questions about the flow of the site and its impact on conversion. You will be asked about orders and products. You will be asked questions about customers and their data—and you will have to work with ecommerce platform data or related data, and perhaps the ecommerce platform itself, to do so.

Understanding the Business Functions Supported by an Ecommerce Platform

The ecommerce platform supports the operation of business functions that an analyst will be asked to help with via research and analysis. However, the businesspeople you interact with will have varying knowledge of the ecommerce platform. Some will work directly and daily with it, whereas others will work only infrequently and indirectly with it. What's certain, from an analyst's perspective, is that these people will all want data to inform their business activities and will have varying abilities in their capacity to understand and analyze the data you present. It's also unlikely that the businesspeople will have full knowledge of an ecommerce platform. They may not even understand that term. Your role is to understand how they use the platform (however abstractly), determine what data they generate and/or want to analyze, and help them answer business questions that guide them in the execution of their jobs and the fulfillment of their business goals.

It is common for an ecommerce platform to have tools that businesspeople can use to participate in business operations and/or the deployment of the site. The tools will vary by platform, but the roles working directly and indirectly with the platform are fairly consistent from ecommerce company to ecommerce company. The business tools supported by the ecommerce platform can include the following:

- **Product management tools.** Crossing both the business and the IT sides of the business, product managers define the look and feel, features and flows, and overall consumer experience for ecommerce. Depending on the size of your business, the product manager may own the entire web site, or a number of product managers at various levels of seniority may be responsible for various functions or applications within it. For example, a product manager might own the entire shopping cart experience and another may own the product catalog and product detail pages. Yet another product manager may own search.

  The ecommerce platform will be well understood by most, if not all, product managers because they defined the functionality. Product managers will likely have some knowledge of how to directly use it to create new pages or modify an experience. However, the product manager will expect IT to build and create the user experience to the specifications and product requirements they create. Thus, although product managers won't directly operate on the platform to build functionality, they will likely use any prebuilt reporting that comes from the platform. That usage may be less than ideal when the data coming out of the platform differs, in some way, from the curated data coming from analytics. Make sure you address this potential point of confusion by effective data governance and meet the data and analytical requirements from product managers— or else they will get it themselves and go around the analytics team.

- **Merchandising planning tools.** The "merchandising" team is responsible for promoting products so they get sold. The brands, products, promotions, and other aspects of the ecommerce experience that impact products are in the domain of merchandising. This team may use the ecommerce platform to enter orders and check the status of inventory on-order, in-site/ store, in-flight, and so on. They will want data about inventory turnover, sell-through, inventory aging, stock outs, and more. The merchandising team will expect you as an analyst to help them find, source, analyze, report, and visualize data that supports their deep understanding of the products sold, including buying behaviors, current trends, seasonality, and promotional impact.

- **Inventory and warehouse management tools.** This role may not exist at your company because the work may have been contracted out to a third party, and that third party provides data and reporting related to supply and inventory levels back to your company. For those companies that operate or manage their own inventory and warehouse operations, the analytics teams may assess the demand side of the business using data mining and predictive analytics to provide detailed insights that can help frame and forecast demand for the supply side. For example, the inventory and warehouse managers will want to understand peak demand times, the biggest supply risks, and the duration from order receipt to warehouse fulfillment. Other managers may want to understand the impact of seasonality and variability in demand on their resourcing and space allocation.

- **Promotional tools.** These are most frequently used by merchandisers and marketers to create, deploy, and change the promotional codes, coupons, and the discounts and offers available. This functionality is typically baked into almost all ecommerce tools. People developing and deploying promotions will expect the analytics team to provide self-service tools and reporting about the usage, sales, profitability, and margins resulting from orders that use a promotional code. In addition, the marketing team will want to dive deeply into the data about customers who take advantage of promotions to understand that customer segment. Marketing and merchandising will want data for determining the best products to discount, for adjusting the frequency and content of offers, and for identifying the right customer segments to target.

- **Content management tools.** The content management system is important to an ecommerce platform. Although a content management system may be a core part of the platform or integrated with it, the analytics team will want to have a strategy that enables tracking of the clickstream, events, and behavior of people within specific content. Data collection should be automatically tagged in your content management system by native features or via tag management.

- **Marketing tools.** Capabilities for marketing are integrated to work with an ecommerce platform. Marketing tools run the gamut from e-mail service providers to marketing automation vendors to digital analytics to campaign management to attribution. Marketing tools in an ecommerce platform can enable testing and optimization of key ecommerce flows and functionality. Marketers will want the analytics teams to help them find, transform, and use the data marketing tools integrated with the platform.

- **Search tools.** Tools that allow for the natural language or operator-based searching and querying of the ecommerce platform can be enabled and tuned within the ecommerce platform. The queries entered into the search experience may be tracked and stored by the ecommerce platform, and the rules that map certain pages, brands, or categories to specific keywords may be established within the ecommerce platform. Naturally, business stakeholders will seek to use analytics to help them understand how customers are expressing themselves about the product mix and what queries are most effective in helping people find and buy specific products.

- **Security and fraud awareness tools.** Although it is common for a large ecommerce sites to have dedicated resources for site security and fraud detection, the ecommerce platform may provide functionality that enables security (like SSL) and have basic business rules baked into it that automatically detect potential fraud and suspicious orders and provide alerts about it. For example, a large amount of orders from specific IP addresses or the creation of new accounts that subsequently have a high rate of credit card declines are types of suspicious behaviors and transactions that could throw a flag or generate an alert to be investigated. The frequency of these alerts and other data and details about the security of the site or fraud on it may be requested by stakeholders from the analytics team.

- **Mobile tools.** These are tools for creating and rendering mobile ecommerce experiences on mobile devices, smartphones, tablets, and even apps. Mobile browsing, as opposed to shopping and buying, can be a primary use-case for an ecommerce mobile site or app. As such, people such as product managers and merchandisers will seek to understand data from the analytics team about the types of devices, what functionality is used on mobile, and the difference in the behavior of mobile browsers versus mobile shoppers. Mobile can also be a way to drive online users to physical store locations or enable collaboration with customer services (via mobile chat).

- **Social tools.** Tools for embedding social media functions into ecommerce experiences are provided to business users in ecommerce platforms. Simple integrations via a code snippet may be supported. Other ecommerce platforms provide deeper integration with common social networks, such as Pinterest, Twitter, Facebook, Instagram, and Snapchat. Although inbound traffic, behavior, and conversion resulting from tagged social media campaigns will be primarily tracked in your digital analytics tool, the ecommerce platform may also track some of this data and potentially merge it with known customer data from CRM.

Determining an Analytical Approach to Analyzing the Ecommerce Platform

Given the different levels of knowledge that businesspeople will have about the ecommerce platform—from mostly none to a deep level of understanding—it is necessary for an analyst to have an approach for analyzing the usage of ecommerce platform, the core functionality embedded within it, and other integrated technologies and tools. Presented next is an approach the analyst can take for figuring out what to do next. You will note that this process is aligned with the processes described in Chapter 2, "The Ecommerce Analytics Value Chain":

1. Start with the business questions.

2. Identify the type of analytical output required from the platform and the timelines for it.

3. Determine the user experience and functionality created by the platform that needs to be tracked.

4. Ensure that the data model exists or the tools deployed are sufficient to support the analytical need.

5. Instrument the platform and its functions, as necessary, to collect the data.

6. Create a data model, implement it, store the data, and govern it to ensure accuracy.

7. Apply analytical and data science methods to analyze the data, and then socialize the analysis.

The ecommerce platform is central to the functionality of an ecommerce site. It contains data for analysis and will integrate with other systems that contain data. While it is an abstract technology that will "look" very different at different companies, it is important for ecommerce analysts to understand and work with it.

13

Integrating Data and Analysis to Drive Your Ecommerce Strategy

Integration refers to the process of bringing together data from different systems into a unified data set and providing views of that data. It is technical work typically executed by data engineers and other IT professionals under the guidance of the analytics team and/or the people using the combined data set. Integration will be largely driven by the mission and vision of the leader of your analytics team and the needs of business stakeholders. Technical analytics teams that manage and maintain infrastructure and technology for data collection, storage, processing, modeling, reporting, and visualization, will do data integration. These teams will combine data to create new data sets and views, which will be delivered in various applications. Technically focused data analytics teams may also do systems integration, connecting and stitching together technical tools to support analytical business processes. Take the case in which a CMO wants to bring together customer relationship management (CRM) data with third-party–provided demographic data and web behavioral data and mobile application behavior. Four different data sets are required to be joined into one common dataset. These different data residing in different systems would be brought in an existing or new system, such as an enterprise data warehouse or via data virtualization in-memory caching technology or perhaps they would be stored in their raw form in a data lake.

As you can imagine if you have worked in highly technical environments, various inputs to technical processes (i.e., requirements and scope) must be in place before work activities for integration can begin. The data sources, detail of the data, and available options for extracting, transforming, and loading that data will all need to be carefully considered. The overall scope, the analytical deliverables (such as reports, visualizations, and dashboards), as well as the proposed timeline must be communicated. In agile analytics environments, epics or stories must be written and aligned with measurement requirements before sprints and scrums. In waterfall environments, technical design documents and other requirements and specifications must be provided before the integration work can be scoped and interpolated in a long-before-determined waterfall schedule. In companies that manage their own data using their own machines, hardware may need to be ordered, racked, provisioned, and made available before the project can even commence. Or for those companies using private or public, single or multiresident clouds, the servers need to be configured and made available. Whatever the processes are for executing technical work to support analytics in your company, you need to follow them. IT and engineering processes to support the business are necessary for the appropriate control and management of complex technical environments. IT can be slow, but they are deliberate. Corporate processes always win, so try to adhere to them. When they don't work, invent new ones for analytics. Even when revenue is at risk, having technical analytics teams go around existing processes or use alternative environments or hardware is a hard-pressed case to prove in more mature corporate environments. Thus, data integration, for a technical analytics team or a team named "analytics" embedded in IT, can have long lead times and may require additional work that a business user may not be aware of or respect. Be sure to set proper expectations with other teams and the business.

For analytics teams that are more business-focused and use the data and tools supported by other teams to interpret data and communicate findings, insights, and recommendations, the data and systems integration work will be largely supportive by coordinating, guiding, and ensuring the work done meets analytical needs and business goals. Analytics teams that are more business-focused will also create and participate in the creation of artifacts, such as data specifications and other requirements (functional, reporting, and so on), to support integration. When new processes need to be created, the analytics team may lead the development of those that impact their work. Analytics also becomes the "users" of integrated data and systems, and, thus will participate in the UAT (user acceptance testing) of inte-grated data and systems to ensure they meet requirements. When data exists outside of the jurisdiction or control of IT and internal engineering, analysts and the analytics team will have a much larger role to play—for example, when analytical data exists in one or more SaaS vendor tools. In these cases, the analytics team may lead projects to bring second- or third-party data together into a single SaaS sys-tem, including determining the requirements, managing or doing the technical work, ensuring UAT, and rolling out the results to the busi-ness—for example, adding custom dimensional data to Google Ana-lytics or sending various data to Domo for visualization. Data and systems integration can be important to delivering successful ecom-merce analytics.

Defining the Types of Data, Single-Channel to Omnichannel

Data can come from many different sources. When data comes from one activity, such as paid search or internal inventory data, it is said to be single-channel. When data is analyzed across one or more areas of the business separately from each other, it is considered to be multichannel. For example, analyzing affiliates and organic search data is considered to be multichannel. When a business wants to look at more than two channels in a way that combines elements of the customer, brand, or transactions (orders) so that the different types of data can be looked at as one combined data set (joined either directly or indirectly), then the data is considered to be omnichannel. Another way to think about omnichannel is to understand that "omnichannel analytics" require the analyst to consider every data source that applies to the ecommerce business and can be connected by the brand and its customers. An "omnichannel analyst" analyzes ecommerce data with a unified approach for determining common relationships and insights about customers, segments, behaviors, and transactions in all available data sources. Omnichannel analysis considers all sources as one giant source, in a business-focused approach similar to the technical idea of data warehousing. When you are integrating data, either single-, multi-, or omnichannel data, the types of data you may run into will include **first-party data, second-party data**, and **third-party data**. *First-party data* is created/generated and owned by the company; it is usually proprietary data that is business-critical and includes customer, transactional, and financial data. *Second-party data* is about your customers and business, specific to your company, but owned by a third party, which they sell or license back to you. For example, the data known about your customers by advertisers, publishers, and social networks, which you can buy and reuse in your company, is second-party data. *Third-party data* is data that you do not own and that is stored outside of your company, which you may or may not buy access to or use within your business. Research and data collected about your customers, audience, or business from other companies is considered third-party data. It is possible, depending on the company, to have similar data that is both first-, second-, and third-party data. Take the example of an ecommerce site that has a social feature popular with users. The social data on their network is first-party data. If the company advertises on Facebook, then the data collected by the advertiser is third-party data. If the company uses elements of Facebook's social graph to augment their internal, first-party data within their first-party data, the data extracted and loaded from Facebook is second-party data. The types of data frequently used by an ecommerce analyst are listed here:

- **Internal data** is the type of data created by systems within your data centers or controlled by your company. Typically, owned media falls into this category. First-party data owned by your company falls into this category. Second-party data provided by another company that you have purchased and loaded into your environment is also internal data. Some companies may have even integrated third-party data into their internal systems, like DMP (data management platforms).

- **Digital analytics data** is behavioral and transactional data from web sites, owned social networks, e-mail, mobile, connected devices, IoT, IoE, and other new, emerging, and future digital formats.

- **Social data** is also digital data collected about people from their inputs, behaviors, and transactions in social media. This data can be first-, second-, or third-party data depending on whether your company owns, advertises, or pays to access the data.

- **Syndicated research data** is often surveyed, sampled, or panel data about the behaviors, propensities, attitudes, and beliefs about an audience. This data is typically second- or third-party data.

- **Audience data** is household-level and geographic information about people in a specific area; for example, attributes of an audience such as household income, family size, race, religion, and so on. This data is usually first-party data but can be second- or third-party data.

- **Financial data** is information related to the cash on hand, investments, credit and credit worthiness, credit scores, household financial, and other bank-owned and investment-related information derived from available public and private sources. This data is most often first-party data but can be second-party data (or even third-party data).

- **B2b data** is business to business data, sometimes called firmographic data. It is structured data about companies and businesses across regions, countries, markets, cities, and so on. The information may include profile data, company size, revenue, and other corporate data. This data is typically third-party data but may be integrated internally as second-party data.

- **Specialized and customized research data** are insights provided by out-of-the box or customized, primary or secondary research areas about audiences, prospects, and customers. Specialized data may be focused on particular products, lifestyles, markets, behaviors, geographies, and other vertical segments of desired populations. This data is usually first-party data, when the research is done in-house, or third-party data when externally created.

- **Television and cable data** is specifically tied back to subscription and customer record data that identifies what content and advertisements people were shown, and when. Depending on the company, this data can be first-party data (for TV networks) or second- or third-party data.

Integrating Data from a Technical Perspective

An ecommerce business can have a lot of data to integrate—behavioral, customer, marketing, finance, merchandising, order, product, inventory, supplier invoice, tax, shipping data, and more. When the data from these different sources is brought together via data integration, analysis can be created by analysts that is more detailed and richer in business insight and potential action. The technical work involved in data integration needs ownership. Integration work can't be done haphazardly or consistently ad-hoc. The sources, systems, formats, and movements of data across an enterprise, in order to support business process, require process, transparency, and accountability. Thus, for an ecommerce analyst and the ecommerce analytics team, it is absolutely necessary to identify a technical partner that can run point and help ensure data integration is executed successfully. Project or program management may be necessary. When you're partnering with IT and technology teams, it is in your best analytical interest to create a positive and functional working relationship by working within their processes (but calling out bottlenecks or improvements needed in processes). Follow this guidance to set the right frame for working with technical teams doing integration:

- **Identifying the types of data and source systems that need to be integrated.** Working with IT to map out the topology and architecture of the systems that contain data and the data that is housed in these systems is useful for informing IT about what data and systems analytics uses, how they use them, why, and what they do with them.

- **Establishing the level of effort required to support analytics projects.** Estimating the level of effort, in terms of number of hours, and the skill set needed to support analytical work is a solid input to help guide IT. From this estimate, you can work with IT to translate the need into an allotment of support hours or, more ideally, a dedicated IT liaison who works alongside analytics to marshal resources to support analytics projects. Level of effort estimates are helpful in both agile and waterfall analytics environments.

- **Reviewing planned projects ahead of the need for IT or technology team involvement.** It's useful to get IT and technology teams involved as soon as you determine there is a real need for their services. Do not wait until the last minute. Advanced notice is extremely important in environments that follow a waterfall approach to development in which insertions into planned work can be difficult—and may even require a "change request" (if they are heard at all). In Agile environments (discussed shortly), the interpolation of new work into existing schedules will be easier to accommodate. It's agile, after all, right? That said, let the people whose help you need know that their help is needed as soon as possible.

- **Accommodating for and operating within IT and technology ways of working.** Although IT and technology teams may claim to use the same development methodology, process, artifacts, and ways of working as other companies, the reality is that no two organizations develop software or deploy technology in the same way. There are commonalities and similarities, but everywhere is different to a degree. Analysts can't expect the same process or approach to data integration that they've used in the past to be adopted quickly if it dramatically differs from the way their current company works. A good rule is that the analytics team must align with and work within existing processes and adapt. Of course, calling out areas where delivery of analytics may be problematic or compromised by the current ways of working is important—just remember that if you present a problem, you should also present the solution.

Agile Versus Waterfall Delivery

Agile is the name for an approach to the development and delivery of software solutions in which fast iterations to deliver incremental functionality ready for use is preferred over longer development cycles. The core of an Agile approach is collaboration between team members, ideally on a daily basis (called a scrum), first thing in the morning, to align on key work to be delivered that day to support short-term goals (usually over two weeks). Each increment of time during which software is developed and delivered is called a sprint.

Typically, sprints are two weeks long or so. Resources are allocated to Agile sprints through a quantification; each resource may have 200 points of effort available for each sprint. The level of effort and amount of time to deliver on a business requirement is also enumerated. For example, larger efforts may be allocated 100 points whereas smaller efforts may require only 25 points. Who works on what feature and when is assigned based on comparing the available resources to the level of effort needed to deliver. Central to the calculus of resourcing an agile project is the idea that the teams assigned to work in each sprint will be self-organizing and autonomous, and will include the necessary cross-functional talent.

Agile can be powerful when executed correctly, but it can be challenging from an analytics perspective because as sprints iterate, less attention can be given to ensuring correct data versus the correct functionality and flows. Effort to code and deliver features and functionality will take priority over analytical needs. Remember to sound-off in the scrum when analytics needs are being deprecated. As soon as the project is released, then people want to look at the data (so be ready). In Agile environments where analytical work requires data collection, whether through APIs, database writes, JavaScript, or another method, the analytics team will work with engineering to provide the right inputs in sprints, such that each iteration or sprint will progress toward the right solution. Agile's flexible and iterative nature can frustrate the analyst who wants the same consistent and standard set of inputs across every project before beginning work. That said, the artifacts such as epics, stories, chapters, and themes that can be authored and approved before Agile sprints begin are excellent sources to review to begin to understand analytical requirements. Remember, Agile development can require Agile analytics. Ecommerce analysts must understand Agile.

Waterfall approaches to development are different in that they are defined well in advance, typically one year or more. The waterfall approach prioritizes projects as a sequence of scope that must be created to deliver capabilities over time. Although projects may occur simultaneously, when resources allow, waterfall roadmaps sequence projects linearly one right after the other. The entire schedule and sequence of projects to deliver is approved by management ahead of time. Resources are made available and allocated to the projects based on the temporal sequence identified. Unlike Agile, waterfall projects are inflexible to accommodate for new feature requests or business urgencies to reallocate resources to new projects or to cater to new initiatives. In such cases, complicated and even burdensome change request procedures may need to be followed to address new items or modifications to the approved roadmap scope, sequence, and schedule. Waterfall approaches are structured so that standard artifacts are delivered to support the different teams. Most commonly, Product Definition Documents (PDD), Functional Requirements Documents (FRD), a Technical Design Document (TDD), and a Project Plan and Schedule (PPS) are produced by various stakeholders to define each waterfall project. These artifacts are useful for analysts to understand the required analytics and develop an analytical plan and data specification.

The way analysts and analytics teams will work with technology teams will depend greatly on whether they take a pure Agile, pure waterfall, or some combined hybrid approach (which I refer to jokingly as "agilefall" or "waterfragile"). Regardless of development method, there are commonalities in how an analyst should approach their work and coordination with other teams. The analysts have to participate in project elaboration from the beginning on the first day of inception. The analysts need to act as the voice of the business and keep an eye on the data and how it aligns to and supports business goals. They will ensure that the analytics work gets done well and is acceptable for the desired use. Following are helpful ways that analysts and the analytics team can effectively work with and participate in both Agile and waterfall development methodologies.

In Agile environments, the analyst should work to do the following:

- **Attend the daily scrum.** Companies that are serious about Agile often have hired or trained one or more "scrum masters." Typically in engineering or project management, scrum masters hold a daily "stand-up" meeting in which work done the prior day is confirmed, current work for the day is assigned and allocated, and current issues or blockages are addressed. Many companies hold a scrum daily, whereas others may not hold them as frequently. Scrums provide a daily activity for project-managing an Agile project in a way that allows for all participants and stakeholders to be aware, coordinated, and on top of project progress, known issues, and current work.

- **Establish roles and responsibilities.** Part of onboarding and elaborating an Agile project is the identification of a clear set of roles and responsibilities for each team member. This information identifies the expectations for contribution and work efforts by each team member—from the most senior leader involved to the most tactical worker.

- **Lock down data requirements and data collection methods early.** One of the primary responsibilities of the ecommerce analyst will be to capture business requirements related to the data, functionality, outputs, and outcomes necessary to be perceived as having delivered successful analytics work. Then the analyst will identify the detail of that data, as well as how to generate, create, or access the data, and other methods and approaches for handling the data.

- **Lead discussions about how the data will be used by the business.** Whether in a scrum, in an ad hoc meeting, or in working sessions with other team members, the ecommerce analyst will be the primary representative for advocating for data and for how the business will use it. Analysts must remain steadfast and resolute in their decisions about what is the best treatment and handling of the data, especially when challenged by other voices whose role isn't ensuring data accuracy, utility, and alignment to business goals.

- **Approve or be a voice in the approval of data models.** As data requirements are identified and approved, the analyst will lead or participate in working sessions that define the conceptual data model and the logical model that includes keys, and will ultimately review the physical implementation of the data model in a database, which the company will use for storing and accessing the data (see Chapter 5, "Ecommerce Analytics Data Model and Technology"). In environments where data models are denormalized (like the data lake, discussed later in this chapter), the analyst will ensure that the appropriate data is available and may not necessarily model it until it leaves the data lake.

- **Ensure that people mock up the reports, dashboards, and visualizations they want.** One of the outputs of analytics projects is data in reports, which can be used to feed and create visualizations, or as the detail to drill down or explore from dashboards and KPIs. Whether the output is a report, a dashboard, or a visualization, it is the job of the analyst to work with stakeholders to confirm, align, and gain approval on what those outputs look like. One of the easiest ways to do that is to have stakeholders draw the columns and rows they want to see in a report or draw the mockup of how they would like the data visualized.

- **Be a data steward.** Although formal data stewards may have been defined at your company (or not; see Chapter 14, "Governing Data and Ensuring Privacy and Security," for information about data governance), most analysts fulfill a de facto, if not de jure, role as data stewards. Data stewards are people responsible for the management of data, in order to ensure its accuracy, ownership, and business applicability. In Agile projects, analysts will act as data stewards and ensure that any appointed data stewards outside of the analytics team are aware of the implications of the project on existing data.

- **Lead user acceptance testing (UAT).** Analytics projects continue long after the technical work is completed. After the ecommerce experience is deployed, people will want to learn about the data. But if the technical work done during an Agile sprint hasn't supported analytics requirements, it will be hard to deliver the data and analysis required. In this case, the project would not pass UAT. The analyst must do UAT to ensure that the data is suitable for the business purpose—and if it is not, reject the delivery and work to ensure that it is acceptable.

In waterfall environments, the analyst should work to do the following:

- **Attend required project meetings.** Because waterfall projects are planned well in advance, it is common for weekly or periodic meetings to occur during the project lifecycle in which all stakeholders get on the phone or in a meeting room, review the delivered and in-progress work, get feedback from each stakeholder, address urgencies and criticalities, and generally ensure that the project is on track. The analytics team needs to be in these calls to provide input and guidance on data-related issues that can impact analytical outcomes.

- **Establish roles and responsibilities.** Most PMP-trained project managers will create a project artifact named something like a "Mission, Vision, and Roles and Responsibilities Overview." In this document, these concepts are defined and team members are listed. The analog in Agile, to some degree, is the epic. Realize that project managers, in most cases, don't fully understand how analytics work, so you don't want to let them define your responsibilities. The best analysts will tell the project managers what they will do and, perhaps even more importantly, what they will not do. That way, the analysts can frame their own work activities, efforts, and destiny—and not get surprised by finding out that their role was different with different outputs/outcomes than expected. Manage your peers or they will manage you.

- **Define the data collection, data definition, and data reporting requirements.** The analyst will create a plan, often called a "data specification," that will identify and define the data needed, the definitions for the data, how the data will be collected, what systems may be used, and, at a high level, what types of reporting requirements are necessary. Make sure the analyst and analytics team review this document—and that the work delivered meets the requirements expressed in it. If requirements aren't being met, despite best efforts, then escalate. In fact, scream at the top of your lungs. You need the data to do your job, and no one should prevent you from getting the data you need. Only your leadership decides to deprecate analytics work, not people in projects or peers who may not "get it."

- **Create and follow an analytical plan.** Following the data specification, the analyst will create an analytical plan. This plan will identify the business questions to answer, as well as the overall analytical approach to answering them. It can also include sections of the data specification. For more information about analytical plans, read the discussion about them in Chapter 2, "The Ecommerce Analytics Value Chain."

- **Verify how QA (quality assurance) on the data will be performed and by whom.** This action is more of something an analyst should always do regardless of the project or type of delivery style. Who is going to verify that the data collection was instrumented correctly? In other words, who is going to ensure that one action generates one entry in a database table or populates one line in the log file, which then increments a count of one in the report? Who is going to ensure that the data is correct at collection, through pipeline processing, and all the way into the final deliverable? In some cases this may be the analyst, but in other cases the analyst may not have access to the systems or the technical knowledge to do so. Make sure to determine who will test and perform quality assurance on your data—because it may not be you! Be relentless in expressing the requirement that data quality isn't just the analyst's job; it is everyone's job who worked on that project.

- **Participate in user acceptance testing (UAT).** Critical to any project is ensuring that what has been delivered to support analytics and analysis is suitable for doing the job. For data-intensive projects, the analyst and the stakeholders will be the primary end users; thus, it is necessary for the analyst to participate in UAT overall, and even take leadership and ownership for UAT for the analytical output from the project.

Integration with Operational Data Stores

An operational data store (ODS) is a database that is designed to integrate data from different operational systems. It typically contains record-level detail, at the individual or atomic level, that is populated in near real time or real time by operational systems. In an ODS, the data is not meant to be stored for long periods, but rather to represent the current data as it has occurred and is occurring in operational systems, such as a CRM system, the front-end ecommerce platform, or back-end inventory and transactional systems. The generalized function of an ODS is to prepare different data sets by joining them in order to use the data for reporting and visualization, and to move the data into an enterprise data warehouse (EDW, discussed shortly) so that the long-term history of the data can be stored and accessed.

Part of the analyst's job of working with an ODS, if the analyst does so, is to verify that the data within it is clean and accurate to definitions, complies with business rules, and is nonredundant with other data. An analyst will query the ODS for short-term data, connect business intelligence tools to it, and work with the data within it, when that data is not present at the frequency or granularity required for analysis. Just keep in mind that ODSs contain only small amounts of data as a snapshot in time—and thus can be queried only over short time periods. ODSs are also commonly used as a logical storage area for data to load into an EDW, and the data within them can be part of a data lake (also discussed in this chapter). When an ODS is used outside of an EDW, it is used for small queries on current data across one or more sources—as opposed to the complex queries over long time ranges and against many disparate data sets combined into one representation in an EDW.

Integration with On-Premises Enterprise Data Warehouses

An enterprise data warehouse (EDW) is a software system that unifies data from many different and disparate sources and arranges it in a manner that enables relationships to be made across the unified data set. The EDW stores historic and current data in a particular data model and makes the data available for reporting or analysis or usage by other systems (via extracts). Reports that come from a data warehouse may be financial reports, such as quarterly earnings, or reports about inventory levels or the promotional sales and margins. An EDW is an abstracted representation of business data that is highly structured and transformed to meet specific data definitions.

An EDW is usually fed from an operational data store (ODS), discussed previously in this chapter, or from copying data from other source systems. The process for loading data into an EDW is named ETL (extract, transform, and load). ETL is an easy mnemonic for remembering the process for integrating data into an EDW. ETL is still a dominant integration paradigm, but in the light of big data processing and data lakes (discussed later), it is not the only option in 2016. When data is loaded into an EDW via ETL, the first step is called "staging." In staging the rows and columns are moved from the source into a staging environment (which may write to disk or be stored in-memory), and the different, disparate source data is then transformed and most frequently stored as a unified data set, often an ODS. In that sense an ODS may be the source of the data for the EDW or the ODS may be created as part of the ETL process.

The now-integrated data in the ODS is then loaded into what is called a "data warehouse database" and arranged into dimensions, facts, and measures (see Chapter 5). The resulting data and the relationships are represented in a schema model, with the Star and Snowflake schemas being the most common ways to represent combined data. You will also be exposed to "denormalized schemas," which are discussed in the "Integration with Data Lakes" section of this chapter.

The EDW is structured to support the data definitions and relationships you have identified. All the data is cataloged and made accessible for use by business intelligence, data visualization, data analytics, and data science tools. Because the definition of the data is important, as well as the referential integrity and accuracy of the data, data governance is employed to manage the data residing in an EDW. Although an EDW is really a unified data storage and access system, other tools such as ETL, reporting, visualization, and governance are often associated with it. See Chapter 14 for more information about governing data.

Integration with Cloud Data Sources

Over the past several years, SaaS vendors have provided externally hosted infrastructure for storage and tooling data. Prime examples of cloud-based data stores are Amazon Web Services, Rackspace, and even Google Analytics. In some cases, the cloud vendor may provide only infrastructure in which you deploy and use the software tools you bought. Instead of deploying your EDW in an on-premises data center owned and managed by your company, you deploy your EDW on someone else's hardware and then simply access it to manage and use it. Other cloud vendors, like Amazon, have created their own EDW technology (Redshift) and a host of supporting tools for managing and using it. A vendor-hosted cloud solution requires you to send your data to the vendor, typically through an API, in a batch process via SFTP, or possibly via the installation of a proprietary data loader that sits on your database, queries the data automatically, and then sends the data to the cloud vendor in near real time.

As an analyst, you will need to understand how to access the data in the cloud and how to plug your tools into it, and will want to work with your IT and data governance teams to ensure that the data going to the cloud conforms to expected data definitions and analytical needs. Cloud environments can be public or private and single or multitenant. In a public cloud, servers are available to the multiple companies, so your data may be physically located on the same hardware as someone else's data. Public clouds are considered to be "multitenant." In a private cloud, the servers are available only to your organization and contain only your company's data. Private clouds are said to be, in most cases, "single-tenant." In the case of a single ecommerce company with multiple sites, the private cloud could be multitenant.

Integration with Data Lakes

Data lakes are very new to ecommerce environments. You are more likely, in 2016, to find enterprise data warehouses, standalone RDBMSs, or cloud databases underlying an ecommerce experience. That makes sense because of the transactional nature of an ecommerce site where data must be available to support real-time business processes, such as checking available inventory levels and sending and receiving payment and shipping information. On the other hand, when there is a need to bring together data from many sources, in many different formats, so that the data can be accessed and made available to other systems such as an enterprise data warehouse, a data lake may be created.

A data lake contains all source data from whatever system it originated from. The data does not need to be defined before it enters a data lake, which is a key difference from an EDW. All data in your corporation can be put in its original format into a data lake—a file, a spreadsheet, a database, an image, and so on. Nothing is off-limits and nothing needs to be defined. If an EDW is a nicely packaged bottle of filtered water, a data lake is the well from which the water is drawn.

Data in a data lake is stored as a "leaf" in an untransformed or lightly transformed state. This gives the analyst the ability to examine the data in its original state and then transform it later when it needs to be used for a particular purpose. In other words, you extract, load, and then transform in a data lake, whereas in traditional EDWs you extract, transform, and load. This difference is necessary for you to understand. Data lakes are ELT, not ETL. This paradigm shift has big implications for democratizing data and making it available for analysis. Data lakes can make it simpler to introduce and work with new data sources, because they don't need to go through the staging, integrating, and transformation processes required by an EDW.

Data lakes are powerful business constructs for data integration because they retain all data in whatever format it was originally created and make it available to all users of data. The data in a data lake doesn't need to have purpose immediately to be included, whereas in an EDW it is unlikely you will get the support to load data you don't need right away. Because data lakes are created on commodity hardware as opposed to specialized hardware or appliances, the cost of scaling the data in a data lake is diminutive compared to doing so in an EDW (Campbell 2015).

A data lake will contain standard, structured, and traditional data sources resulting from transactional systems and related metrics, and nontraditional data sources that may be nonstandard and unstructured can be added to a data lake. Sensor data, web server logs, social network feed, images, video, text, and other multimedia can be added to a data lake. Remember, data lakes contain all sources you want to load into them. The raw data is kept and transformed when needed (remember, ELT not ETL), and schemas are generated on read ("schema on read") as opposed to when written at load time as in an EDW ("schema on load").

Data lakes may still be aspirational for most ecommerce companies in 2016, but the largest ecommerce companies are already deploying or experimenting with them. From an ecommerce analysis perspective, because data lakes can contain all the data you want, they are well suited for supporting the needs of analytics. You can work with IT or transform the data in the lake for use in analytical systems if you are a power analyst, or you can place self-service tools on top of the data in a data lake to enable business users. For data scientists who want to combine data from different sources, the data lake is a more flexible repository for creating data science sandboxes for experimentation and modeling (Campbell 2015).

Integration with Data Federation

Another approach to data integration is named data federation. In a federated approach to integration, multiple databases from different systems—often in different locations—are mapped into one "meta" database. A single query can be written and processed against all the different databases in the federation such that a single results set for that query is returned. To do this, a federated approach to integration may include "wrappers" that handle the query language for each database. In this sense a federated database needs to be able to break down a query into its constituent parts (i.e., decompose), retrieve data from the different databases in the federation, and provide the query results. To do this, federated databases typically have a user interface that allows for querying the federation, and the routines and wrappers that enable the unified querying of the federation are abstracted from the user. In environments where multiple data sets will never be brought together in an ODS in the short term or stored in the long term in an EDW, a federated approach to data integration may be worth exploring. On the other hand, a federated approach means creating a single-data model across all sources that you query, so it imposes a structure that may not support all information needs all the time. For example, in ecommerce you may want to make a request like "Show me the customers who bought these products in these sizes and used this promotion and received their order within two days in which the order size was more than $300 and the order was placed on a mobile phone"—a federated database across your CRM, inventory, fulfillment, and shipping databases would answer that question.

Integration with Data Virtualization

Data virtualization is a newer approach to integration that enables an analyst to pick and choose data that resides in different databases and replicate it without knowing the lower-level technical details. The data is copied and joined, often as an in-memory cache of data, and then made available to whatever tool wants to use the data. The data in a virtualized data environment never truly leaves the source system. Instead it is replicated in another location and accessed by the tool you point at it. In other words, there is no ETL; also, unlike with a federated database, there is no single data model, so you can create custom data models for your specific analytics applications.

Taking the sample pseudoquery I proposed in the data federation discussion, you may want to make a request like "Show me the customers who bought these products in these sizes and used this promotion and received their order within two days in which the order size was more than $300 and the order was placed on a mobile phone." You would then use your virtualization software to select and populate a data model that contains just this data for only this purpose. You wouldn't wrap the database and map querying language as you would do in a federated model, nor would you ETL or ELT anything. You would simply copy the data you want, define your joins, and link the virtualized data to the tool you are using to do analysis.

Integrating Analytics Applications

Analytical applications can be integrated together with the data from tools provided by other vendors. Usually an analytics application vendor will have a partner ecosystem. Each partner may have had the opportunity to integrate their technology together through some sort of technical method. Take the case of Domo, Tableau, Microsoft BI, Adobe, Webtrends, Google Analytics, Tealium, Ensighten, and many other vendors that have a set of prebuilt connectors that allow for data from other vendors' tools to be brought into their software. These connectors are built, in part, based on server-to-server connections that receive credentials (i.e., username/password), access the data you want, and pass it back to the application requesting it. Other software has custom data import features that allow you to import a specific file type or mark up your data into some format (such as JSON or XML) and then send it to be loaded. Take the example of Adobe Genesis, RJMetrics Pipeline, or the product linking that Google does between Google Analytics, Google AdWords, and other Google Advertising products.

For those of you who have been in the analytics business for some time, you will recognize that I am talking about enterprise application integration (EAI) specific to analytical products. As you may know, in EAI, there are different patterns for integration. Mediation is a design pattern for integration in which the integration is done by some software sitting in between the applications and the data to be integrated. Adobe Genesis is mediation software that sits between Adobe and source systems. Another pattern is called federation (not to be confused with data federation), in which the system for integration is at a layer above the applications to which it sends data, and the design is such that the data is sent as needed to each application by the federated integration layer. These technical design patterns are largely outside of the realm of the ecommerce analyst but it is helpful to understand them.

These are the primary methods for application integration from an analyst's perspective:

- **Server-to-server connections** are a type of federated application integration in which the machines connect to each other synchronously and share data between the two applications, usually based on a public application programming interface (API). Public APIs are available for many technologies in 2016, and thus a programmer can often write a server-to-server connection using these public APIs. You will find cases in which you can't code your own integration to a source because there is no public API. Yet other vendors may offer technology to integrate with that source. When the integration is proprietary between the two applications, a private API may have been used to create the integration between the two sources. You may see server-to-server connections being used in ecommerce for tag management, for permissioning, for multivariate testing, and for online advertising.

- **Data loaders** are a type of middleware (i.e., mediation) in which the loader is a software process (often a daemon) that operates with a named user account or a service that is permitted to connect to a data source, issue one or more queries for which to retrieve data, and then pass back the data to the vendor, usually asynchronously.

- **Batch processing** (often via SFTP) is mediation and occurs when a file type or other markup is generated by some process (such as a stored procedure in a database). The stored procedure is executed and the output file containing the data is created in a location where it can be accessed by the tool or vendor, moved to the software environment, and loaded into the application.

Integrating Data from a Business Perspective

Although much of this chapter has reviewed what data integration is, the systems and architectures that contain data, and the types/approaches to integration, the chapter has been perhaps overly heavy on technology discussion—although I wrote the chapter in such a way for a business user to understand. As a business leader, I've found that in order to ensure that the technical work gets done to scope and on time, it is helpful for the business stakeholders—from analyst to managers—to provide input in framing, justifying, and guiding integration projects to completion. Following are the high-level steps that an analyst can follow when executing integration projects:

- **Gather requirements.** The analyst will speak with project sponsors, stakeholders, and users to gather and document requirements.

- **Act as a business voice within technical meetings.** The analyst should adopt the mindset of the business user when providing input in technical meetings.

- **Document and socialize data definitions and participate in data governance.** The analyst will ensure data is defined and adheres to data governance mandates and standard practices.

- **Provide updates on the current project status and work with project management.** The analyst should keep their manager up-to-date and be available to work with the project manager.

- **Escalate critical concerns in order to mitigate them.** The analyst is accountable for ensuring integration projects meet analytical needs, so issues need to escalated and remediated.

- **Collaborate on user acceptance testing.** The analyst should verify the project meets requirements and, when it does, sign off on UAT.

- **Analyze the data post-release.** The analyst has done the hard work, and now is the time for the fun work. Analyze the data timely and accurately and tell people stories that help to improve the business.

Supporting data and systems integration projects by being aligned with both the business and IT is the job, to some degree, of the ecommerce analytics team. More technical analytics teams will do more integration work hands on, while business analytics teams will help to guide integration projects to completion and acceptance. Regardless, working on integration projects is part of what ecommerce analysts do in 2016—and they also, of course, analyze the data resulting from integration projects. In 2016, most companies don't simply want to derive insights from a single source of data. They want to combine multiple sources and do analysis in unison across all of their business data whether first, second, or third party and regardless if the data is stored in internal or external systems. The only way to combine data into these unified data sets is by integrating the data using the systems, technologies, and approaches outlined in this chapter.

14

Governing Data and Ensuring Privacy and Security

Successful ecommerce companies convert prospects to new customers and create customer loyalty because they have built a relationship based on trust. People trust that Amazon will not share their personal data, lose their credit card information, or fail to adequately protect their cloud services from bad people. Less-known brands and smaller ecommerce sites can't rely on the power of a global brand like Amazon's to generate trust. Instead, trust can be established based on the tone in their content, the brands and products sold, through referrals from existing customers (often incentivized by discounts), privacy and data handling/sharing policies, and even from badges and editorial copy that indicate the site is trustworthy and secure. When building customer trust, most companies go through the necessary process of creating content that communicates trustworthiness to their audience, including artifacts like privacy policies and clear statements about data usage and how personally identifiable information (PII) is handled. Many companies provide their customers detailed information about data collection, storage, and retention, as well as the details of how user and customer information is applied to their business practices and shared (or not) with other entities and companies. All of these approaches can be helpful for trying to instill confidence in a person such that they are willing to provide their personal data in order to buy a product.

Communicating about how data is used, stored, retained, and handled by your ecommerce company is important to the analytics team's operations and ways of working; however, such communications are not generally catalyzed, defined, or formalized by the analytics team. But the analytics team may review and approve any internal or external policy about data usage or storage. For example, the team leading the writing, review, and verification of a privacy policy may be the legal team. IT may be responsible for data usage policies. Companies with adequate resources to staff privacy teams may include those experts when drafting data policies. Various business stakeholders from lines of business impacted by privacy, security, and data governance will be involved. Marketing will help define rules around advertising campaigns. Customer service will participate in discussions about customers. The work of the analytics team, of course, is impacted by the decisions about data usage, privacy, and security that are made by these teams. Thus, it is important for analysts to participate in the creation, development, enhancement, maintenance, and practice of the policies that relate to data. In light of the EU's disagreement on Safe Harbor for data, there has never been a better time for analysts to participate in data governance, privacy, and security initiatives.

In today's ecommerce companies, there are few teams as well informed and aware about the technical, business, operational, and financial impact of data on a company as the analytics team. In fact, the Ecommerce Analytics Value Chain discussed in Chapter 2 includes phases related to data collection and data governance. These activities are essential to successful analytical execution and delivery, and they also apply to privacy and security of ecommerce data. Ensuring the highest and proper use of data and its application to guide understanding of the business and to safeguard it is the responsibility of the analytics team. Analysts and analytical leaders alike benefit from being involved in initiatives related to data governance, privacy, and security.

Data governance can help to protect privacy and help to secure your data. The goal of data governance is to provide a set of processes, procedures, and even tools and technology for managing the overall availability, usability, integrity, and security of the data used by a company. When a data governance program is established, it should include a governing body or council, a defined set of procedures, and a plan to execute those procedures. The analytics team will benefit from being involved, as necessary, in data governance activities.

Within the concept of data governance exists the idea of data privacy. Although the notions, ideologies, and regulations regarding privacy are beyond the scope of this book, the idea of privacy is well within it. Data privacy (or data protection) is defined by Wikipedia as "the relationship between collection and dissemination of data, technology, the public expectation of privacy, and the legal and political issues surrounding them." As an ecommerce analyst, you will likely be exposed to some level of personally identifiable information that is associated with an order. This personally identifiable information is legislated and regulated, but when it is combined with a log of transactions and orders for specific merchandise over time, the sensitivity of the information is heightened. For example, knowing your address is one level of privacy; knowing where to send your prescriptions and what type of prescription you have requires ensuring a legally compliant level of privacy.

To provide for data privacy, an ecommerce company requires comprehensive and state-of-the art data security. Governed data is secured data that provides the required level of privacy to the customer in order to protect the business. Data security, another gigantic topic, is outside of the scope of this book, but there are elements of data security that relate to ecommerce analytics. Managing user accounts for data and tool access, extracting data for use in other tools, sending data to and from the "cloud," and using second- and third-party data from providers of social and advertising platforms all require the analyst to work within proper corporate protocols for data security. Fortunately, within a governed collection, storage, processing, use, and retention of ecommerce data, the analyst has a privileged view and opportunity for keeping an eye on the appropriate and secure usage of data.

The data to be governed will vary based on the ecommerce site for which you work. In other words, the type of activities that you execute to define or support data governance will vary depending on where you work. For analysts who work in more technical environments, the data governance work will involve more of defining the technical definitions and data lineage from differently sourced data. Analysts who work on the business side, in contrast, will concentrate more on informing the technical activities of data governance and ensuring compliance with data governance policies and usages.

Analysts who work on the business side can also function as data stewards and work alongside business partners to ensure that the data they need is governed appropriately.

In that context different types of data have different requirements for data governance, privacy, and security:

- **Anonymous customer data** is defined as data that cannot be related or linked back to a known individual. Anonymous data does not contain personally identifiable information (PII). In many cases, aggregate data summarized by combining the details of individual records may be considered anonymous. Other times, data that is encrypted or encoded in a way that obfuscates the actual detail can be considered anonymous. The risk of negative consequences from leakages or unauthorized distribution of anonymous data is lower than with other types of data because it can't be tied back to people. For example, the count of sessions on your mobile app and the amount of in-app purchases are anonymous data. But remember data encrypted with the best of intentions can certainly be unencrypted by people with bad intentions if they get access to it. Financial data is anonymous data, but it is a special kind of anonymous data (discussed in more detail later) because it can be regulated and can require legal compliance, which can be enabled by data governance, security, and protection.

- **Mostly anonymous customer data** is data that does not contain PII about an individual, but may contain pointers or keys to PII. For example, an account ID or user ID is mostly anonymous data. Although it references an individual, the ID in and of itself cannot be used to identify someone. Of course, mostly anonymous data, especially in the case of IDs, can be joined with other data to form a picture that can be less than anonymous—and an ID is a key to finding PII, so mostly anonymous data also needs rigorous governance, privacy, and security.

- **Personally identifiable information** is any type of data that can be used to explicitly define and recognize an individual or be used to de-anonymize data to make it PII (like a person's public key). PII isn't just a technical or analytical concept; it's a legal concept whose definition varies by geography, country, and jurisdiction. The National Institute of Standards and Technology defines PII in Special Publication 800-122 as "any information about an individual maintained by an agency, including (1) any information that can be used to distinguish or trace an individual's identity, such as name, social security number, date and place of birth, mother's maiden name, or biometric records; and (2) any other information that is linked or linkable to an individual, such as medical, educational, financial, and employment information." Obviously, protecting PII is critical to consumer privacy. And since PII is often the target of bad people, it is a primary emphasis for data security. Thus, governing PII data is of utmost importance to the ecommerce analyst.

- **Transactional and behavioral data** is event-based data about the orders, merchandise, invoices, and payments, as well as non-PII data about events engaged in by customers. The product identifier, product brand, product category, transaction type, marketing channel, promotions used, and counts of various metrics related to reach, frequency, engagement, revenue, cost, shipping, tax, content consumption, and conversion rates are examples of types of event data related to transactions and behaviors. These types of data certainly need to be governed, and can represent proprietary information that, of course, should be secured adequately with privacy ensured. The proliferation of cloud-based tools that provide data about some aspect of ecommerce transactions—whether for site analytics, testing, research, or abandonment and recapture—requires the analytics team to verify appropriate configuration, permissions, and definitions from tools that may not be centralized, authorized, or widely used.

- **Financial data** is data that contains information about the revenue, costs, and investments of a company. It can be private or public data. Data governance helps to ensure that the definitions, stewardship, ownership, and usage of financial data conform not only to regulatory and compliance requirements but also to internal stakeholder perceptions. Data governance of financial data within the company, and not just outside of it,

ensures that line-of-business owners and executive stakeholders receive, see, and use consistent financial data that accurately represents business performance.

The data to govern can reside either outside of the company in
cloud-based environments owned and run by other companies or
within on-premises data centers within your company. For more
information about the different architectures for storing data, like
data warehouses and data lakes, see Chapter 13, "Integrating Data
and Analysis to Drive Your Ecommerce Strategy." The different
approaches to managing systems and data infrastructure will impact
the way you govern data—and will greatly impact the data security
and data privacy. In managed environments that are hosted, whether
in a private cloud or multitenant, the host vendor will have sold to
your company services and support for data security and rules for protecting data privacy. Even within your company, unless you are building the environment from scratch, the analytics team will be told the
rules and guidelines. But if you are operating your own analytics environment, you have a greater opportunity to influence change to these
guidelines. In both cases the way you govern the data will be based on
your understanding of data governance and how you insert yourself as
an analyst or the analytics team into it.

Applying Data Governance in Ecommerce

The application of data governance is nuanced and complex, especially in regulated business environments with compliance requirements, such as financial services and insurance. In other industries,
such as ecommerce, there are fewer regulatory standards; thus data
governance may be more straightforward and simpler to formulate,
yet it will still be challenging. Laws and governments may not drive
the challenge of data governance as much as it does in finance; instead,
the rapidity of new data may be a primary driver for ecommerce data
governance. Take, for example, the milieu of data that is constantly
growing, shifting, and being used at marketing agencies and media
companies. Ecommerce data governance falls between these two
spectrums. On one hand, ecommerce companies must govern data
to standards supported by finance institutions, payment providers,

suppliers, and shippers. These data sets are regulated, structured, and standard, and ecommerce data governance must support them. Yet ecommerce data resulting from the customer experience, merchandising, and marketing lacks the same formal frameworks to guide governance as industries beholden to legislation. Thus, the ecommerce analytics team is in a superior position to participate in and even guide data governance. Following are some helpful practices for creating or evolving data governance for ecommerce:

1. **Start contextualizing your data.** By putting into writing the definitions of your data in technical, operational, and business context, you begin to govern your data to conform to those definitions. Technical definitions may include the names of fields, tables, SQL, specific query language for NOSQL, consistency semantics, and other definitional information related to technology. Operational definitions relate to the usage of the data and may include the lineage of the data, metadata about where it is stored, its subject, information about taxonomy and ontology, and so on. Business definitions explain, in human language, the business usage and application of the data.

   To contextualize data, definitions are documented in a data dictionary, which includes the technical and operational information, and a business glossary with the easy-to-understand business language for expressing the data. Contextualization means identifying critical data elements and ensuring that the staging for those elements supports definitions. Mapping data across systems to create and resolve relationships and understanding crosswalk tables to inform an enterprise view of referential data integrity are part of context. All of this work ensures that the data surfacing in reports and dashboards is fit for the business purpose and not misleading.

2. **Identify and assign ownership of data and related roles and responsibilities.** Associating technical, operational, and business owners to groups and sets of data, and even your key data elements is useful. Assign ownership of conversion rate, lifetime value, cost of customer acquisition, churn rate, and so on. Assign ownership of the systems and processes used to collect, count, and measure these metrics. Develop a metrics

catalog that lists the metrics and the key performance indicators. Next, create processes that allow for data owners to modify the data for which they are responsible. Data owners must create policies for appropriate data usage and stages for approving modifications to data and the introduction of new data. Violations of policy must be captured with consistent notification and escalation. The process and handling of data ownership must be transparent and traceable throughout.

3. **Gain an understanding of data quality.** Rules applied to the data within business processes must be understood. For example, if only one "user" or "visitor" is counted per deduplicated cookie, how do you know that the software you are using to count that data is accurate? How do you ensure the quality of the data? Periodic and incremental auditing of data against business rules is one way. Tracking the lineage of data from source to business output assists in monitoring data quality. Establishing thresholds and monitoring available data against those thresholds are helpful. Data governance teams may build dashboards that track the number of available data objects, their current status, the owners, and the usage. It is possible to even provide software that enables collaboration to discuss concerns and escalate issues about data quality.

4. **Appoint stewards and committees to monitor and manage your data from a business perspective.** Data steward is a title aligned with data governance. A data steward is the person, or people, in the case of larger companies, who is/are responsible for ensuring the accuracy, usability, and readiness of critical data elements. Typically, each line of business will have a data steward who participates on a data governance steering committee. The analytics team should have a data steward on the team. All these people form the data stewardship committee, which is a formalized group of assigned data stewards, often led by the data governor, who meet periodically to discuss, align, and make decisions about governing data. The data governor, in some cases, may be the chief data officer, and in other cases may be a formal role, such as vice president or director of data governance. Larger enterprises that govern many critical data elements across an entire global business

may have a data governance committee for each business unit and one top-level data governance committee.

Regardless of the number and structure of your steward(s) and committee(s), central to the mission of the data steward are the creation, agreement, and rollout of the data-sharing agreement across the company. Different data owners must agree on the treatment and handling of their data such that it flows consistently and accurately through standard processes and systems. Data stewards will define for their business unit the data ingestion and extraction process and data standards—with an eye toward aligned governance of all data across the company. After data is ready for use, the data steward may promote the data across controlled zones. For example, new data generated or sourced may be hosted in a "raw" zone until metadata is associated with it and it is authorized as ready to use, at which point it may be moved to a "curated" zone until the data steward may eventually "certify" it for use. When context needs to be added to data, when new metadata needs to be associated, and when new users need access to different data, the data steward can help. It's a good idea to appoint a data steward for an ecommerce analytics team.

5. **Use technology to help drive data governance.** Data governance tools, according to Forrester's definition, "provide capabilities that support the administrative tasks and processes of data stewardship." Tools that assist data governance "support the creation of data policies, manage workflow, and provide monitoring and measurement of policy compliance and data use." These capabilities most frequently take the form of features for automating the processing of data or monitoring it against known standards. Some tools offer features in which data glossaries can be defined, associated with visualizations about lineage, and provide methods to communicate and collaborate with the business and other data stewards. Technology can help an enterprise understand data quality and ensure that references to data are accurate. Dashboards within these tools can provide security/privacy information and link to metadata.

6. **Create dashboards that provide insight into governance activities and data attributes.** An emerging feature in newer and more powerful data governance tools is the capability to view dashboards about key governance activities. A dashboard might list the top data sources and profile their data. The number of data assets may be identified and itemized across various stages (i.e., 346 "raw" assets and 12 "curated" assets). The number of data stewards may be listed and associated with the data for which they are responsible, along with quality metrics. Critical data elements may be profiled. The analytics team is well-positioned to use its expertise to help determine the metrics for data quality dashboards and may even work to help build and roll them out.

Applying Data Privacy and Security in Ecommerce

Ecommerce analysts are responsible for ensuring privacy and maintaining the security of the data they use. The maturity of an ecommerce company will dictate the level of participation the analytics team will have in privacy and security. More mature companies may want less involvement from analytics or more and vice-versa; it really depends on the company. As mentioned earlier in the chapter, the analytics team is most likely to be held to using data in a way that adheres to existing privacy standards within established security frameworks. Teams that exist outside of analytics in other parts of the company, from legal to technology, may have created these standards. In start-up ecommerce companies and less organizationally mature or elaborately structured companies, the analytics team may function without known safeguards for consumer privacy, or in the worst case little or inadequate data security. News of cracking into business networks where bad people abscond with personally identifiable information and other digital corporate assets, knowledge, and intellectual property is common. Companies get hacked. There are many bad people. And the data generated by analytics or contained within analytics systems can be a prime target. For publicly traded companies, the analytical data and even printed data tables, dashboards, and reports derived from analysis can contain information that can be used to capitalize on market opportunities. Imagine that the quarterly sales data report just happened to be left at Starbucks. Imagine what would happen if the lists of the most popular products, brands, and styles for your ecommerce site—or your marketing and merchandising performance—were shared with your competitors. Analytical data is the lifeblood of a company; its value is inherent in how it can be used and misused. Thus, the ecommerce analyst does have an important role to play in data privacy and data security. Here are business activities the analyst can sponsor, initiate, manage, execute, and deliver to help ensure privacy and security:

1. **Ensure alignment with existing policies and procedures.** Unless you're building an ecommerce site from scratch, it is very likely that you have existing policies and procedures for privacy and security. These need to be followed to a T by the analytics team. In particular, for ecommerce, an analyst can be exposed to personally identifiable information, the types of products a person purchased, and other information collected by the site. For example, if the site offers credit, the analyst may be exposed to personal financial details and other information. Fortunately, if the analyst follows the policies and procedures of the company, if they exist, then they will be in compliance with legal considerations, properly handling customer data correctly.

2. **Create appropriate policies for data collection, storage and retention, and appropriate usage.** If you are building or working at a newer ecommerce site, then you must create a privacy policy that provides information to consumers about how their data will be collected, processed, stored, and used. The privacy policy must be authored in clear and concise English or the primary language in which the site was created. Critical to a privacy policy is identifying what consumer information is shared and with whom. In addition, it is important to provide detailed and explicit information about how consumers can opt out from any data collection and tracking—especially digital environments. Of course, the privacy policy must be easily located on the site, up to date, and viewable on different screen sizes and devices.

3. **Set and train on guidelines related to data privacy and security.** Many ecommerce companies offer their new employees the opportunity to take training about privacy and security and conforming to the company's rules. Some companies mandate it and make employees sign off or take tests to verify employees understand the rules. In other companies this training does not exist. In either case, it is the responsibility of the analytics team to identify this policy, adhere to it, and help to evolve it as needs and the law dictate. Allies in the quest for privacy will include the corporate legal team, the security team, the privacy team, the database team, and even the finance team. Why finance? They will be able to model the implications of a data breach or loss of key performance data. The guidelines you establish will vary by role, line of business, and the goals for data usage. These rules will also vary by whether the data will be used externally or only internally by the company. Of course, these rules should be brought to the data governance team, if it exists, and formalized as your company requires; see the next item.

4. **Establish and participate in data governance by understanding data lineage.** The preceding section defined and described the process of data governance and how an analyst can work within it and evolve it to ensure that the needs of the ecommerce team are taken into account. In companies that don't have data governance, the ecommerce analytics team should begin to establish the guidelines for what data is available, what definitions the data has, who the data owners are, and what data can be shared with whom and under what conditions. These types of decisions will help inform data privacy and security and vice versa.

5. **Set and practice clear rules for permissions to different kinds of data.** To enable data security, you must define who has access to specific data, under what guidelines, and with what permissions. Privacy is an outcome of having the right data security. To foster these concepts, the ecommerce analytics teams must set clear rules for permissions on each type of data. Typically this activity is part of establishing ownership and lineage of data. For each piece of ecommerce data, permissions

need to be set that give people the right to read, write, extract, transform, and use it. Rules and permissions can be established at both the data element level and tool level. It can help to define a set of user groups, as opposed to individual-level permissions to do so. Working with IT or other teams (or vendors) may be necessary for defining permissions at the corporate level for data outside of the systems that the analytics team manages.

6. **Set up monitoring frameworks to ensure compliance and existing need.** Part of the process for ensuring privacy and security is setting up tracking of how data is being used, by whom, and how, throughout the company. Some analysts may set up "analytics on analytics" by providing a view into how users of data are using it. For example, the analytics team may set up a report that shows how many users have logged in to a particular tool, what reports they viewed, what data they used or extracted, and so on. These monitoring approaches and more elaborate frameworks, auditing logs, and procedures for reviewing how data is shared help to ensure that compliance is verifiable. In fact, software tools for "data cataloging" can provide some of this functionality.

7. **Establish discipline for violations.** When you are dealing with data, the idea of disciplining people who mishandle, misuse, or go around policies for privacy and security is standard operating procedure. Discipline can be as simple as informing the offender of what privacy or security protocol he violated. More harsh penalties for violators that have been taken by analytics teams include permission revocation, retraining, and—in the worst case, of a financially impactful data breach—job termination. Of course, if the ecommerce company sets up the right data governance to inform privacy and security, then the chances of these negative events occurring is diminished. Data governance, privacy, and security reduce corporate financial risk (i.e., unsystematic risk).

8. **Work with IT to ensure data encryption.** In contemporary and cutting-edge data environments, all data can be encrypted. Newer approaches such as Secure Function Evaluation make it possible to perform analysis, and apply algorithms, on

encrypted data—and receive encrypted output viewable only by those who have the key to decrypt. Although not all ecommerce data would make sense to encrypt, certain data does. Passwords, right now, are commonly encrypted, but other data such as consumer preferences and PII are not generally encrypted. Of course, encryption is only as good as the algorithm used to encrypt—and much evidence exists about data breaches that shows certain types of encryption to be more suitable than others.

Governance, Privacy, and Security Are Part of the Analyst's Job

It is not only your goal as a data analyst but your responsibility to protect every person's analytical data from misuse. Data analysts in many ecommerce companies can be largely left to self-regulate their analytical activities—in much the same way the analytics tool vendors are left to self-regulate their innovations. That is why it is important to apply ethical principles to analytics, to ensure privacy and the application of analytics in a way that positively promotes, protects, and safeguards both global ecommerce and human society. Following are several helpful guidelines for ecommerce analytics teams to apply when dealing with ecommerce data—whether behavioral, transactional, qualitative, quantitative, first or second or third party, or private or anonymous:

- **Be absolutely transparent about what data you collect and how you collect it by creating and frequently updating a "privacy and data usage" policy and prominently displaying it on your site.** Write it in English or the country's language, not legalese, and keep it simple, comprehendible, and summarized. If needed, link to a more formal legal document.

- **Understand and be able to provide, on request, a list of the tracking and measurement technologies currently deployed on your site.** Such a simple idea is hard to execute and deliver—especially at globally distributed enterprises—but smart companies should create and maintain a list of all tracking and measurement technologies deployed within an ecommerce site and have that list ready for review when requested. Centralizing digital data collection using tag management tools can help.

- **Publish a simple metadata document that people both externally and internally can review that describes the data being collected and how it will be used.** For every technology deployed, the vendor should be providing a document answering the following questions: (1) What is this technology? (2) What data is being collected? (3) How is the data being used? (4) How do I view, modify, and prevent my data from being collected? These answers, and others relevant to your business, can be used to craft your policy and privacy statements relevant to ecommerce analytics.

- **Create formalized governance around analytics data.** As described in this chapter, formalize the processes that support data and its usage. Involve cross-functional representatives from teams across your company to ensure they have a voice in the decisions.

- **Enable easy and logical "opt-out."** Ecommerce sites should enable people to opt-out of data collection specific to their behavior, customer data, and orders. Technologies that use data to do things like targeting should be "opt-in."

- **Eliminate all unnecessary data collection while regularly reviewing the data you have collected, and delete unneeded data.** So much data can be collected, and not all of it will be used. Some data will certainly be more viewed and used; it will be more useful, insightful, and actionable (UIA). Figure out what data is UIA in generating profitable revenue and reducing cost, and then minimize the collection and storage of the rest.

- **Don't exploit new technologies in tricky ways that attempt to circumvent a user's choice or perception of privacy.** In other words, do not use technologies to reset or force the persistence of cookies after the user deletes them. Do not use hacks to store cookies forever. Handle your user and customer data like you would want your own personal data handled.

By following the guidelines I've established and understanding topics discussed in this chapter, you can provide for data governance, security, and privacy in your ecommerce analytics work. Governance, privacy, and security are important foundations and underpinnings that not only protect consumers and their data, but also protect your company and your job.

15

Building Analytics Organizations and Socializing Successful Analytics

Successful analytical outcomes that are well regarded by business stakeholders are primarily the result of empowered people applying processes to deliver analysis and are not simply the result of deploying technology. Although technology and tools are critical and necessary for enabling analytics, it is the people on the analytics team who are the primary users of analytics tools. People apply their analytical knowledge and analysis experience to answer business questions. Technology and tools by themselves do nothing to create value—and can be, in fact, overhead in many businesses. Most ecommerce analysts have run into the baggage of legacy and minimally supported systems containing data for analysis. To work with legacy and new systems, analytical processes need to be established to access and use the data. People who aren't provided guidance on the process for doing analysis within an established company or who don't develop process in a new company will not be able to maximize analytical effectiveness. A lack of analytical process impedes success. It's cliché to say that the triumvirate of "people, process, technology" is important for success with analytics, but that's actually a very accurate meta-concept. However, it's not just having people, process, and technology alone that makes for successful analytics. Companies that succeed with ecommerce analytics organize, manage, align, work, communicate, and socialize differently. What successful companies do is build analytics organizations. They create analytics teams, appoint leadership, and resource the group. Successful analytics teams do not concentrate entirely on technology but instead focus on the output and outcomes of analytical work. It's not the tools that are the largest factor in success in these teams; it's the way people team up, organize, define analytical roles and responsibilities, operate, interact, and communicate analysis, which makes for success.

This chapter is about how you build an ecommerce organization, though the principles suggested in this chapter are almost universal for analytics in general. We will review the set of activities necessary for building analytics teams across ecommerce companies. The use-cases, goals, and activities for doing ecommerce analytics are similar, if not identical, across companies; therefore, it is possible to identify universal steps for building an ecommerce analytics organization. In fact, I wrote a book titled *Building a Digital Analytics Organization,* in which you can read hundreds of pages on the subject. What follows in this chapter is a perspective on a universalized approach for building analytics teams, which aligns with my previous work and has also been updated with a few more years of my professional experience.

Suggesting a Universal Approach for Building Successful Analytics Organizations

The universal approach for building successful analytics begins outside of analytics—in the minds and ideations of business leaders. These top-level business executives will have recognized and understood the value and importance of analytics, and they desire to use accurate data and expert analysis to guide and inform their business activities, decisions, and goals These executive leaders will make a decision to hire an analytics leader to run the analytics function. In 2016, the role of Chief Analytics Officer (CAO) is increasingly common as is the Chief Data Officer (CDO). The CAO is a business-focused role that ensures analytics are applied at their highest and best use in the business, while the CDO is a more technically focused role responsible for ensuring data is governed, available, and accurate. The responsibilities of these two roles may be collapsed into one role in charge of using data and analytics as an asset, including all related analytics technology and tools, data governance, analytics engineering, analysis and data science, team management, and strategic leadership.

After a leader is hired, the work to build an analytics organization becomes focused less on why the analytics team is needed and more on internal work to identify what the team will actually do. This leader will be tasked with a lot of work that crosses business, technology, management in order to build an analytics team. The leader may have the luxury of creating the team and the analytics function from scratch, or they may have to work with existing baggage from previous attempts at analytics. In that context, a universal process for building analytics organizations is presented here:

1. **Determine and justify the need for analytics.** Typically, senior leadership will make the decision based on business need.

2. **Gain support for hiring or appointing a leader for analytics.** Whoever determines the need for analytics will also "drive the bus" and ensure that they have the right support and authorization to command the function to be created.

3. **Hire the analytics leader.** In an industry with a dearth of leadership expertise, this process can take a long time and require substantial salaries.

4. **Gather business requirements.** The analytics leader will run point to gather business requirements and understand the business catalyst driving the need for analytics.

5. **Create the mission and vision for the team.** The analytics leader will work to create these statements, which define what the team does and what success looks like.

6. **Create an organizational model.** Aligned with requirements, the analytics leader will determine the staff needs along with the roles and responsibilities.

7. **Hire staff.** Analysts command and deserve higher salaries than other workers with the same amount of experience and can be hard to find.

8. **Assess the current state capabilities and determine the future state capabilities.** The team will map requirements to what is feasible, determine the gap, and identify what needs to be done to deliver them.

9. **Assess the current state technology architecture and determine the future state architecture.** The team will determine if the technology can support requirements and, if not, figure out what should be done.

10. **Begin building an analytics road map.** The analytics road map sequences over the time the work that will be delivered.

11. **Train staff.** By training staff, you can ensure they know what to do in the current state—on top of the experience they bring to work.

12. **Map current processes, interactions, and workflows.** The team will need to document current processes and fix, evolve, and create new processes when needed.

13. **Build templates and artifacts to support the analytics process.** The team will create the format for work products that support the analytical processes.

14. **Create a supply-and-demand management model.** This model will help to match analytical demand from stakeholders to available supply of human and technical resources.

15. **Create an operating model for working with stakeholders.** This model documents how the team will work with stakeholders to initiate, execute, communicate, escalate, and close project work.

16. **Use, deploy, or upgrade existing or new technology.** As need arises, the team will work with technical partners to ensure the technology needed is available and operational.

17. **Collect or acquire new data.** The team will work to collect new data as needed to support analytics requirements.

18. **Implement a data catalog, master data management, and data governance.** The team will act as helpful data stewards of their data and apply data management and data governance practices.

19. **Meet with stakeholders and participate in business processes.** The team will work with peers and other groups to do their jobs.

20. **Do analysis and data science and deliver it.** At the heart of the function is the production and delivery of analysis that is helpful to people.

21. **Socialize analysis.** The analysts must go to stakeholders and communicate to them what the data says and answer their business questions.

22. **Lead or assist with new work resulting from analytical processes.** The team will initiate new work to answer questions that occur from their excellent analysis.

23. **Document the financial impact and business outcomes resulting from analysis.** It is important to quantify the financial impact of analytical work to justify the team's existence.

24. **Socialize the business outcomes and highlight the financial impact.** Once the positive financial impact is documented, the members of the analytics team should use data to advocate for themselves and show how they have positively impacted the business.

25. **Continue to do analysis, socialize, and manage technology to emphasize the business impact ad infinitum.** Analytics work is ongoing. There is always more to do.

26. **Manage change and support stakeholders.** Business goals change and the nature of the business questions will evolve. The analytics team needs to stay on top of the business to maintain alignment.

Determine and Justify the Need for an Analytics Team

Analytics teams don't just appear in corporations out of thin air. They are often conceived in boardrooms and in meetings between senior leaders and executive and senior vice presidents. These teams can develop organically when business leaders realize that they have resources performing the analytics function and decide to align them under one team or across a line of business. Other times, an analytically savvy manager takes a solo initiative to embed analytics into the business function and enlarges someone's job or jobs to support. There are several signs that indicate a need for analytics in an ecommerce company:

- **Senior management does not have any data to make decisions.** A lack of visibility to the key data that is perceived to be accurate or helpful is a primary driver for analytics team formation.

- **Senior management has too much data to make decisions and needs help working through it.** Analysis paralysis can result from too much data that is deemed to be relevant but isn't because of the lack of interpretation and analysis.

- **Senior management has conflicting data that can't easily be identified.** When data is not controlled, it can seep through many different pathways in an organization. This can result in ungoverned data proliferation without data definitions or standards. The end result is conflicting data that confuses people.

- **Business goals demand careful attention to tracking data that informs business goals.** In goal- and performance-driven and incentivized cultures, measurement and analytics is a necessity. The old adage applies: "You can't manage what you don't measure."

- **Competitors are determined to have analytics teams and are benefiting from the work.** The competitive intelligence team may have identified that a competitor leads with data, has advanced analytical capabilities, uses data sources, or applies data and analytics in innovative or new ways, thus creating competitive advantage that the company wants to counter.

- **Line-of-business leaders need help setting strategy or managing programs that can be tracked quantitatively.** Teams in ecommerce companies, such as merchandising, customer service, and marketing, benefit from enhanced data analysis, whether tracking the impact on conversion of particular brands or marketing programs.

In all of these cases, it is important to justify the investment in analytics, document and socialize your rationale for investment into staffing the analytics function with all the key stakeholders, and then present it to senior management. This approach is bottom-up (i.e, it comes from middle management to senior management). The alternative is the top-down approach, where senior leadership commands the function be created and resources it. In either case, it can help to justify the investment and develop a business case specific to ecommerce:

1. **Specify the ecommerce business problem or challenge or initiative.** The business issues, concerns, needs, requirements, or, ideally, business questions must be established, documented, and agreed on. This detail provides the foundation for which to map needed future state capabilities and helps to frame the type of resources—from hardware to software to human—that you will need.

2. **Indicate the financial impact that would result from the problem not being solved.** Missed opportunities or ways to generate new or incremental revenue or decrease costs can be quantified. If you frame the business problem monetarily, the impact is clear.

3. **Identify how analytics can help solve the problem or augment the company's ability to execute.** The analytical capabilities you map to the business area and its goals must guide decisioning or provide input to solve the business challenge. In some cases the work may be solely led by the analytics team, and other times analytics will assist, guide, or advise other teams.

4. **List the investment needed in terms of the fixed and variable costs, including head count, software, and hardware.** Be specific about the investment required. Put it in clear financial terms and extend the analysis to incorporate all cost factors. Don't try to hide or diminish the investment.

5. **Create a financial model, using NPV or IRR, that identifies the financial impact of the investment.** After you have all the inputs outlined previously, it will be possible to calculate the impact of the investment in today's dollars (using a net present value method) or to evaluate if the investment would exceed the company's cost of capital (the internal rate of return).

Gain Support for Hiring or Appointing a Leader for Analytics

If you are at this point in building an ecommerce analytics team, congratulations, your investment decision was improved. You may need to hire a Chief Analytics Officer or other appropriately entitled expert, such as a VP or Director of Analytics. What's important at this stage is where you will source candidates from three areas. Let's explore each:

- **Have the line-of-business ecommerce leader or senior executive who justified the investment lead the analytics team.** In some cases, the executive who got the budget to hire for analytics will run the team. This person might be in marketing, finance, or merchandising and will simply add "analytics" or some derivative (consumer analytics, marketing analytics, data science, and so on) to their title and then lead the analytics function. You can appoint someone internally who already works at the company to lead the function, or you can hire someone externally to run the team. The decision point here is whether the existing employee can handle taking on a larger role from an expertise, capability, and efficiency perspective and whether he has the skill set to deliver. In some cases, an executive may be empire building: When commanding analytics falls under his jurisdiction, he takes on the role as the analytics leader, on top of his other work, and then hires a subordinate who does the real analytical work while he manages his empire.

- **Promote from within the organization.** In companies whose staff have analytical ability and may be fulfilling analytical roles either part-time or full-time, it may be logical to promote them. This path to hiring an analytical leader is helpful because existing staff can have a strong understanding of the business and its drivers, the data, and the technology in-house. On the other hand, employees can become entrenched in ways of working and may suffer from learned helplessness that diminishes their ability to excel as analytical leaders. Politics may exist and carry into the newly established analytical function.

- **Hire from outside.** For analytical roles, this is easier said than done, because as of 2016 there is still an acute insufficiency of analytical leadership, especially at the more senior levels. Although the rank-and-file analysts and data scientists who work in ecommerce are found more frequently than in years past, it is still a difficult role for which to find talent. The benefit of hiring from the outside is that someone external can bring perspectives on what has worked in the past, may have business accelerators and ways of working that advance the analytics function, and is removed from politics.

Ultimately, the best path for your company is choosing from one of these alternatives. If you exist in a corporation heavy with politics, where divisions don't collaborate, or where there is little analytical management expertise, you want to hire from outside. If you have an analytical leader in your midst to appoint, in many cases, the company already knows who that is, so enlarge, broaden, or create a new role for them.

Hire the Analytics Leader

Hiring an analytics leader requires the prerequisite of writing and posting a job description, The description can be created from the requirements that justified the investment. The job description should express the job title, the role and responsibilities, the analytical expertise, including the concepts, methods, and technology the leader should be skilled in. The job description should also advocate for the company and give helpful information about the culture, benefits, and salary. After the job description is created, there are several choices for filling the role:

- **An internal human resources team hires from outside via referrals or by surveying the available market.** Most mid-size and large companies have one or more human resources staff who work via established processes for hiring human capital.

- **The hiring manager sources candidates from their network or social media.** In this approach the hiring manager gets no or minimal support and is just told to hire the person. They look for staff on LinkedIn and on employment sites, consult their social networks, and attend industry conferences and events.

- **Recruiters and employment search specialists are used.** For-pay recruiters can be contracted on an individual job-hire basis or for a period of time to find analytics candidates.

My experience has been that recruiters in analytics are generally more successful in finding candidates, but internal human resources teams can be better at getting people to take the offer. Recruiters often work across geographies and have a deep network of experts and a large database of potential candidates. Human resources teams use traditional channels, such as job boards and employment-based social networks. It's a lot to ask hiring managers to find a suitable candidate who is available from their social networks without other support from HR or recruiters. After all, they have their own job to do.

Of course, the right path to hiring an analytics leader depends on the company, the role, the recruiter, the HR team, and the hiring manager. In start-ups, it not uncommon to see hiring managers bring their team from other jobs. Or for some companies to choose not to work with recruiters. Other large brands that are common household names cast a wide net and have HR teams that are better suited than external recruiters to land candidates. Your mileage will vary from mine—and I prefer to use all the channels: myself, my network, the HR team, and recruiters if I can get the budget.

Gather Business Requirements

At this point, the executive who created and gained approval for the business justification to staff for analytics has hired the leader for the analytics team. The primary function of the leader initially will be to understand the business and the needs of their peers and stakeholders and to gather business requirements that will define the scope of work for the analytics team. The business requirements must capture specific business questions, data sources, data sets, and the in-scope deliverables that will prove success when provided. Gathering business requirements at the leadership level requires meeting with people in-person or virtually. To gather business requirements, you can interview people one on one, do large workshops, or small focus groups (Liles 2012). Whatever your method of choice, you must create the materials for eliciting and documenting business requirements, and then you must do the work to capture the requirements, socialize them, and gain approval and sign-off.

Create the Mission and Vision for the Analytics Team

One of the first actions of the analytics leader is to define the team's mission and vision statements. A mission statement is an unwavering declaration made to the key stakeholders that defines the ultimate goal and core purpose of the analytics team over time. It defines what type of work the team will do (and by proxy, what work the team will not do) and sets the frame for what the team will accomplish. The mission statement is often elaborately articulate but could be as simple as "the analytics team mission is to increase gross revenues via conversion analysis and optimization." On the other hand, the vision statement declares the aspirations of the team to accomplish over time. A vision statement could be "the analytics team vision is to embed data-informed decision making in all aspects of the company." The mission statement and vision statement are symbiotic and accompany one another to define the purpose of the team and the outcomes of it (Liles 2012).

Create an Organizational Model

An organizational model is the hierarchical organization chart that defines the management structure and employee roles and responsibilities. It will reflect standard operating procedures and, by virtue of the stated roles and responsibilities, indicate who manages the team, who makes the decisions, and who does the work. There are many ways to create an organizational model for analytics (Davenport et al 2010):

- **Centralized.** This model is essentially what I am laying out in this chapter. One leader owns the function for the entire ecommerce company. This person may be a senior leader, in the case of the CAO or CDO, or may report to one. All aspects, both technical and business, flow through this team; however, the technical resources to support a centralized team will likely, for the most part, live in IT. The centralized team will own the vendor relationships and the budget for business analytics tools.

- **Decentralized.** Decentralized models involve a lack of corporate structure and alignment. An analyst or a team of analysts is under some management structure in each line of business: merchandising, buying, planning, shared services, fulfillment, warehousing, marketing. products, finance, legal, privacy, customer service, IT, and so on. These analysts have self-sustaining capabilities to generate analysis specific to their line of business. Across the company the analysts rarely talk to each other or collaborate. There may be little logic to the size and function of each team.

- **Center of excellence.** This model requires a team of people who act as advisors to other business units in the form of methodologies, tools, technologies, capabilities, models, and expertise that can help the company do analytics and embed it into their daily operations. The center of excellence model works well for large companies, and parallels the centralized model, but the centralized team has a larger responsibility for analytical delivery and outcomes. The center of excellence team, on the other hand, provides reusable components, training, best practices, and other guidance to help lines of business use data and analytics.

- **Functional.** Functional models exist when one or more lines of business hire analysts and analytics managers to serve their function. It's like a decentralized model except the lines of business have the same organizational footprint or size with minor differences. Collaboration occurs across functional areas and shared systems may exist.

- **Consultative.** As in a centralized model, in a consultative model the analytics team is "hired out" by other business units and deployed to address a particular program or project.

- **Hub and spoke.** These models are centralized and consultative at the same time. There is an analytics team that is recognized as a formal corporate structure where all analysts work, but each analyst is assigned to navigate a primary line of business and help the team to which they are assigned use the data.

Hire Staff

After the analytics leader has determined and prioritized business requirements, it is time to start writing job descriptions that identify the key needs for ecommerce analysis. A formal approval process will occur, and after approval the leader will work with an internal human resources team, use a recruiter, or find the hire through her own professional networks. Hiring staff means having a plan for what they will do when they start working. The business requirements and the analytics team mission and vision will guide this work. But there is some other core and foundational work the first hires onto your ecommerce analytics team will do. You want them to have bought into or soon buy into your strategy. Thus, you want these resources to evaluate the current state, assess gaps, and plan for the future state, as discussed in the next few sections.

Assess the Current State Capabilities and Determine the Future State Capabilities

A current state assessment is a core deliverable from the nascent, newly formed analytics team of more than one person. The current state assessment should rank the company on some maturity curve and identify the difference between the company's current capabilities and what the future capabilities could be. Assess the current state maturity against these criteria:

- **Scope** can be assessed in terms of the areas of analytical coverage ranging from individual projects to across the enterprise.
- **Sponsorship** may be from a single person as the sponsor or ranging up to C-level executive sponsorship.
- **Funding** for analytics may not exist or may be self-funded in the case of analytics teams who can justify their business impact.

- **Value** comes from increasing revenue or reducing cost, so analytics teams vary from being immature with no financial contribution to being very mature such that the analytics team monetizes the data in some way and creates new revenue streams—for example, selling the data about the sizes bought for popular clothing back to manufacturers or using the analytics data to power personalization.

- **Architecture** manifests itself in mature companies as self-service analytics based on a data lake or an enterprise data warehouse. The most immature architectures are built-in tools like Excel or loosely cobbled-together data structures and sources that are ungoverned.

- **Governance** like architecture may not exist or it may be cross-enterprise and steered by committees.

- **Data** ranges from untrustworthy to highly trustworthy across the entire company.

- **Communication** in terms of whether any consistent standards are practiced, such as regular meetings, newsletters, office hours, and so on. The most immature analytics teams have no standard cadence for producing or communicating analysis. The most mature companies do.

- **Delivery** can range from people sending data in Excel to elaborate automated architectures that use artificial intelligence and machine learning to produce analysis.

- **Analytical outcomes** may not exist, in the sense that people just release reports, or they may range all the way to predictive and prescriptive analytics that provide insights and make recommendations that guide decision making and positively impact financial performance.

Assess the Current State Technology Architecture and Determine the Future State Architecture

A current state technology assessment begins by identifying the technical architecture used for analytics. This work will be done in coordination with IT. You want to find out what software has been bought, by whom, and under what license and terms. The hardware, if in a data center, or the cloud infrastructure must be understood. The technology for collecting and acquiring, governing and mastering, transforming and preparing, reporting and analyzing, optimizing and predicting, and prescribing and automating must be mapped to an architectural diagram of considerable detail. It is common for an analytics stack to contain the following components, which will be evaluated and examined in a current state architectural assessment:

- **Storage:** The systems like databases and big data processing platforms that house and provide access to raw data.

- **Data management and governance:** The systems and processes that move data from a raw state into a state usable by the business such that all data is consistently defined and accurate, such as master data management (MDM) tools.

- **Analytics platform(s):** The tools and technology used primarily by the analytics team. These tools may be part of one vendor's offerings and may include the functionality for connecting to data, extracting and transforming data, preparing and cleaning data, defining custom data models, unifying and joining data, building reports, visualization, and KPI dashboards, doing data science, and feeding good data to other systems for automation and artificial intelligence.

- **Models:** The scientifically rigorous way of analyzing the data such that statistics and math are applied. In other words, data science! A model may also include data collection, ingestion, processing, and transformation for use in data mining, machine learning, and artificial intelligence.

- **Visualization:** Visual representations of key data elements that are presented in an intuitive way that exposes and illustrates relationships, patterns, outliers, and relationships in the data, including the ability to explore the visualization by filtering, using dimensions, drilling up and down, and applying custom metrics.

- **Self-service:** The tools that stakeholders, outside of the analytics team, use to work with data and analytics. The analytics team, of course, will also use these self-service tools.

Begin Building an Analytics Road Map

The analytics road map is a detailed, multiyear plan that shows conceptually how the analytics team will deliver against business requirements. A road map is often done by fiscal quarter or within periods as short as a week to as long as a year. The technology, data, people, and projects are mapped over a timeline and sequenced in priority order. In this way, a person who looks at the road map will know, for the most part, what work is being done and will be done in the future, when, and for how long until completion; who is doing the work, using what data; and what the projected financial impact could be.

The road map must be constructed from multiple data points. Use the business requirements that were gathered and contextualize them against the known current state capabilities and technical architecture. By triangulating the type of work needed from the predecessor work outlined in this chapter, you can plan the projects to execute to deliver business requirements and know what technology and data you will need, and when to deliver.

A road map is still supported by Agile analytics approaches. The road map, in Agile, is at a very macro level and is used to guide the sequencing of scrums and sprints as work is integrated. Programs become epics. Projects become stories. Road maps, of course, are central to waterfall methodologies.

Train Staff

Although it is expected that analysts who join an ecommerce company will understand the basics of ecommerce analytics, that is not always the case. "Entry level" employees need training, as do people who may have worked in different industries before ecommerce. All employees need training about the company, what it does, how the analytics team fits in, who the stakeholders are, what the supporting processes and teams are that impact analytics, the types of analytics deliverables, and even training on how to use specific technology and tools. Dedicating time to training people how to do their jobs effectively and use the tools provided can only be helpful. Training may

be costly or time-intensive, but it is most often a net positive investment that generates team collaboration and leads to better analytics
outcomes more quickly.

Map Current Processes, Interactions, and Workflows

As your analytics team begins to do analytical work, analysts must
pay attention to the processes they use, the interactions they have
with people, and the workflows in which they are asked to participate alongside other teams. These processes must be documented
and mapped out using process diagramming techniques. The ways
to interact with the team, specifically the handoffs of work to and
from other teams, must be defined. Workflows for interacting with
supporting teams and stakeholders must be created. Processes are a
series of steps that must be executed to accomplish a goal. You may
want to map the following processes:

- **Request for data collection process.** How is data requested
  and what inputs are needed to begin data collection?

- **Prioritization process.** How are different projects prioritized
  so they can be delivered in a sequence that is timely and meets
  requirements?

- **Analytics escalation process.** How are the concerns of analytics escalated to leadership when necessary?

- **Data science model creation process.** How is data science
  accomplished?

The analytics team should map out the following interactions they
will have with other teams and people:

- **Requirements gathering and project elaboration with
  stakeholders.** How are requirements gathered? What is the
  process? What are the artifacts?

- **Communicating and prioritizing projects with IT.** How
  are analytical needs and projects communicated, prioritized,
  and delivered by technology partners?

- **Delivering analytical work.** How is analysis delivered to end users and communicated to stakeholders?

Workflows are sequences you will want to document, including these:

- **Data sourcing from raw to curated.** Who does this work; what stakeholders are involved; what technology is used by whom?
- **Requesting work and responding to work requests.** What is the process for requesting work from the analytics team? What should the team do when a work request is submitted? How should the team respond? What inputs should people requesting work provide to the analytics team?

Build Templates and Artifacts to Support the Analytics Process

Templates are standard formats for analytical deliverables; artifacts are procedural documents that support processes. Templates can be used to communicate analysis and can include items such as reports, dashboards, visualizations, PowerPoints, and related presentation tools. Artifacts can include items such as the analytical plan, report wireframes, visualization mockups, and the documents that support processes, such as the analytics specification, the data specification, and epic and story templates that support Agile analytics.

Create a Supply-and-Demand Management Model

This activity is crucial to newly formed and existing analytics teams. The team needs a model for taking in requests from the business and delivering accepted results back to the business. In practice, such a simple-to-understand set of activities can be very hard to execute for a number of reasons: resources, politics, complexities, technology, priorities, and so on. The activities for managing supply and demand must be mapped out into a model that does the following:

1. Intake requests for demand for work.

2. Capture sufficient details of the demand.

3. Guide the team in how to respond to the work.

4. Prioritize accepted requests and backlog rejected ones.

5. Understand available supply to match against project demand.

6. Align resources to execute and manage them.

7. Manage change, urgencies, and escalations.

8. Communicate status to management, the work team, and requesting stakeholders.

9. Deliver analysis.

10. Gain stakeholder acceptance.

11. Close the work requests after delivery of analysis that has been accepted by the person or team initially requesting the work.

Create an Operating Model for Working with Stakeholders

An operating model is an abstraction of how the analytics team works to accomplish its functions. You build the operating model based on the organizational chart, process, interactions, and workflows you have previously identified and documented. An operating model stitches together all of these items in a way that can be understood by people outside of analytics. The operating model is usually expressed as an authored document or as a presentation that encapsulates a business view of how the analytics team operates as a functional entity and how it interoperates with other business and technology teams. An operating model explains the following about the analytics function:

- Who is the leadership and how do they manage and govern analytics?

- What is the organizational chart and the names, titles, roles, and responsibilities of people on the analytics team?

- What are the processes, workflows, and interactions for analytics and who or what teams participate in them?

- How is demand for analytical work from the business mapped and managed to the available supply of analytical time, resources, and technology?
- What are the analytical services, deliverables, and outputs provided by the team; what are they and why are they important; what is timeline and frequency for delivery?
- What are the success measurements and benchmarks that indicate the analytics team is or has been successful in creating business value?

Use, Deploy, or Upgrade Existing or New Technology

Analysts use tools. All sorts of tools—from operational business intelligence tools, to conversion testing tools, to digital analytics tools, to data preparation tools, to data visualization tools, to data science tools. The list of tools for different analytical work is extensive. New tools are released or updated almost every day. Because you are an analytics leader who has mapped your current toolkit to business requirements and trained people on how to use the tools (assuming you are following the suggested work in this chapter), now your team will be using the tools. The tools will need to be maintained; thus, upgrades will be required. To accomplish these tasks, you will need strong alignment with IT, which you should have had because you created processes, mapped workflows, and socialized your well-conceived operating model for the analytics team. On top of this, you should consider establishing service-level agreements (SLAs) with your company's internal technology teams—and verify the existence of acceptable SLAs for your cloud infrastructure and tools.

Collect or Acquire New Data

One of the ongoing, never-ending 24/7 activities in analytics is the process of data collection. Sites and mobile apps are instrumented with data collection tags and other methods to track behaviors, events, interactions, transactions, goals, and so on. All this data is being captured in one or more databases. Data is being created from purchase orders, fulfillments, inventories, warehouse, and shipping. All this data is part of the overall ecommerce data pipeline, and the analytics team will likely need to expand that pipeline to include new data from existing sources or from new sources entirely. When building a team that is responsible for collecting data, you must hire expertise that can identify the target data to collect, determine how to collect it, implement the data collection, store the data, load and transform the data, and make it available to the system used to do analytics.

Implement a Data Catalog, Master Data Management, and Data Governance

A data catalog is a software system that can contain definitions of data, queries, metadata, and information about values of the data in the database, including database information such as tables, views, indexes, and users. This information is helpful to ecommerce analysts who want to discover what data exists, what values the data has, what other team members created or use the data, the query for the data, and other information to use to navigate the data. Data catalogs also have a management layer where data or queries can be deprecated, the usage understood, and lineage visualized.

Master data management is the name for a set of methods for creating a master set of data residing in one database or file. This master data or master data file is considered to have validity, integrity, and accuracy. It is used as a reference when creating derivative data or to validate new data created. Master data management provides the single source of truth that many companies aspire to create.

Data governance is the name for a set of activities related to the management of all data within a company. Usually governed by committees that are made up of data owners and data stewards, the practice of data governance requires the creation of defined procedures for managing data that is aligned with a plan for continually governing data. The goal of data governance is closely related to the goals of master data management such that a data governor would use master data management principles to ensure the accuracy, usability, integrity, lineage, security, and consistency of data within the organization.

For more information, see Chapter 14, "Governing Data and Ensuring Privacy and Security."

Meet with Stakeholders and Participate in Business Processes, and Then Socialize Analysis on a Regular Cadence and Periodicity

The positive perception by stakeholders of the value and benefit of the analytics team helping them drive their business goals is crucial to success. Stakeholders get value from analysis by being in the loop. The only way to keep people in the loop is for the analytics team to communicate with them on a regularly scheduled cadence. It sounds easy enough; you just need to talk to people, right? But it can be difficult based on work schedules, project demands, and other distractions. It may sound obvious, but there are several ways to communicate analysis, such as in-person, virtually, on the phone, via e-mail, SMS and text, business social networks, the intranet, and so on. The cadence for analytical communication by the analytics leader could be daily with team members, weekly with technology partners, biweekly with your manager, and monthly with business stakeholders. Of course, the right cadence for your team and your company could be totally different. Cadence is less important than delivering excellent work that people like and value. This perception is what will make or break the analytics team. Perception is reality—and you want all stakeholders across the company to perceive the analytics team as experts who do valuable work that helps people improve the business.

Do Analysis and Data Science and Deliver It

Your job is to do analysis and data science and deliver it to people in a timely manner when they want and need it. The primary outcome of successful analytics is the creation of business value. The value is created by people taking action from recommendations based on information found or knowledge learned through analysis. Many times it is not even the analysts themselves who take action on the data. As you can read in this book, there are many types of ecommerce analysis that can be done for different lines of business and stakeholders. At a macro level, Jeffrey Leek, Professor at Johns Hopkins University, identifies several analytical archetypes, which can be applied to many types of ecommerce analysis:

- **Descriptive analytics** does just that. It describes a set of data so that basic statistics are known about it. Usually applied to a larger data set, descriptive analysis involves interpreting data and then describing it. Think of the U.S. Census.

- **Exploratory analytics** attempts to find hidden, unseen, or previously unknown relationships. You explore data to find new linkages and connections between data points just by looking at the data. Correlation may be used to uncover relationships, which may not be casual but associated or dependent. Data visualization is often used to guide exploratory data analysis.

- **Inferential analytics** uses sampling to tell the analyst something about the larger population; thus, statistical error can have a dramatic impact on the meaningfulness and utility of this type of analysis. Inferential modeling is routed in statistics.

- **Predictive analytics** is a set of mathematical and statistical methods that attempt to predict an outcome from a set of data. The outcome is not caused by the variables in the data set; it is dependent on them. In that sense, the proper construction of the model, including dimension reduction and variable weighting, can have a material impact on the predictive power of the model.

- **Prescriptive analytics** uses predictive techniques and other methods to automatically suggest the best possible decision to take based on all available options. It is probably the most complex and challenging type of data science to do.

- **Causal analytics** attempts to understand the influence or impact of one variable or set on another variable. Causality is a difficult concept to prove, and thus great lengths are taken to use random data to determine causality.

- **Algorithmic or mechanistic analytics** seeks to explain the relationship, influence, and interdependence of a set of variables such that changes to one variable are understood in the way they impact other variables. Algorithmic approaches to analysis can involve machine learning that uses deterministic approaches with no randomness. Any randomness is considered to be error. As you might imagine, algorithmic analysis is complex (Smith 2013).

For more information, see Chapter 3, "Methods and Techniques for Ecommerce Analysis."

Lead or Assist with New Work Resulting from Analytical Processes

Analytics teams don't just want to "live on an island." There will certainly be times when the team must cloister itself away and have long uninterrupted periods to do analytical work. And there will also be other times when the analytics team must lead or assist in leading with new work resulting from analytical outcomes. To ensure that analytics is focused on the stakeholders and not just on doing analytics, it is suggested that you do the following:

- **Set up regular checkpoints.** In these checkpoints, collaborate with team members and talk to stakeholders to find out what analytical work will be needed in the future.
- **Get involved with recurring business planning meetings outside of analytics.** Go to meetings hosted by other teams. The analytics team has a right to be there if that team wants the analytics team to do work for them or with them.
- **Create a queue in the ticketing system you use.** If your company uses a ticketing system, like Jira, then you should create a way for people to "ticket" analytics work. While work tickets can be cumbersome at first, they make work transparent. Ticketing systems also have reports that can show what's been done by whom and for whom and what still needs to be done.
- **Host office hours.** Open up the doors of your office or book a conference room in which the analytics team and the experts on it can meet with stakeholders. In these office hours, analysis can be discussed, data can be reviewed, and future work

determined. Office hours are also helpful when stakeholders need more guidance or benefit more from "higher touch" analytics services.

Document and Socialize the Financial Impact and Business Outcomes Resulting from Analysis

To prove the impact of data, ironically, you need data. In this case the data you need is financial data that demonstrates that analytical work has been used to improve the business and create net positive outcomes. In the optimal world the financial estimates you create to justify your company's investment in analytics must be tied back to actual outcomes. You must quantify the financial outcomes of business programs and projects in which analytics contributed in some way. To influence people with analytics, you need to socialize your analysis. Analytical outputs and deliverables must be made available to the wider corporate audience; project status and results must be communicated; stakeholders must be updated on progress toward their expectations. Some of the ways to document and socialize analysis include publishing successful work on the intranet, holding meetings to highlight business impact of past work, creating an efficacy dashboard that shows what the analytics team has done and the impact, creating infographics to show key data, doing periodic business reviews with stakeholders, and so on.

Continue to Do Analysis, Socialize It, and Manage Technology While Emphasizing the Business Impact Ad Infinitum

Analytics is an ongoing process that continues day by day, week by week, month by month. The analytics team must continue to analyze data, socialize it, and manage the technology that supports it. Because you have business requirements and an organizational structure including an operating model, as well as the artifacts to support the development, creation, and rollout of analytics, you simply need to continue to do what you said you would do—and make sure you are answering the key questions that can help stakeholders do their jobs more effectively. Here are some tips that work for guiding how you continue to do analysis, socialize, and prove the effectiveness of the analytics team:

- **Double down on what's working.** If people like the work and it is providing business benefit, consider doing more of it more frequently. Or model and apply the successful approaches to analytical work in one line of business to another.

- **Pay attention to industry and technology trends.** Keeping up to date with what thought leaders, experts, and practitioners are saying about the industry keeps the team current in their methods.

- **Publish a newsletter.** Sending out a companywide e-mail or an e-mail to a smaller set of stakeholders that contains a newsletter is helpful. The newsletter can contain data, analysis, visualizations, a list of available analyses, the team's business impact, and so on.

- **Do periodic education sessions.** Meeting with employees and explaining to people what the analytics team does and how to work with the team is important.

- **Demonstrate best practices for self-service tools.** The team may want to train people or guide them on how to best use analytical tools to get the data they need without requesting work from the analytics team.

Manage Change and Support Stakeholders

In the best of times, there will be change to manage. In the worst of times, there will be escalations and critical urgencies and even crises to manage. Change management refers to a methodology or set of techniques that enable a team to transition to a new state. The new state may result from the introduction of new products, new promotions, new customer types, and marketing externalities that impact ecommerce (such as various holidays and seasonality). When managing change, the leader of the analytics team needs to take a top-down approach that focuses on helping people adapt to the change. Change is handled differently based on your company's approach to delivering analytics. For example, Agile analytics processes are more flexible to adapt to change than are annual, quarterly, or waterfall planning processes. When considering how to manage change and support stakeholders, consider how the following concepts can help you:

- **Change management process.** Document the change management process for analytics.
- **Quarterly analytics reviews.** Review what the data is saying about the business quarterly.
- **Project postmortems.** Explore why projects and analytical work were successful (or not) so you can reuse what worked and fix what didn't work.
- **Agile sprint and scrum masters.** Appoint analytics team members to work Agilely and even to learn how to be scrum masters.
- **Planning committees.** Create planning committees to align the work of the analytics team with other teams and business plans.

While I have discussed a universal process for building an analytics team and organization, it is even harder to build analytics culture. My friend, Gary Angel, in his book and blog *Measuring the Digital World*, put some thought into how to build analytic culture. His take is that there are work and work products that the analytics team creates and manages that help create analytics culture. Gary believes, and I tend to agree, that things like analytics reporting and dashboards, a cadence of communication, having an advisor work with the C-level, and "walking the walk" are all helpful. In addition, he cites having tagging standards, metadata, "rapid" VoC data, testing plans, doing segmentation, annotating data with narratives, and a focus on continuous improvement are useful. Other activities like having an independent expert audit the analytics function yearly and having frameworks that define the data to be used to evaluate success can be beneficial.

The process for building an analytics team involves each of the steps I've outlined previously. The order in which I've presented these activities, though linear, is a good sequence to follow but you may do it differently. And that is okay. Of course, all companies are different, and some of the activities I've identified may already be occurring or, if not, may be occurring in other business areas. In this case, the analytics team should leverage past work and not do something different. For example, there may be standard business justification templates and models for justifying investment or proving the financial impact. Overall, however, the universal approach I've outlined captures how to build an analytics organization in ecommerce and even in other industries. For more information, please read my book *Building a Digital Analytics Organization.*

16

The Future of Ecommerce Analytics

The future of ecommerce analytics is challenging to predict, but it is bright and ever-evolving. As you've read in this book, there are many ecommerce subject areas and approaches to analysis, which future technical, academic, and scientific progress will continue to advance and expand. Although the future will inevitably lead to the creation of new technologies, architectures, tools, models, algorithms, and methodologies for advanced analysis, this chapter lists what could be on future road maps for ecommerce analytics. The chapter is framed less on how to analyze data. Instead, I present new themes, leitmotifs, concepts, and capabilities that will assist in infusing analytics across an ecommerce business.

By talking to practitioners and business leaders and from professional work, one can begin to see the signals of what the future may hold. We live in a cluetrain world where analysts are increasingly required to seek out and use data that exists in many different sources both inside and outside the company. The data isn't only quantitative; it's qualitative. Data volumes can be enormous, and many ecommerce companies have "big data." This huge amount of data collected is not usually ready for immediate use; it needs to be cleaned and prepared, which is why data scientists spend inordinate amounts of time getting data ready to analyze. Meanwhile, the demand for analysis in ecommerce business continues to grow, and people have higher expectations than ever that data can help them. As a result, analytical projects are numerous and increasingly complex. Today's ecommerce analytics projects require cross-functional team collaboration and the reuse of existing data and analysis. Increasingly analysts are, quite correctly, tasked with identifying financial impact. I hope you've gathered by reading this book that I strongly believe analysis done for business-people must be tied back to improving the financial performance and the health of the business. Meanwhile, there is an expectation not only that analysis will be descriptive, exploratory, explanatory, and inferential but that it is possible to predict outcomes and use algorithms to prescribe the best course of action to take. Although theoretically true, in order to do advanced analysis, you need to have the right data to do it. And companies sometimes don't have the data or the data they think is applicable isn't. To course-correct, analytics projects can be handled like IT projects, but that is not optimal. Analysis projects, unlike IT projects, may not produce an outcome that is expected; sometimes you have to experiment and fail before you find the right data to analyze or the right model and algorithm to use. Fortunately in analytics, like in life, failure can be the mother of success. Thus, collaboration and socialization of analysis is important to ensure the business, technology, and the analytics team are aligned on work, expectations for output, and what the desired outcomes for analytics could be, including the possibility to learn from failure. Meanwhile, analysts are required to use multiple technologies to do their work. No one tool does it all. In fact, there are hundreds of software tools and technologies for doing analytical work—from collection, to metadata, to processing, to data modeling, to data preparation and cleaning, to reporting, visualization, analysis, and data science. Future software capabilities must accommodate enabling analytical work in these disparate, global heterogeneous environments that contain assorted data types.

But we need to keep in mind that technology is not the panacea for analytics. People are the solution for advancing ecommerce analytics in such a fast-growing, rapidly evolving ecommerce ecosystem. In this ecosystem, there are companies of all sizes—from major brands, smaller companies, start-ups, and even individuals selling products online in most industries. Competition makes ecommerce a challenging industry in which to win customers for the long term. All but the largest brands are fierce competitors to each other using discounts and razor-thin margins to grow market share and a share of wallet. Ecommerce companies start up, try to build excellent and creative experiences across different devices, and either succeed or wither and then fail. The global ecommerce market is international, with ecommerce brands popular in some countries and unheard of in other countries. For example, Taobao in China lists 800 million products and has 500 million customers; Tmall in China has 181 million customers; Flipkart, Jabong, and Snapdeal in India are massive ecommerce companies (Joson 2015). There are small players selling specialized goods on sites they own, and marketplaces where multiple vendors offer their products and services, and then, of course, major players in ecommerce most people know as household brand names, like Amazon, eBay, Walmart, BestBuy, Alibaba. The future of ecommerce analytics must address global, large-company concerns and also the needs of medium, small, and individually owned ecommerce businesses.

As the future progresses, the ecommerce companies, user experiences, and even device form factors will change in new ways that need to be measured. For established companies that have physical stores, omnichannel analytics requires understanding customers wherever they shop both online and also back at the store. For example, there is a trend in being able to pick up online orders at nearby physical store locations. This merging of the offline and online customer experiences requires the analyst to consider new methods of fulfillment and how they impact path to purchase and the consumer mind-set. To compete with in-store pickup, online-only ecommerce providers are speeding ordered products into the home with extremely quick delivery—one hour or less shipping from Amazon is being tested right now. Traditional shipping processes in which delivery is made by vehicles owned by a shipping company could shift toward drones or even self-driving cars ready to deliver core products. All these new methods for fulfillment will need to be tracked and analyzed. Predictive delivery based on customers' purchasing patterns for core goods may be offered as part of new subscription models. When ecommerce features are integrated into products that are connected to the Internet, new channels for ecommerce become a reality. The Internet of Things and the even more ambitious concept, the Internet of Everything, will create new behaviors related to products and the ability for customers to interact with the products, even buying replacement parts or related products directly from within the product. The ecommerce experience itself will become virtual when virtual reality begins to be mainstream; trying on and buying a shirt will never be the same with Facebook's Oculus. The dynamic personalization of most aspects of ecommerce based on knowledge derived from behavioral, transactional, and other customer data will create new experiences that are truly individualized. These experiences will be augmented with virtual assistants that use conversation to drive commerce. You will be able to tell robots what to buy for you in the brave new world. Intent and context will be in deep learning and used by artificial intelligence to create new commerce opportunities both in the physical and virtual worlds. The future of commerce isn't in *Minority Report*; it's right now in the apps on your smartphone and in the pervasive Internet and home networking, and it's being thought up as you read by innovative companies, including but not limited to Facebook, Google, and Apple.

To understand and make sense of all these potential new changes and advances in ecommerce experiences and functionality, a solid data and analytics foundation is of course required. This foundation must take into account privacy, security, governance, and management of data, while enabling analysis of behavior, marketing, products, orders, and customers within an analytical-driven and informed organization. The entirety of this book discusses and describes the what, why, and how of starting, building, and/or evolving your approach to ecommerce analytics. Following are ways to think about how to extend or build analytical capabilities for the future, categorized as follows:

- **Data collection and preparation.** New technologies that increase the efficiency and effectiveness of collecting, ingesting, cleaning, and unifying data will increase in importance and change the work done by analytics teams.

- **Data experiences.** Ecommerce experiences will be driven from data in ways beyond current personalization and collaborative filtering. These include guided buying experiences driven by Chatbots and artificial intelligence, augmented reality, virtual reality, wearables, the IoT, and the IoE.

- **Future analytics and technology capabilities.** These capabilities will change the role of the analyst, including the type of work analysts will do in the future, the emphasis of how tools enable people to do analysis, and the role of data mining, machine learning, and artificial intelligence on replacing and augmenting human work.

The Future of Data Collection and Preparation

Analysts in 2016 are commonly asked to analyze different sources of data in order to answer a single business question. As I've described in this book, systems that generate and store data can exist inside and outside the ecommerce company. Traditional ways of dealing with all this data were to replicate some or all of it using operation data stores, ETL software, and data staging environments to create a data warehouse from which governed data could be extracted and used. As described in Chapter 13, "Integrating Data and Analysis to Drive Your Ecommerce Strategy," the long durations it can take to load and extract data from traditional data warehousing technologies are causing companies to rethink their approach. The future could hold these possible realities:

- **Ecommerce data lakes will rise in importance.** Instead of storing data in raw formats that need to be extracted, transformed, and loaded in centralized databases, ecommerce companies will manage data by keeping it in raw formats within a data lake. Data will then be accessed from the data lake and enabled for business use by data storage and processing technologies such as Hadoop and Spark. Ecommerce platforms, of course, will still underpin and provide the operational foundation for ecommerce sites to work. But the volumes of data generated by the various components in ecommerce architectures beyond the platform, such as digital analytics, product databases, social media, audience data, and market research, will be pooled into data lakes, so the business is aware of the existence of the data and is ready to begin the process of preparing it for use. This could lead to ecommerce DMP (data management platforms) as a layer on top of the data lake.

- **Data cataloging and data profiling will become a concept to consider for ecommerce.** If all the data is stored in a data lake and contemporary big data technologies allow the analysts to work with it, then how does the analyst know what data is available? The answer exists in building capabilities for ecommerce analysts to create data catalogs of the data, which include data definitions, canonical queries, and data lineage back to the original source before the data laking. In addition, data that is available must be profiled in raw and curated states to make its content and other statistical measures understandable. In this way, data profiling helps an analyst understand whether the data in the data catalog is relevant and applicable to the analytical effort.

- **Data preparation will be done by the analytics team.** Currently it has been anecdotally claimed that 80% of a data scientist's time is spent not on modeling, testing, refining, and operationalizing advanced analytics, but rather on cleaning data so that the data can be used. A related challenge upstream is that technology teams are often faulted for not having accurate data for business purposes, or data availability is latent and comes too late for business usage, or the data can't be joined or unified in the desired way. In the future, ecommerce analytics teams will take, in the worst case, raw data, and in the best case, curated data, from technical systems that are governed. They will use data preparation tools to clean data, join data, and script the data cleaning and joining processes so that the prep work can be reused again and again on the same data set. Machine intelligence, data visualization, and learning algorithms will assist the analyst in finding missing values, integrity issues, and other data problems in huge data sets, in ways that just can't be done in Excel or using SQL. No longer will analytics teams have to work with data of questionable quality or be reliant on IT or insufficient software that can work only in aggregate. The analytics team, instead, will have data preparation tools that enable them to access data, create a copy, and clean and prepare data in a systematic and reusable way suited to analysis and data science.

- **New data sources will arise from which data will be generated and collected.** The rise of the Internet of Things and the Internet of Everything will be embedded in consumer goods, from appliances to wearables, to augmented reality and virtual reality. This will of course change how customers interact with products. These interactions are behavioral data to be captured and shared, when chosen by the user, with ecommerce companies that can do something to use and act on the data. Waterproof shoes get wet? The sensor starts the warranty process. Temperature changing as detected by your wearable shirt? Render an experience in which warmer clothes are suggested on the next login. These examples may seem futuristic, but such use-cases are feasible in 2016.

The Future Is Data Experiences

In the future, people will generate behavioral data from engaging in ecommerce, and products will generate data that ecommerce companies will want to collect and analyze in order to act on it. Suppliers will generate data. New data types in the future, when combined with available data types now, will enable the creation of data experiences. The combination of customer data, behavioral data, biometric data, mobile data, profile data, customer service data, transaction data, demographic data, and so on opens up avenues of innovation to build consumer experiences based on data.

Data experiences are machine-driven interactions with ecommerce functionality, regardless of device or location, in which the user's experience is generated or guided from data known about the customer. The simplest example of data experience in 2016 is personalization. Personalization can be driven by recommendations and predictions of what products a known customer may buy next, or the look and feel of a site may be rendered based on preferences. The more an ecommerce site knows about a customer, the richer the types of data experiences can be. To drive these experiences, ecommerce will continue to personalize, but the experiences will be hypercontextual. That means that the ecommerce experiences will appear at the right place, at the right time, with the right offer. Amazon's Dash Button is a physical example of this Internet of Things–based hyper-contextuality that leads to data experiences. Say that you are nearing the end of your bottle of detergent. You push the Dash Button to order the detergent. Doing so may order the product, but it will also give data to Amazon that enables them to understand your purchasing frequency such that predictions could be made about when you might run out of detergent. So in the future Amazon can start to automatically send you detergent delivered just-in-time before you run out. Or your refrigerator detects that your water filter is low, so it prompts you on the touch-interface on the door to reorder. Your coffeemaker and refrigerator share data that estimates when you might run out of coffee, so it gets ordered. Your thermometer detects a rise in your basal temperature, so your mobile phone suggests a remedy. Just-in-time delivery won't just be made by suppliers; ecommerce sites will use analytics to deliver needed products just-in-time to customers.

These types of data experiences are possible only if many data sources can be stitched together, and only if patterns and behavior can be modeled, predicted, and prescribed and then integrated into business rules and operationalized into ecommerce functionality. This area is rich for innovation. Virtual reality and augmented reality are examples of technologies in which data and analysis renders the experience, and of course commerce will evolve on these platforms. Artificial intelligence will continue to push into ecommerce. Commerce will become conversational, in the sense that you can order products by speaking to a virtual buying assistant. The ecommerce experience could, theoretically, converse with the customer using AI or virtual reality during the browsing, buying, or customer service experiences.

Data experience management will emerge to complement customer experience management. As ecommerce companies create data experiences, analysts will become leaders, managers, and participants on the ecommerce teams that are defining, creating, and ensuring these future capabilities.

Future Analytics and Technology Capabilities

New capabilities for analytics tools and technologies will continue to evolve and be released in the future. That's an easy call to make. What's harder to identify is what the features and capabilities of these new tools and technologies will be. It's clear to me that privacy and data security will be a foremost global concern. Data breaches and customer data losses can't occur, and analytics tools will comply with initiatives and laws in these areas. Business stakeholders and even analytical teams will rely less on information technology professionals for assistance with tools that create data pipelines and data flows to other systems. Enhanced abilities to use natural language, both as a voice-activated method for retrieving data and as a query language, will emerge. Collaboration features to bring together people across geography in both real and virtual environments will grow in importance. The emphasis on predictive will move toward prescriptive recommendations to enable the prediction. Machine learning will continue to be involved in higher-level analysis that touches the business, such that machines will do some of the grunt work of analysts—and eventually artificial intelligence and the analytical automation that will result will change what it means to be an analyst. Let's dig into some of these future themes here:

- **Abstraction of data flows and data pipelines.** Currently, the data pipeline from collection to storage to ingestion to curation and governance to cleaning and preparation to analysis, visualization, and data science is fragmented across systems. Although it is unlikely that one tool will be released that does it all, future analytics technology will enable analysts to create a visual abstraction of data flows and the data pipeline. From this abstraction of systems, business rules, analytical methods, and a topology of the objects necessary to create a data flow and analyze the data will exist. Each node in the flow will be an object that can be worked with and defined for use to yield the end result. For example, you might have an object representing a file, another representing the database, others representing data transformations, and others representing applied analytical models through which the data is analyzed. Each object can be explored, configured, and made interoperable and integrated with other objects to weave and stitch together data flows into data pipelines that enable analytics. Objects could be interacted with in augmented or virtual reality.

- **Encryption.** SSL usage is widespread today for processing ecommerce transactions. Customer data, on the other hand, may not be encrypted, which can represent a security and privacy risk. Analysts in the future will deal with more encrypted data, especially when related to the customer. Even fairly innocuous data like geographic data may be encrypted. Analysts will have to understand the implications of encryption on their work—from a consideration for data availability to the requirement to have a decryption key. As Secure Function Evaluation

(SFE) scales and runs faster, it's conceivable that various types of customer analysis could be supported by SFE.

- **Natural language search and conversational speech-enabled features.** Querying languages will become simpler and more abstract in the future. The requirement for less technical businesspeople to be able to explore data will create capabilities that allow for the use of natural language and even speech to analyze data. At the simplest, these voice commands will be structured sufficiently to retrieve data, such as "What products are most popular today?" In the future it is entirely possible that speech can be used to direct the type of analysis applied, as in "Run a polynomial regression on data set one." For now in 2016, the ability to enter queries in natural language to retrieve data and analytics is a step in this direction.

- **Automation for self-service and guided-service.** Business will continue to demand timely data—that is, data when absolutely needed. The trend for self-service will go beyond giving users the ability to use filters and drill up and down on data. Future tools will take data preferences, business rules, and behavior as input to automate the delivery of reporting and analysis. Business users will specify the data they want to see. The rules for using the data will be understood from an existing semantic layer. Natural language generation technologies will create complex and relevant written reporting in far less time than a human could. Analysts will become less authors of narratives but more of curators and editors of machine-generated narrative analysis.

- **Collaboration.** Features for collaboration are increasingly more common in analytics tools in 2016. Most typically, these features enable analysts to enter comments and provide qualitative feedback (like star rankings), threaded discussions, and forums. Some tools may enable a person to be designated the business owner of a particular report. New forms of collaboration in analytics tools will include virtual collaboration rooms, including video, audio, and visual immersion into data leading to virtual-reality environments.

- **Ease of using predictive analysis.** The application of pre-built models for analyzing data to answer a specific business question will require less data science. Instead of having to solely rely on a data scientist or data science team, analytics models will be prebuilt and then customized to use-cases. Data will be mapped to the models, and the output in its simplest form will be narratives providing predictive results, in formats easily understood by businesspeople. Tools will scan data and use artificial intelligence to determine the best model to apply and may even start testing data in models to refine the predictive power—with the data scientist as a higher-level shepherd of automated processes as opposed to coding them.
- **Artificial intelligence and machine learning.** These advanced and powerful innovations in computer science will enable prescriptive analytics for ecommerce to become mainstream over the next ten years. Cognitive computing will impact customers, analysts, and employees. Prediction of what might happen will evolve into applications that suggest the best decision to make. Customer experiences will learn customers' preferences and go beyond personalization to interaction and guided intelligence as part of "data experiences." You will be able to tell your ecommerce provider to buy you specific items at specific prices, and based on your expressed preferences and some machine-guided interactions, items will be bought for you and sent to you (without your providing a real-time approval or choosing to buy them). The brain of your house will know when something needs to be replaced and will automatically order it for you. Within an ecommerce site, an artificial intelligence will be able to select or identify the best products, promotions, and offers and render them in real time to prospects and customers. Chatbots for ecommerce browsing, purchasing, and servicing will be built on top of AI frameworks.

As you work in ecommerce and use analytics in a noble quest for the truth, you must keep an eye on the future to guide how you evolve today's innovations into tomorrow's capabilities. Ecommerce analysis is critical to companies that sell online. It is a capability achieved through more than just tagging a site and looking at the data and reports using one tool and then extracting that data into Excel. The best ecommerce analytics collect raw data, prepare and curate it, understand the data's profile and lineage, and govern it so it can be analyzed and applied to the highest and best business purpose. Defined data governed by committee, often led by a chief data officer, is managed by line-of-business stewards. Analysts work within an organization structure, which when centralized or constructed as a center of excellence can be led by a chief analytics officer. Controlled data foundations yield usable and accurate data, which can then be ingested in analytical sandboxes where descriptive analysis, reporting, data visualization, and data science can be done. The resulting analysis, prepared automatically through AI and natural language generation or manually, is then socialized through in-person meetings and delivered in online collaborative environments. Raw, curated, or analyzed data may also be streamed into models that automate prediction, guide toward prescriptions, and enable machine-driven, intelligent data experiences. Within the innovative and fascinating current and future ecommerce environment, analysts have an important role to play in creating business value. The data collected, defined, governed, and analyzed by analytics teams is crucial to ecommerce success. Skillful analysis maximizes ecommerce opportunities, creating business value today and promising to create even more future value. Good luck.

Bibliography

Adams, Ben. "eCommerce Platforms." Function 22. www.slideshare.net/benadams12/e-commerce-platforms. Accessed June 20, 2015.

Agrawal, R., A. Somani, and Y. Xu. "Storage and Querying of E-Commerce Data." In VLDB. Morgan Kaufmann, 2001. N.p.

Ash, Tim. "Taguchi Sucks for Landing Pages." May 15, 2008. http://searchenginewatch.com/article/2054202/Taguchi-Sucks-for-Landing-Page-Testing. Accessed February 7, 2015.

Ash, Tim. *Landing Page Optimization.* Indianapolis, IN: Wiley, 2008.

Bain and Company. "Customer Segmentation." June 10, 2015. www.bain.com/publications/articles/management-tools-customer-segmentation.aspx. Accessed July 18, 2015.

Banerjee, Debajyoti. "Pricing Strategies." www.spookybin.com/study-zone/marketing-for-beginners/pricing-strategies/. Accessed September 20, 2015.

Barotocha, Kamil. "The Path to Enlightenment in Ecommerce." July 18, 2015. www.kbartocha.com/2015/07/18/the-path-to-enlightenment-in-e-commerce/.

Berger, P. D., and N. I. Nasr. 1998. "Customer Lifetime Value: Marketing Models and Applications." *Journal of Interactive Marketing,* 12: 17-30. doi:10.1002/(SICI)1520-6653(199824)12:1<17::AID-DIR3>3.0.CO;2-K.

Bokman, Alec, Lars Fiedler, Jesko Perrey, and Andrew Pickersgill. "Five Facts: How Customer Analytics Boosts Corporate Performance." July 2014. www.mckinseyonmarketingandsales.com/

five-facts-how-customer-analytics-boosts-corporate-performance. Accessed August 22, 2015.

Brohan, Mark. "Mobile Commerce is Now 30% of All US Ecommerce." August 18, 2015. https://www.internetretailer.com/2015/08/18/mobile-commerce-now-30-all-us-e-commerce. Accessed January 4, 2016.

Campbell, Christopher. "Top Five Differences between Data Lakes and Data Warehouses." January 26, 2015. www.blue-granite.com/blog/bid/402596/Top-Five-Differences-between-Data-Lakes-and-Data-Warehouses. Accessed October 17, 2015.

Campbell, Kunle. "14 Key Ecommerce Events to Track in Google Analytics" October 8, 2014. www.practicalecommerce.com/articles/74215-14-Key-Ecommerce-Events-to-Track-in-Google-Analytics. Accessed May 21, 2015.

Chatterjee, P., D. L. Hoffman, and T. P. Novak. "Modeling the Clickstream: Implications for Web-Based Advertising Efforts." *Marketing Science* vol. 22, no. 4 (2003).

Chen, P. P. "The Entity-Relationship Model: Toward a Unified View of Data." ACM Transactions on Database Systems. January 1976.

Cohen, Steve, and Paul Markowitz. "Renewing Market Segmentation: Some New Tools to Correct Old Problems." ESOMAR 2002 Congress Proceedings. ESOMAR, pp. 595-612.

Comscore. "Final 2015 Desktop Online Holiday Sales Reach $56.4 Billion, Up 6 Percent vs. Year Ago." January 8, 2016. http://www.comscore.com/Insights/Press-Releases/2016/1/Final-2015-Desktop-Online-Holiday-Sales-Reach-56-Billion-Up-6-Percent-vs-Year-Ago. Accessed January 12, 2016.

Converto. "Choosing an Attribution Solution." www.convertro.com/wp-content/uploads/2013/12/Choosing-an-Attribution-Solution.pdf. Accessed September 13, 2015.

Croarkin, Carrol, Paul Tobias, and Chelli Zey. *Engineering Statistics Handbook.* Gaithersburg, MD: Institute, 2001.

Crook, Thomas, Brian Frasca, Ron Kohavi, and Roger Longbotham. "Seven Pitfalls to Avoid When Running Controlled Experiments on

the Web." 2009. N.p., n.d. http://dl.acm.org/citation.cfm?doid=
1557019.1557139. Accessed September 5, 2015.

Croxen-John, Dan. "Step-by-Step Guide to Online Merchandising."
June 30, 2011. www.awa-digital.com/blog/step-by-step-guide-to-
online-merchandising. Accessed April 12, 2015.

Cutroni, Justin. "Tracking Ecommerce Transactions with Universal
Analytics." March 22, 2013. http://cutroni.com/blog/2013/03/22/
tracking-ecommerce-transactions-with-universal-analytics/. Accessed
April 12, 2015.

Davenport, Thomas H. "Realizing the Potential of Retail Analytics—
Plenty of Food for Those with the Appetite." 2009. Babson College.

Davenport, Thomas H., and Jeanne G. Harris. *Competing on
Analytics: The New Science of Winning.* Boston, MA: Harvard
Business School, 2007.

Davenport, Thomas H., Jeanne G. Harris, and Robert Morison.
Analytics at Work: Smarter Decisions, Better Results. Boston, MA:
Harvard Business, 2010.

DeNale, Rebecca. "Quarterly Retail E-Commerce Sales." November
17, 2015. https://www.census.gov/retail/mrts/www/data/pdf/ec_
current.pdf. Accessed November 29, 2015.

De Vries, Andrie. "Using Survival Models for Marketing Attribution." July 23, 2013. http://blog.revolutionanalytics.com/2013/07/
using-survival-models-for-marketing-attribution.html. Accessed
March 28, 2015.

Digital Analytics Association. "Standards Committee Deliverables."
www.digitalanalyticsassociation.org/?page=standards. Digital Analytics Association. N.p., n.d. CC BY. Accessed February 8, 2015.

Dorian, Alicia. "50 Mobile Facts And Stats Every Merchant Needs
To Know." May 19, 2015. https://www.payfirma.com/blog/
50-mobile-facts-and-stats-every-merchant-needs-to-know/.
Accessed January 15, 2016.

Eisenberg, Bryan, Jeffrey Eisenberg, and Lisa T. Davis. *Waiting for
Your Cat to Bark? Persuading Customers When They Ignore
Marketing.* Nashville: Nelson Business, 2006.

Emarketer. "Top-Down vs. Bottom-Up Attribution." December 27, 2013. www.emarketer.com/Article/Top-Down-vs-Bottom-Up-Attribution/1010479. Accessed May 23, 2015.

Few, Stephen. "Common Pitfalls in Dashboard Design." https://www.perceptualedge.com/articles/Whitepapers/Common_Pitfalls.pdf. Accessed May 9, 2015.

Fitzgerald, Craig. "Special Report—Inbound Marketing: The 4 Stages of Engagement." May 1, 2014. www.targetmarketingmag.com/article/top-10-inbound-marketing-tactics-mapping-content-marketing-customers/. Accessed October 25, 2015.

Frank, Ulrich. "Modeling Products for Versatile E-Commerce Platforms—Essential Requirements and Generic Design Alternatives." University of Kobelenz.

Friedman, Vitaly. 2008. "Data Visualization and Infographics." in Graphics, Monday Inspiration. January 14, 2008.

Google. "About Enhanced Ecommerce." https://support.google.com/analytics/answer/6014841?hl=en. Accessed August 10, 2015.

Google. "Attribution Model Overview." https://support.google.com/analytics/answer/1662518?hl=en. Accessed December 30, 2015.

Gross, Phil. "Top-Down vs. Bottom-Up Attribution: Why Meeting in the Middle Is Just Right." September 23, 2015. www.cmo.com/articles/2015/9/14/topdown-vs-bottomup-attribution-why-meeting-in-the-middle-is-just-right.html. Accessed November 1, 2015.

Guest, Gregory, Steven Guest, Kathleen MacQueen, and Emily Namey. *Applied Thematics Analysis.* Thousand Oaks, CA: Sage, 2011.

Gupta, Sunil, Dominique Hanssens, Bruce Hardie, Wiliam Kahn, V. Kumar, Nathaniel Lin, Nalini Ravishanker, and S. Sriram. "Modeling Customer Lifetime Value." *Journal of Service Research* vol. 9, no. 2. Sage Publications: November 2006.

Halbrook, Michael. "Advanced Web & Store Attribution in Insight." March 29, 2012. http://blogs.adobe.com/digitalmarketing/analytics/advanced-web-store-attribution-in-insight/. Accessed July 12, 2015.

Hastie, T., R. Tibshirani, and J. Friedman. *The Elements of Statistical Learning: Data Mining, Inference and Prediction, 2nd ed.,* New York: Springer, 2009.

Hillstrom, Kevin. "Ecommerce Buyer Behavior." 2015. https://rjmetrics.com/resources/reports/ecommerce-buyer-behavior. Accessed December 6, 2015.

Hirschman, E. C. "People as Products: Analysis of a Complex Marketing Exchange." *Journal of Marketing* 51 (1987): 98-108.

Hughes, Chase. "Customer Acquisition Cost: The One Metric That Can Determine Your Company's Fate." https://blog.kissmetrics.com/customer-acquisition-cost/. Accessed November 15, 2015.

Isson, Jean Paul, and Jesse Harriott. *Win with Advanced Business Analytics: Creating Business Value from Your Data.* Hoboken, NJ: John Wiley & Sons, 2013.

Jirafe. "Ecommerce Demo." http://demo.jirafe.com. Accessed October 17, 2015.

Joson, Linjo. "Top 10 E-commerce Sites in the World Based on Visitors." June 2, 2015. http://www.dollarfry.com/worlds-top-10-ecommerce-sites-alexa-rank-basis/. Accessed December 22, 2015.

Kimelfeldt, Yaakov. "Optimize Digital Touchpoints: Attribution or Path to Purchase?" May 20 2013. https://blog.compete.com/2013/05/20/optimize-digital-touchpoints-attribution-or-path-to-purchase/. Accessed: September 19, 2015.

Kotler, Philip. *Marketing Management: Analysis, Planning, Implementation and Control.* Prentice Hall, 1999.

Kumar, Sanjay. "eCommerce Platform—Components Overview." http://thinking.edynamic.net/ecommerce-platform-components-overview. Accessed April 11, 2015.

Lacey, Michelle. "Statistical Topics." N.d. www.stat.yale.edu/Courses/1997-98/101/stat101.htm. Accessed January 24, 2015.

Laja, Peep. *How to Build Websites that Sell: The Scientific Approach to Websites.* Markitekt, ConversionXL: February 2013.

Laja, Peep. *Master the Essentials of Conversion Optimization: Experts' Approach to Optimization.* Markitekt, ConversionXL: January 2013.

Laja, Peep. "Quick Course on Effective Website Copywriting." https://www.smashingmagazine.com/2012/05/quick-course-on-effective-website-copywriting/. Accessed January 24, 2015.

Latham, Steve. "Interactive Musings: Attribution and Engagement Mapping." July 10, 2013. www.attribution101.com/tag/engagement-mapping/. Accessed August 9, 2015.

Liles, Jill. "Methods for Eliciting—Not Gathering—Requirements." May 14, 2012. www.batimes.com/articles/methods-for-eliciting-not-gathering-requirements.html. Accessed June 13, 2015.

Lindauer, Nick. "How to Choose the Right Attribution Model." November 19, 2014. www.forthea.com/choosing-attribution-model/. Accessed July 18, 2015.

Looker. "Data Modeling in Looker." www.looker.com/resources#ufh-i-121344443-data-modeling-in-looker. Accessed August 29, 2015.

Maamar, Zakaria. "Commerce, E-Commerce, and M-Commerce: What Comes Next?" Communications of the ACM, vol. 46, no. 12. December 2003.

MarketingSherpa. "The MarketingSherpa E-commerce Benchmark Study." 2014.

McCarl, John. "The Smart Way to Calculate Your Share of Customer Wallet." January 28, 2013. www.lighthousemktg.com.au/the-smart-way-to-calculate-your-share-of-customer-wallet/. Accessed June 21, 2015.

McMullan, Siobahn. "An Introduction to Online Merchandising." October 2013. www.smartinsights.com/ecommerce/merchandising/online-merchandising/. Accessed June 7, 2015.

Moffett, Tina. "The Forrester Wave: Cross-Channel Attribution Providers, Q4 2014." November 7, 2014. Forrester.

NetBeans. "The NetBeans E-commerce Tutorial—Designing the Data Model." https://netbeans.org/kb/docs/javaee/ecommerce/data-model.html. Accessed May 30, 2015.

NIST/SEMATECH e-Handbook of Statistical Methods. www.itl.nist.gov/div898/handbook. Accessed January 20, 2015.

Novo, Jim. "Customer Response, Retention and Valuation Concepts (RFM Model)." www.jimnovo.com/RFM-tour.htm. Accessed March 28, 2015.

Olsen, David H. "GEM: A General E-Commerce Data Model for Strategic Advantage." IACIS 2001.

Pepelnjak-Chandler, John. "Modeling Conversions in Online Advertising." May 2010.

Peppers, Don, and Martha Rogers. *The One to One Future: Building Relationships One Customer at a Time.* Currency/Doubleday, 1996.

Peterson, Eric T. *The Big Book of Key Performance Indicators by Eric Peterson.* Portland, OR: Scribd Free Version.

Phillips, Judah. *Building a Digital Analytics Organization.* New York, NY: Pearson/Financial Times, August 2013.

Phillips, Judah. *Digital Analytics Primer.* New York, NY: Pearson/Financial Times, October 2013.

Ratner, Bruce. *Statistical and Machine-Learning Data Mining: Techniques for Better Predictive Modeling and Analysis of Big Data.* Boca Raton, FL: Taylor & Francis, 2012.

Rogers, Adam. "Huge Growth Potential in the Global E-Commerce Market." November 17, 2015. http://marketrealist.com/2015/11/huge-growth-potential-global-e-commerce-market/. Accessed November 28, 2015.

SEC and Amazon. 2015 Q3 Quarterly Report from Marketwatch web site. http://www.marketwatch.com/investing/Stock/AMZN/SecFilings?subview=secarticle&sid=41519&guid=10965974&type=4. Accessed January 13, 2016.

Sentell, Jason. "Inventory Analysis Simplified: Turnover, Customer Service Level, and Stockouts." July 2013. www.waspbarcode.com/ buzz/inventory-analysis-simplified-turnover-customer-service-level-stockouts/. Accessed February 15, 2015.

Shao, Xuhui, and Lexin Li. "Data-Driven Multi-touch Attribution Models." August 21-24, 2011. www.turn.com.akadns.net/sites/ default/files/whitepapers/TURN_Tech_WP_Data-driven_ Multi-touch_Attribution_Models.pdf. Accessed April 5, 2015.

Singh, Siddarth, and Dipak Jain. "Measuring Customer Lifetime Value: Models and Analysis." Insead: 2013.

Smale, Thomas. "How to Apply Psychological Principles to Boost Your Conversion Rate." August 12, 2014. http://blog.crazyegg. com/2014/08/12/psychological-cro-principles/. Accessed December 23, 2015.

Smith, Jerry. "Six Types of Analyses Every Data Scientist Should Know." January 29, 2013. http://datascientistinsights.com/ 2013/01/29/six-types-of-analyses-every-data-scientist-should-know/. Accessed July 25, 2015.

Song, Il-Yeol, and Kyu-Young Whang. "Database Design for Real-World E-Commerce Systems." Drexel: March 2013.

Underwood, Jen. "Data Visualization Best Practices 2013." www.jenunderwood.com.

Weber, R. *Basic Content Analysis: Quantitative Applications in the Social Sciences.* Thousand Oaks, CA: Sage, 1990.

Wikimedia Foundation. "Analysis." Wikipedia. http://en.wikipedia. org/wiki/Analysis. Accessed January 1, 2015.

Wikimedia Foundation. "Attribution (Marketing)." Wikipedia. https://en.wikipedia.org/wiki/Attribution_(marketing). Accessed September 12, 2015.

Wikimedia Foundation. "Cluster Analysis." Wikipedia. https:// en.wikipedia.org/wiki/Cluster_analysis. Accessed October 10, 2015.

Wikimedia Foundation. "Customer Analytics." Wikipedia. https://en.wikipedia.org/wiki/Customer_analytics. Accessed October 25, 2015.

Wikimedia Foundation. "Customer Attrition." Wikipedia. https://en.wikipedia.org/wiki/Customer_attrition. Accessed June 27, 2015.

Wikimedia Foundation. "Customer Lifetime Value." Wikipedia. https://en.wikipedia.org/wiki/Customer_lifetime_value. Accessed April 25, 2015.

Wikimedia Foundation. "Data Governance." Wikipedia. https://en.wikipedia.org/wiki/Data_governance. Accessed October 26, 2015.

Wikimedia Foundation. "Data Lake." Wikipedia. https://en.wikipedia.org/wiki/Data_lake. Accessed October 25, 2015.

Wikimedia Foundation. "Data Model." Wikipedia. https://en.wikipedia.org/wiki/Database_model. Accessed June 13, 2015.

Wikimedia Foundation. "Data Modeling." Wikipedia. https://en.wikipedia.org/wiki/Data_modeling. Accessed June 13, 2015.

Wikimedia Foundation. "Data Virtualization." Wikipedia. https://en.wikipedia.org/wiki/Data_virtualization. Accessed November 1, 2015.

Wikimedia Foundation. "Data Visualization." Wikipedia. https://en.wikipedia.org/wiki/Data_visualization. Accessed September 19, 2015.

Wikimedia Foundation. "Data Wrangling." Wikipedia. https://en.wikipedia.org/wiki/Data_wrangling. Accessed August 22, 2015.

Wikimedia Foundation. "E-commerce." Wikipedia. https://en.wikipedia.org/wiki/E-commerce. Accessed November 14, 2015.

Wikimedia Foundation. "Exploratory Data Analysis." Wikipedia. https://en.wikipedia.org/wiki/Exploratory_data_analysis. Accessed July 18, 2015.

Wikimedia Foundation. "John Tukey." Wikipedia. http://en.wikipedia.org/wiki/John_Tukey. Accessed January 13, 2015.

Wikimedia Foundation. "Market Segmentation." Wikipedia. https://en.wikipedia.org/wiki/Market_segmentation. Accessed October 25, 2015.

Wikimedia Foundation. "Merchandising." Wikipedia. https://en.wikipedia.org/wiki/Merchandising. Accessed September 12, 2015.

Wikimedia Foundation. "Metadata." Wikipedia. https://en.wikipedia.org/wiki/Metadata. Accessed November 22, 2015.

Wikimedia Foundation. "Multivariate Testing." Wikipedia. http://en.wikipedia.org/wiki/Multivariate_testing. Accessed January 6, 2015.

Wikimedia Foundation. "Next Best Action Marketing." Wikipedia. https://en.wikipedia.org/wiki/Next-best-action_marketing. Accessed August 30, 2015.

Wikimedia Foundation. "Non-parametric Regression." Wikipedia. http://en.wikipedia.org/wiki/Non-parametric_regression. Accessed January 7, 2015.

Wikimedia Foundation. "Operational Data Store." Wikipedia. https://en.wikipedia.org/wiki/Operational_data_store. Accessed August 8, 2015.

Wikimedia Foundation. "Personalization." Wikipedia. https://en.wikipedia.org/wiki/Personalization. Accessed June 20, 2015.

Wikimedia Foundation. "Price Optimization." Wikipedia. https://en.wikipedia.org/wiki/Price_optimization. Accessed September 26, 2015.

Wikimedia Foundation. "Regression Analysis." Wikipedia. http://en.wikipedia.org/wiki/Regression_analysis. Accessed January 13, 2015.

Wikimedia Foundation. "Student's *t*-test." Wikipedia. http://en.wikipedia.org/wiki/Student%27s_t-test. Accessed January 18, 2015.

Wikimedia Foundation. "Student's *t*-distribution." Wikipedia. http://en.wikipedia.org/wiki/Student%27s_t-distribution. Accessed January 22, 2015.

Williams, Barry. "Retail Merchandise Authorization." February 21, 2009. http://databaseanswers.org/data_models/e_commerce/index.htm. Accessed October 17, 2015.

Yankelovich, Daniel, and David Meer. "Rediscovering Market Segmentation." *Harvard Business Review,* February 2006. pp. 122-131.

INDEX

Numbers

4-5-4 retail calendar, 28

A

abandon cart rates (KPI), 63-64
abandonment rates (behavioral analytics), 125
ACID (Atomicity, Consistency, Isolation, Durability), 179
acquisition costs (customer analytics), 168-169
acquisition marketing, 112
action logs, 24
activation marketing, 111
ad hoc reporting, 76
administrating data in analytical environment, 19
advertising
  advertising analytics, 103-105, 112-113
    affiliate analysis, 114
    attribution, 115
    audience analysis, 115-116
    campaign analysis, 113
    conversion optimization, 134
    customer journey analysis, 116
    Customer Origin reports, 116-117
    ecommerce and user experience, 3
    email analysis, 114-115
    focus groups, 107
    goals of, 105-108
    interviews, 107-108
    marketing goals, 105-108
    marketing mix-modeling, 115
    necessary data in, 116-117
    online display ad unit analysis, 116
    panels, 108
    projective techniques (stimuli), 108
    qualitative analytics, 107-108
    SEM, 113
    SEO, 113-114
    social media analysis, 114
    surveys, 108
  display advertising and attribution, 218
affiliates
  analysis of, 114
  marketing and attribution, 218
  orders and, 182
Agile environments (software solutions), 248, 250
  dashboards, 251
  data models, 250
  data stewardship, 251
  data visualization, 251
  reports, 251
  scrums, 247-250
AI (artificial intelligence), 317
Aksoy, Lerzan, 172-173
algorithmic (mechanistic) analytics, 302
analytical dashboards, 79
analytics, 4-8
  analysis techniques
    action logs, 24
    capital budgeting models, 25
    confirmatory analysis, 22
    descriptive analysis, 22-23
    explanatory analysis, 22
    exploratory analysis, 22, 31-33
    predictive analysis, 22
    prescriptive analysis, 22-23
    revenue/cost tracking, 24-25
    socializing analysis, 23-24